THE PHILADELPHIA CAMPAIGN

1777–1778

Gregory T. Edgar

HERITAGE BOOKS
2012

HERITAGE BOOKS
AN IMPRINT OF HERITAGE BOOKS, INC.

Books, CDs, and more—Worldwide

For our listing of thousands of titles see our website
at
www.HeritageBooks.com

Published 2012 by
HERITAGE BOOKS, INC.
Publishing Division
100 Railroad Ave. #104
Westminster, Maryland 21157

Copyright © 1998 Gregory T. Edgar

Other Heritage Books by the author:
Campaign of 1776: The Road to Trenton
"Liberty or Death!" The Northern Campaigns in the American Revolutionary War
The Philadelphia Campaign, 1777–1778
Reluctant Break with Britain: From Stamp Act to Bunker Hill

All rights reserved. No part of this book may be reproduced or transmitted in any form or by any means, electronic or mechanical, including photocopying, recording or by any information storage and retrieval system without written permission from the author, except for the inclusion of brief quotations in a review.

International Standard Book Numbers
Paperbound: 978-0-7884-0921-9
Clothbound: 978-0-7884-9174-0

"Howe has taken Philadelphia? No, Philadelphia has captured General Howe!"

- *Benjamin Franklin, replying to a Parisian who informed him that the British had taken Philadelphia.*

ALSO BY GREGORY T. EDGAR

Available from Heritage Books:

"Liberty or Death!" The Northern Campaigns in the American Revolutionary War. Nominated for the 1995 Cincinnati Prize.

Campaign of 1776: The Road to Trenton. Nominated for the 1996 Fraunces Tavern Museum Book Award.

Reluctant Break with Britain, From Stamp Act to Bunker Hill.

Available directly from Gregory T. Edgar, at 131 Pinnacle Road, Ellington, CT 06029:

"Are the Yankees Cowards Now?" A Story of Bunker Hill.

Gone to Meet the British, A Novel of the American Revolution.

CONTENTS

Introduction   vii

Maps   xi

1	Philadelphia Beckons, July - August 1777	1
2	Brandywine, September 1777	17
3	Massacre and Loss of a Capital, September 1777	41
4	Washington Counterattacks: Germantown, October 1777	55
5	Fight for the Delaware, October - November 1777	71
6	Valley Forge, December 1777 - June 1778	105
7	The Conway Cabal	139
8	The British in Philadelphia	161
9	The British Retreat Across New Jersey	183
10	Monmouth, June 1778	201

Bibliography   227

Index   233

ACKNOWLEDGEMENTS

The author extends his grateful appreciation for permission to quote from the following books:

Yale University Press, New Haven, CT, for excerpts of Captain Johann Ewald, taken from *Diary of the American War, A Hessian Journal*, edited by Joseph P. Tustin, 1979.

The Huntington Library, San Marino, CA, for excerpts of Ambrose Serle, taken from *The American Journal of Ambrose Serle, Secretary to Lord Howe, 1776-1778*, edited by Edward H. Tatum, 1940.

Heritage Books, Bowie, MD, for excerpts of Lieutenant Heinrich Feilitzsch, Ensign Carl Rueffer, the Jager Corps Journal and the Platte Grenadier Journal, all taken from *Enemy Views, The American Revolutionary War as Recorded by the Hessian Participants*, translated and edited by Bruce E. Burgoyne, 1996. Also for excerpts of Thomas Sullivan, taken from *From Redcoat to Rebel: The Thomas Sullivan Journal*, edited by Joseph Lee Boyle, 1997.

Excerpts of Major Carl Bauermeister are taken from *Revolution in America, Confidential Letters and Journals 1776-1784 of Adjutant General Major Bauermeister of the Hessian Forces*, edited by Bernhard A. Uhlendorf, published by Rutgers University Press, New Brunswick, NJ, 1957.

Excerpts of Jeremiah Olney and Stephen Olney are taken from *The Pennsylvania Navy 1775-1781, The Defense of the Delaware*, by John W. Jackson, Rutgers University Press, New Brunswick, NJ, for e1974.

Excerpts of Captain Friedrich Muenchhausen are taken from *At General Howe's Side 1776-1778*, translated by Ernest Kipping, edited by Samuel Smith, Philip Freneau Press, Monmouth Beach, NJ, 1974.

INTRODUCTION

This, my fourth book on the American Revolution, focuses on the operations of the principal armies during the period from June, 1777 through June, 1778. The first book in the series, *Reluctant Break with Britain, From Stamp Act to Bunker Hill*, covered the formative political crises, and the outbreak of war at Lexington and Concord on April 19, 1775, up through the first major engagement eight weeks later, the misnamed Battle of Bunker Hill. There, the British General William Howe discovered that the Yankees were in earnest, and it would not be an easy task subduing the rebellious colonists. The Yankees' courageous stand that day also convinced patriots outside of New England to join them in forming a truly continental army, under the Virginian Congress chose to lead it, George Washington.

The army's first major offensive (covered in *"Liberty or Death!" The Northern Campaigns*), was the failed invasion of British Canada, an attempt to gain a bargaining chip at the negotiations table. In 1775, most Americans expected the war to end soon, differences would be reconciled, and America would remain within the British Empire.

Attitudes changed, though, in 1776, as Americans came to realize that King George III was in agreement with Parliament and would not intervene on their behalf. The King was not interested in a peaceful settlement; he sought a military solution, and total submission by the American colonists to the will of Parliament. To that end, he provided General Howe enough reinforcements, including Hessian mercenaries, to aggressively push the war.

Campaign of 1776, The Road to Trenton covered Howe's efforts to end the war in 1776, and the gradual realization by many Americans that declaring independence was not only logical, but necessary. It would take a recent emigrant from London, a common laborer with an uncommon gift to write, named Thomas Paine, to convince them in his bestselling pamphlet, *Common Sense*.

On a number of occasions in 1776, General Howe had his chances to annihilate George Washington's ragtag army. But he chose not to. He and his brother, Admiral Lord Richard Howe, authorized to also act as peace commissioners, did not want to make martyrs out of Washington and Congress. Military defeat and martyrdom would have produced another Ireland, with periodic uprisings, out of the American colonies. Instead, the Howe brothers sought to persuade the rebels to give up their infatuation with republicanism, and return to their former allegiance to the mother country. So, repeatedly, after defeating the rebel army, rather than press their advantage militarily, the Howes let Washington's army escape in ignominious retreat. Surely, the rebel Congress would soon come to their senses, see the rebellion as a lost cause, and sue for peace on Parliament's terms. The plan appeared to be working well, until Christmas night of 1776, when Washington counteratttacked at Trenton and, a week later, at Princeton. These two signal victories resurrected "the cause."

Onward to the campaign of 1777 and a second try. Britain put two armies in the field, with separate and, regrettably, uncoordinated missions. In *"Liberty or Death!"* "Gentleman Johnny" Burgoyne was seen leading a British northern army south from Canada in an attempt to reach Albany and seize control of the Hudson River. This would have effectively isolated New England (Washington's best source of men and materiel) from the other former colonies, and might have led to Congress suing for peace. General Burgoyne's campaign ended in October with the surrender of his army at Saratoga, New York.

A planned coordination with Sir William Howe's main army probably would have prevented Burgoyne's disaster. But General Howe had also received permission for a campaign of his own design, an attack on Philadelphia. So he kept his army in New York until late July, when, reassured by reports that Burgoyne had easily taken the rebels' strong point, Fort Ticonderoga, Howe finally sailed for Philadelphia, confident that Burgoyne would be able to reach Albany on his own.

Months later, Howe would be as shocked as everyone else to learn that Burgoyne, surrounded by a reinvigorated rebel northern army, had been forced to surrender his entire army. Howe would come under harsh and unreasonable criticism in Parliament for not moving his army from New York up the Hudson River to ensure Burgoyne's success. But Howe, after all, was the commander in chief, and was not going to waste a whole campaign season sitting still in New York, waiting to go to the aid of a junior general who, from all accounts, would not be in need of help. So General Howe set his sights for the rebel capital of Philadelphia.

This new book covers Howe's Philadelphia campaign during that summer and fall of 1777, as well as the winter encampments of the British in Philadelphia and the Americans at Valley Forge, and the concluding Battle of Monmouth, June 28, 1778. Monmouth signaled not only the end of the Philadelphia campaign, but also the emergence of the Continental Army as a legitimate fighting entity.

Howe engaged Washington's main army on more than one occasion in this campaign, and he managed to capture the city that was both the seat of the rebel Congress and the second largest city in the British Empire. But, as with New York the previous year, Howe would find that taking another major city accomplished nothing toward ending the war. Congress simply relocated, and Washington retained a viable force in the field, his army gaining more experience and confidence with each passing year.

The Continental Army would spend a winter of anguish and discontent at Valley Forge, where even George Washington's position as commander in chief would come under intense scrutiny in the mysterious "Conway Cabal." But the army would at last become a competent one, thanks to a superb drillmaster, newly arrived from Prussia, named Friedrich Steuben. The ragtag Continental Army would be better prepared for battle when spring arrived. By then, the winter's losses from death and desertion would be replaced by new recruits.

Washington's aggressive operations in the Philadelphia campaign, coupled with Burgoyne's defeat at Saratoga, would persuade King Louis XVI to bring France into the war on the American side. This would significantly alter British plans for an early conquest of America. With colonies in the West Indies and elsewhere to defend, Britain could no longer dedicate all its military resources to North America. Sir Henry Clinton would replace General Howe in May, 1778 and be instructed to evacuate Philadelphia, bring his army back to New York, and send part of it to the West Indies. This would give the rebel army an opportunity to attack the British while en route, marching across New Jersey. Hardened by their winter ordeal at Valley Forge, they would prove themselves on the battlefield of Monmouth, the last significant action of the war in the North.

By 1779, the war would move to the South, culminating in a Franco-American victory at Yorktown, Virginia, in October, 1781. There, a proud army of veteran British and Hessian regulars would leave their trenches and, to the beat of *The World Turned Upside Down*, march out to the field of surrender, laying down their muskets in front of this ragtag army that they despised, trained by Friedrich Steuben and commanded by George Washington.

MAPS

Howe's 1777 Invasion of Pennsylvania   xii

The Battle of Brandywine, September 11, 1777   xiii

The Battle of Germantown, October 4, 1777   xiv

The Battle of Monmouth, June 28, 1778   xv

American Forces:
British/Hessian Forces:

xiii

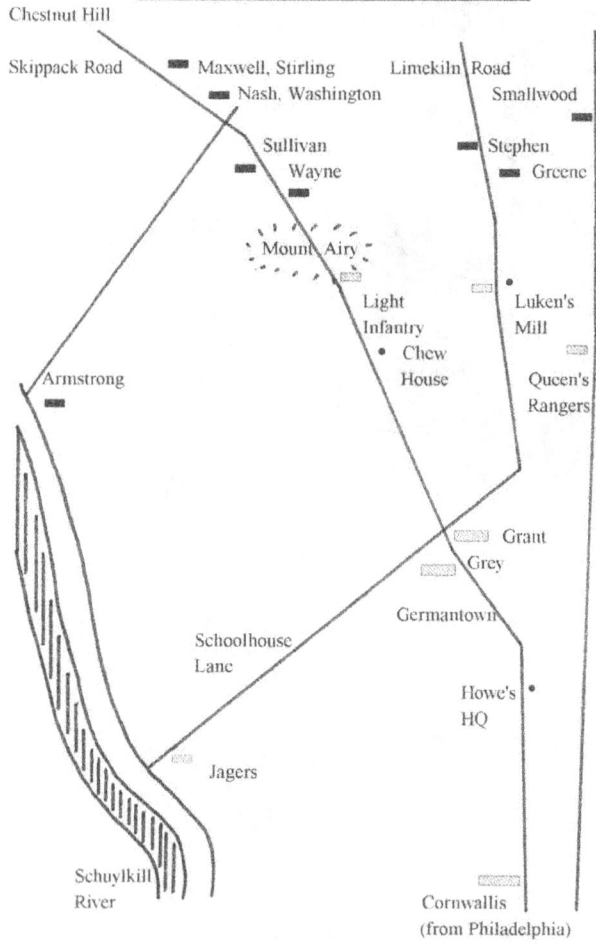

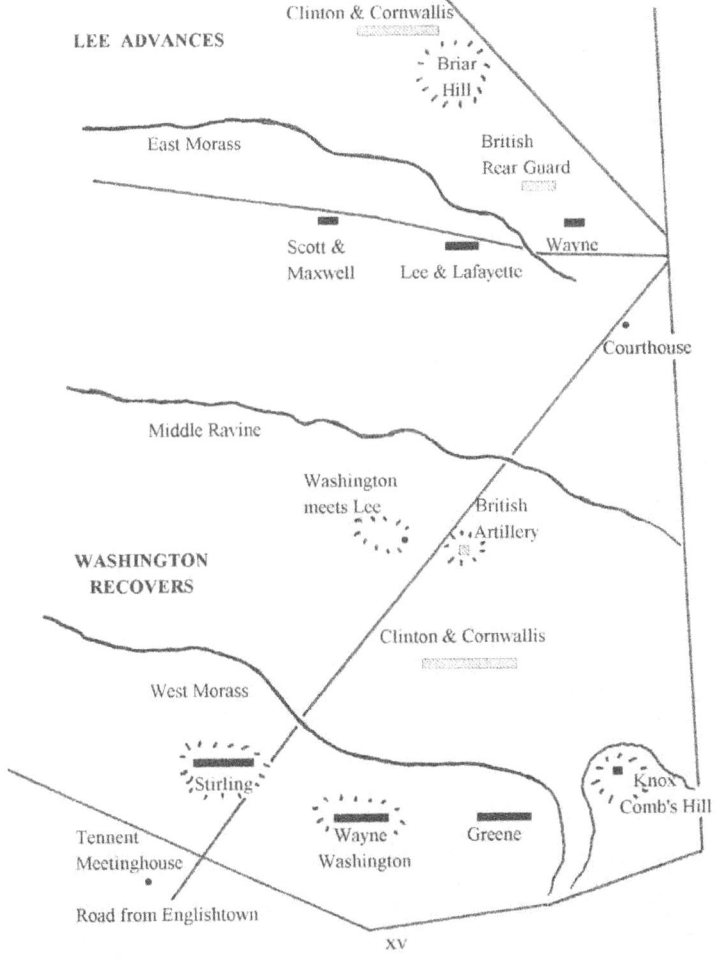

CHAPTER ONE
PHILADELPHIA BECKONS
JULY - AUGUST 1777

"General Howe's in a manner abandoning General Burgoyne is so unaccountable a matter, that, till I am fully assured it is so, I cannot help casting my eyes continually behind me."

- George Washington, on the march to Philadelphia.

The grand British plan to end the war in 1777 called for splitting the colonies in two by seizing control of New York's Hudson River. This would prevent New England from sending reinforcements and supplies to George Washington's Continental Army. The rebel army, stationed in New Jersey close to the main British army at New York, would be starved of men and materiel, and the rebel Congress would sue for peace and a reconciliation with the mother country.

But the British commander in chief in New York, General Sir William Howe, received conflicting orders from London. He was told to cooperate with the smaller British army, which was coming south from Canada along the Lake Champlain-Lake George corridor. He should send a force north, up the Hudson River, to ensure the northern army's successful arrival at Albany. However, in a separate packet, Howe received approval of his own plan, to launch a campaign against the principal American city of Philadelphia, site of the rebel Continental Congress.

When word reached Howe at New York that the northern army's commander, "Gentleman Johnny" Burgoyne, had easily taken Lake Champlain's Fort Ticonderoga, the rebels' strongest obstacle in his path to the Hudson, Howe decided it was safe to head for Philadelphia and leave Burgoyne to fend for himself. Neither Howe nor many others in England or America expected Burgoyne's mission would end in utter failure - the surrender of his entire army to a rebel northern army under Horatio Gates, at Saratoga, New York. This signal victory would, along with Washington's aggressive efforts to defend Philadelphia, convince the French King Louis XVI to finally commit to an open alliance with the fledgling American states.

After his Philadelphia campaign, Sir William Howe would resign his command and return to London to answer his critics in the press, and in Parliament, where he would be interrogated on the floor of the House of Commons. There, Howe would forcefully defend his decision to go to Philadelphia:

> What would have been the consequences of such an expedition [up the Hudson]? Before the object of it would have been attained, the forts in the [Hudson] Highlands must have been carried, which would probably have cost a considerable number of men, defended, as they would have been, by Washington's whole force.
> ... [It] could not have been accomplished in time to [also] have taken possession of Philadelphia that campaign. ... [I would have] wasted the campaign merely to ensure the progress of the northern army which could have taken care of itself, provided I ... [drew] off to the southward the main army under General Washington.

In time, even Colonial Secretary Lord George Germain, the man responsible for directing this war, would admit, in his confidential notes on the campaigns of 1777, that the surrender of the northern army at Saratoga was not the fault of Howe going to Pennsylvania, but of Burgoyne's own "great delay ... [and] total ignorance of the people and country." Rather than finding numerous "friends of government" coming forth to support his army, Burgoyne had encountered an active and hostile people bent on defending their homeland against the invaders.

Let us return to the spring of 1777, the start of the Philadelphia campaign. General Howe was determined to act independently and head for Pennsylvania. But he soon realized that Washington's strong position in the hills at Middlebrook would pose a serious obstacle to a march across New Jersey. He knew the rebel army, or the feisty New Jersey militia, could easily disrupt the progress of a long, strung out column of 17,000 troops, their accompanying wagons, livestock, and camp followers. And he knew Washington could sever the line of communications back to the British supply base at New York.

So Howe spent most of June maneuvering his army on the flatlands between Morristown and New York, trying to engage Washington on favorable terms. Washington came down from the hills to skirmish and harass Howe's army, but he refused to be baited into a general engagement. He knew that, to prolong the Revolution, America must have an extant army. A battle on open ground would put his army at risk; the British and Hessians regulars were simply too disciplined.

Since Washington would not accept his offer of battle, Howe returned his army to New York. This prompted the diarist Nicholas Cresswell, an Englishman visiting America, to criticize the British commander who, after two years of war, had still not captured George Washington and his rabble.

> That a Negro-driver should with a banditti of undisciplined people, the scum and refuse of all nations on earth, so long keep a British general at bay, nay even oblige him ... to retreat, it is astonishing. ...
>
> O! Britain, how thy laurels tarnish in the hands of such a lubber!

On July 9th, General Sir William Howe boarded his army of 17,500 soldiers on the transports of his brother, Admiral Lord Richard Howe. The troops and their horses then spent two weeks sweltering aboard the ships, idly floating at anchor in New York harbor. General Howe delayed his departure until he received the much anticipated news of two favorable events. The first was the imminent arrival of reinforcements from England, sailing for New York. And the second was a letter from Burgoyne, describing his easy capture of Fort Ticonderoga and the precipitous flight of the rebels' northern army. This assured Howe that it was now apparently safe to set sail for Philadelphia.

The Howes kept their destination a tight secret. Colonel Carl von Donop, one of Howe's top Hessian officers, expected his commander to join forces with Burgoyne and punish the people of New England, "the authors of rebellion." Captain Frederick Mackenzie of the Royal Welsh Fusiliers, stationed in Rhode Island, heard that the Bostonians were reportedly "in great confusion as they are apprehensive of a visit from Gen'l Howe." Like Donop, Mackenzie hoped Howe's aim was an invasion of New England.

> Those provinces for their demerits deserve the most severe chastisement. It is to be hoped so severe an example will be made of them as may induce the other provinces to submit without further exertions. ... [Going to Philadelphia] would separate the army too much, and not in the least contribute to the progress of ... [Burgoyne's] army, which certainly should be the great object of the campaign.

But no, Howe was sailing for Pennsylvania, where he expected to defeat Washington and take the rebel capital, and thus discourage the rebels from further resistance. This would also enable loyalists to take control of local government. According to Stephen Kemble, an officer in the loyalist Queen's Rangers, Howe still found "great reason to hope that the inhabitants are much inclined to return to their allegiance." Howe told Germain that, "the opinions of the people are much changed in Pennsylvania ... [they are now] disposed to peace, in which sentiment they would be confirmed by our getting possession of Philadelphia." Like his superiors in London, Howe also expected large numbers of Pennsylvania loyalists to come forward and augment his army, to take responsibility "for the interior defence of the province." He wrote to Canada's Governor Guy Carleton:

> I flatter myself and have reason to expect the friends of government in that part of the country will be found so numerous and so ready to give every aid and assistance in their power, that it will prove no difficult task to reduce the more rebellious parts of the province.

Sir Henry Clinton, Howe's second in command, remained behind in New York with nearly 9,000 troops. According to Clinton's journal, which he edited and published after the war, he was astonished that the Howes were sailing for Philadelphia, instead of up the Hudson. In his journal, Clinton noted that he confided to a friend, "By God, these people cannot mean what they give out." Clinton expected to see Howe feint a southern invasion - to lure Washington into marching his army southward - then abruptly turn about and "return with the first southerly blast, and run up the North [Hudson] River."

On August 16th, while still at sea, Howe received his firmest orders from London about the necessity to cooperate with Burgoyne. Lord Germain informed Howe, he trusted "that whatever you may meditate [for a southern campaign], it will be executed in time to co-operate with the army ordered to proceed from Canada." This, by now, with Howe's typical late start, was impossible. He would have to hope - and he saw no reaon not to - that Burgoyne could take care of himself.

Would Washington set his main army in motion toward Philadelphia, or join forces with the northern army under Gates to pounce on the unsupported Burgoyne just a few days' march to the north? While at sea, en route to Philadelphia, Captain Friedrich Ernst von Muenchhausen, one of Howe's adjutants, expressed a common opinion in his own journal: "I fear that [Washington] will make some forced marches and attack Burgoyne, and after this return to us," at Philadelphia, reinforced by Gates's American northern army. Nathanael

Greene, one of Washington's generals, viewed Philadelphia as "an object of far less importance than the North River." Even General Howe, himself, thought Washington would be a "blockhead" if he followed him to Philadelphia. But here he was, gambling that Washington would do just that.

The American commander had no intention of giving up Philadelphia without a fight. At first, when the British were boarding their ships, Washington, thinking they would sail up the Hudson, had rushed to march his army north to Peekskill, New York. Now his scouts informed him that the British fleet of 264 ships had disappeared over the southern horizon, so he put the army in motion again, marching south from Peekskill to New Jersey. However, uncertain of Howe's true destination, Washington soon sent part of his army north again. A few days later, he reversed that directive when the British fleet was sighted in southern waters. Greene complained that a lack of intelligence concerning Howe's whereabouts "compelled the army to wander about the country like Arabs." A captain from Delaware named Enoch Anderson described the long, hot summer as one spent "marching and counter-marching, and often not knowing which."

By August 5th, Washington was in "a very irksome state of suspense," and felt for his troops, having marched so long in "this extreme heat." He finally halted his army for a few days on the Delaware River's east bank, though he still suspected Howe was "practising a deep feint, merely to draw our attention and whole force to this point. There is still the strongest reason to believe that the North River is their object." From Trenton, New Jersey, Washington wrote to Israel Putnam, who commanded the forts in the Hudson Highlands. He assured the Yankee general that he would not put a major river between his army and Putnam

> till the fleet actually enters the [Delaware] Bay and puts the matter beyond a doubt. General Howe's in a manner abandoning General Burgoyne is so unaccountable a matter, that, till I am fully assured it is so, I cannot

help casting my eyes continually behind me.

Meanwhile, the British fleet had reached the mouth of the Delaware River on July 30th, and halted there while the frigate *Roebuck* sailed upriver to explore. When the ship returned, its captain, Sir Andrew Hamond, delivered a report that did not please Sir William Howe. A subordinate noted:

> The general, receiving intelligence that the enemy had the river on both sides well fortified, and [it would be] dangerous, if not impossible, at this time for the shipping to get up as far as Philadelphia, thought it advisable not to land the troops.

According to Hamond, it was "to the astonishment of both fleet and army," that General Howe instructed his brother, the admiral, to "turn away and steer for the Capes of Virginia," to approach Philadelphia via Chesapeake Bay. This was probably Howe's biggest blunder of the Philadelphia campaign, as it wasted further time at sea, giving his enemy time to further their preparations. True, navigating through the Delaware's many shoals would have been difficult, but surely some knowledgable loyalist pilots could have been found. Furthermore, the shoreline rebel batteries and underwater obstacles were far upriver, near Philadelphia; the navy could have sailed partway up and put "the whole army ashore in 24 hours," at a spot just a few days' march south of the city. This decision of General Howe's, to leave the Delaware in favor of the Chesapeake, probably cost him a month's campaigning time, and would be a focus of the Parliamentary inquiry into his conduct of the war. His accusers would claim that, if Howe had landed along the Delaware, he could have taken Philadelphia in time to send back a sizable detachment to run up the Hudson and help Burgoyne.

According to Ambrose Serle, Admiral Howe's secretary, "the hearts of the men were struck" when they learned that General Howe had decided to put out to sea again, rather than land on the shores of the

Delaware. The troops were already weary of being "tossed about exceedingly" and, at other times, delayed by "continual calms," or "drove out of our course [by] contrary winds." A Hessian lieutenant named Heinrich Carl Philipp von Feilitzsch reflected, on July 28th, that, "Storms here in America are much stronger than in Europe, therefore [it is] much more dangerous ... for ships to sail in company." His words were prophetic, for two weeks later he would be frightened by the sight of a much larger ship approaching his transport. "It did not turn, and it appeared it would run us down." Suddenly, there was "a terrible, frightful cracking," as the "bowsprit or nose of the other ship penetrated about two yards into our cabin."

Even when it was not storming, life at sea was difficult, according to Lieutenant Feilitzsch:

> 6 August - Dull weather and almost no wind. I will very briefly record my thoughts ... concerning life at sea. Anyone who has a desire to experience misery and misfortune should go aboard ship. ... when I am again in Europe, should the opportunity arise for another such trip, I would certainly not go. 1) There is no bread except for zwieback which is spoiled or full of worms. 2) Stinking water with all possible impurities mixed in, because ... we have not had one drop [of rain]. 3) The meat is miserable and frightfully salted so that it can hardly be eaten, and then one nearly dies of thirst. 4) The entire ship is full of lice ...
>
> Anyone who has never been to sea can not understand how miserable that can be. It is nearly impossible to take a step without risk of breaking your neck or a leg. Everything has to be securely fastened, and still everything breaks and busts to pieces. If there is no wind the water is generally restless, which causes the ship to sway back and forth in one place in a dreadful manner. ... God will surely help to return me to my fa-

therland.

The weather was so exceedingly hot that Captain John Montresor observed "the pitch melting off the seams of the vessels." It was not a good time to be cooped up in close quarters on a ship. By the time the fleet reached Chesapeake Bay, Ambrose Serle wrote, "Many of our horses perished in the immense heat of this climate." Captain Muenchhausen did not appreciate "the intolerable heat" either. "If I could own the whole of America," he wrote, "I would refuse if I had to live in these hot regions."

When word reached Washington that the British fleet had left Delaware Bay and sailed further south, he immediately called a council of war. His generals concluded, "that the enemy has most probably sailed for Charleston," and the army "could not possibly arrive in time to afford any succor. The army should move immediately toward the North River" instead. Alexander Hamilton, one of Washington's aides, hastened off to inform Congress, which immediately adjourned for two hours to discuss the situation in private. But before they could reconvene, another messenger arrived, saying the fleet had just been sighted "high up in the north east part of Chesapeake Bay." Washington thought Howe's choice of route was, "to be sure, a very strange one."

According to the Marquis de Lafayette, who had just arrived from France to volunteer in the cause, after the British fleet had left Delaware Bay "the Americans amused themselves by making jokes at its expense. These jokes, however, ceased when it reappeared in the Chesapeake." So, on July 31st, General Washington ordered his army "to cross the Delaware with all possible dispatch and proceed to Philadelphia." Before he broke camp, he sent off another note to Israel Putnam, at Peekskill on the Hudson, "Now let all New England turn on and crush Burgoyne!"

The day before they reached Philadelphia, the troops rested a few miles from the city, washing their clothes, shaving off their beards, etc., to make a good appearance the next day. Suddenly, according to Lieutenant James McMichael, they had some curious visitors.

> The largest collection of young ladies I almost ever beheld came to camp. They marched in three columns. The field officers paraded the rest of the officers and detached scouting parties to prevent being surrounded by them. For my part, being sent on scout, I at last sighted the ladies and gave them to know that they must repair to headquarters, upon which they accompanied me as prisoners. But on parading them at the colonel's marquee, they were dismissed, after we had treated them with a double bowl of sangaree.

The Continental Army marched into Philadelphia on the morning of August 24th, aiming to impress both "Whigs" (patriots) and "Tories" (loyalists). Since they lacked uniforms, each man was ordered to wear in his hat a "green sprig, emblem of hope." Wagons, extra horses, and camp followers were ordered to take an alternate route and bypass the city. Washington's General Orders for the army, the day before the march, stressed the need to present a good showing:

> The soldiers will go early to rest this evening. The army is to move precisely at 4 o'clock in the morning. A small halt to be made about a mile [short of the city] till the rear closes up and the line is in proper order. Not a woman belonging to the army is to be seen with the troops on their march through the city. ...
> [The troops to] appear as decent as possible and to carry their arms well ... [Anyone who dares] quit his ranks [will receive] thirty nine lashes. ... Drums and fifes of each brigade are to be collected at the center of it and a tune for the quick step play'd, but with such moderation that the men step to it with ease without dancing along or totally disregarding the musick.

To one observer, the army made "a fine appearance, the order of marching extremely well preserved," though the critical Congressman John Adams felt the men did not have "quite the air of soldiers. They dont step exactly in time ... hold up their heads quite erect ...cock their hats the same way." Philadelphians turned out in large numbers to cheer and wave as the army spent "upwards of two hours in passing with a lively, smart step" before continuing on to the hills south of the city. Before the parade was over, though, the camp followers, resentful at not being allowed to march with the army, left their parallel route outside of town and "poured after their soldiers, hair flying, brows beaded from the heat, belongings slung over one shoulder, chattering and yelling in sluttish shrills, and spitting in the gutters."

Meanwhile, the British fleet was sailing up the Chesapeake. When they passed Annapolis, Ensign Carl Friedrich Rueffer observed two flags flapping in the breeze, and concluded that, "the city's inhabitants, like most Americans, were rebels. Through the telescope it could be seen that there were thirteen red and white stripes in these flags."

The fleet sailed up the Chesapeake as far as they could, then up the Elk River, and finally dropped anchor at Head of Elk. Here, they were informed "by a person who came off" (deserted) that the rebel "army, rendered sickly by their late, long march, was upon the banks of the Schuylkill, much indisposed with a bloody flux" (dysentery). Pehaps, the fifty-seven mile march north to Philadelphia would be an easy one, with the rebel army only able to offer ineffectual resistance.

The next day, August 25th, Sir William Howe's army came ashore "without the slightest interference." After leaving 2,000 behind to finish unloading the munitions and other heavy baggage, Howe would lead the remaining 15,000 troops north. The commander immediately "advanced with the British light infantry and the Hessian *jagers* (i.e., "huntsmen," or riflemen) for three miles and made a halt."

After having spent 47 days on the ships, the troops were glad to finally be on firm ground again. One soldier noted, "We stood around in confusion, without tents because they had been left aboard ship." So they spent their first night trying to stay dry amid terrific thunderstorms, sheltered by huts hastily constructed from "fence rails and corn stalks."

By August 28th, much of the army was in motion, progressing eight miles to the village of Elkton. Ensign Rueffer:

> The army departed Turkey Point and marched to Elkton which had been deserted by all the inhabitants. We had no reports about the enemy, and no maps of the interior of this land, and no one in the army was familiar with this area. After we had passed the city, no one knew which way to go. Therefore, men were sent out in all directions until finally a Negro was found, and the army had to march according to his directions.

The British Army's march northward was slowed by a lack of horses. Like the men, the horses had "remained pent up, in the hottest season of the year, in the holds of the vessels." "Given little space" and "much distressed for the want of fresh water," some 170 had died and been thrown overboard while at sea. Upon landing, another 150 were so "miserably emaciated" that they were likely to be "of little use for some time." These poor animals were let loose in a cornfield that first night, and several dozen "ate until they dropt dead in the field."

General Howe issued a proclamation promising "a free and general pardon" to rebel soldiers who would "voluntarily come and surrender themselves," but very few did. As for the inhabitants, Howe promised "security and protection to all persons who, conscious of their misconduct, return and remain peaceably at their usual places of abode." Despite these assurances, all the inhabitants who could deserted their homes as the British Army approached. Ensign Rueffer:

> 29 August - In this stretch of land we have not seen any females, because they were told by the rebels that the Hessians would have misused them in an unpleasant manner, so they have all fled ...

> 31 August - At every house we passed a pardon letter was nailed, and a watch posted to prevent looting.

The Continental Army was steadily growing in size and confidence. One of the few loyalists who came forward to join Howe's army told him that almost "everyone is anxious to join the force of General Washington in order to be in the great fight." General Howe was surprised and a bit disillusioned at the "prevailing disposition" of hostility among these people he had been led to believe would flock to his banner. He wrote to Lord Germain, complaining that, "excepting a few individuals, the people are strongly against us." Therefore, he did not think he would "be able to act up to the king's expectations" in returning a force to the Hudson River in time to cooperate with Burgoyne.

One British officer would write that, although Howe selected "gentlemen of the first influence" to head the Tory, or loyalist, units, "they met with so little success in raising their quotas of men that many of the battalions were nearly as strong in officers as in privates."

Why were the loyalists, the "friends of government," not coming forward in greater numbers? The answer lies partly in some common personality traits of loyalists - conservatism, caution, an abhorrence of violence - but also in how they had been treated by the British so far in this war. Prominent loyalists who had come forward to serve as officers had been given provincial commissions, rather than British Army commissions, an effort to save money and permanence (for example, half pay upon retirement). This was a reflection of the condescending attitude of the British toward all provincials, even the loyalists. Often, loyalist troops were given menial tasks, such as scouting, foraging, and garrison duty, rather than more active roles in offensive operations. Back in 1776, in New York's Westchester County and in New Jersey, many loyalists who had committed themselves by taking the loyalty oath felt double-crossed when the British Army withdrew from those territories, abandoning them to persecution by vengeful committee--men. Now, after two years of war, most loyalists were wiser, and showed their cautious nature by largely staying at home.

Pillaging by Howe's soldiers further hampered recruiting efforts. Marylanders and Pennsylvanians found out, just as the people of New Jersey had the previous fall, that Howe's pledges of "security and protection" were only words on paper. A Pennsylvanian named John Miller recorded that when the king's soldiers went foraging, they spared "neither friend nor foe, burning, robing, stealing all the way they went." One British officer sadly wrote home about a "soldier of ours who chopped off an unfortunate woman's fingers in order to plunder her of her rings."

Nearly every day, British and Hessian soldiers were noting in their journals their pillaging comrades who strayed too far from camp and were captured by the enemy. Efforts were made to keep the soldiers in line. General Knyphausen had ten of his Hessians run the gauntlet, and Howe had two British soldiers "hanged and five severely whipped for plundering." But these measures had little effect, for, several days later, Ambrose Serle was recording in his journal:

> Forty seven grenadiers and several other parties straggling for plunder were surprised and taken by the Rebels. The Hessians are more infamous and cruel than any. It is a misfortune we ever had such a dirty, cowardly set of contemptible miscreants.

In truth, rations and pay were so meager that the soldiers had to resort to plundering the inhabitants in order to survive. And the practice was by no means confined to the British Army. Washington addressed the problem in his General Orders of September 1st, which he insisted be "distinctly read" to all the troops:

> Why do we assemble in arms? Was it not to protect the property of our countrymen? And shall we to our eternal reproach be the first to pillage and destroy it? Will no motives of humanity, of real interest and of honor restrain the violence of the soldiers? How many

noble designs have miscarried, how many victories have been lost, how many armies have been ruined by an indulgence of soldiers in plundering?

On August 30th, a British officer named Sir James Murray wrote home, "They say that Washington threatens to fight rather than give up Philadelphia." Washington, Murray thought, must be in "a desperate situation, or very little acquainted with the nature of the troops that are to act for and against him." Another officer predicted that when Washington discovers the strength of "the forces that Sir William Howe has under his command" he will wish that he had "gone up the North River" instead of following Howe to Philadelphia.

August 30th was also the day that several rebel officers were captured. One of them, orginally from Germany, was interrogated by Muenchhausen, who recorded what the rebel told him:

> After we landed on August 25 [Washington] called his generals to a council of war. The French generals and also two German colonels urged an immediate attack on us before we could recover from the long voyage. They figured that we would have many sick, and that we would not be able to use our cavalry nor our artillery because of sick horses.
>
> Contrary to this view, an American general, whose opinion Washington finally backed, maintained that it would be much better to remain in the hills.
>
> Others argued against a battle but recommended a plan designed to slow us down and diminish our strength by small skirmishes and harassments to prolong the war, because England would not continue such a costly war much longer ... situations in Europe would very soon lead to war between England and France.

After this heated council, Washington rode forward with Greene,

Lafayette and a small guard to personally observe the enemy. That night a heavy rainstorm forced them to seek shelter at the farmhouse of a "disaffected" couple. Leaving their escort out of sight, the three generals stayed the night in the house, but kept their cloaks on all night to remain incognito. The commander in chief was very fortunate that his imprudence did not lead to his capture, as had happened to his second in command, Charles Lee, the previous December. Years later, Lafayette recalled the night as an anxious one, and even Washington later admitted that he had acted "hastily." Fortunately, it was not until the day after they had left that the British and Hessians arrived, and this loyalist family discovered the identity of their recent guests. The woman of the house was reportedly "much put out with herself" for having made the celebrated George Washington sleep on the floor.

One of those arriving at the woman's house was the Hessian Captain Muenchhausen. Two days before, he and several others had

> observed some officers on a wooded hill opposite us ... one was dressed unobtrusively in a plain gray coat. These gentlemen observed us with their glasses as carefully as we observed them. Those of our officers who know Washington well maintained that the man in the plain coat was Washington. As soon as they observed our advance they retreated.
>
> General Washington ... [had stayed] in the same house where we are now lodging, and did not leave until yesterday. While here, Washington received the pleasant news, though unpleasant to our side ... [of the Battle of Bennington].

Washington returned to his camp, and immediately sent forward a detachment of light infantry to harass the British Army and retard its advance, by "operating without fixed positions, but to skirmish continuously" around the enemy. Both Washington and Howe now sent all tents and other excess baggage to the rear, and prepared for battle.

CHAPTER TWO
BRANDYWINE
SEPTEMBER 1777

"Dear man, George Washington is on the other side, and he has all the men in this world with him."

- A Quaker woman, warning General Knyphausen not to go to Chadd's Ford.

"Never mind, Madam. I have all the men in the other world with me."

- George Knyphausen's reply.

The American commander instructed his brigadiers to dispense rum, "a gill a man" - a sure sign that a battle was imminent. In his General Orders for the day, he informed his army:

> [The enemy's] all is at stake - they will put the contest on the event of a single battle. If they are overthrown, they are utterly undone - the war is at an end. Now is the time for our most strenuous endeavours.

Washington spread out his army of 11,000 along the northern bank of Brandywine River, 26 miles southwest of Philadelphia. The river had taken its name several generations before, when a ship from France, carrying wine and brandy upriver, sank where the stream empties into the Delaware River. Numerous hills, most of them about 200 feet high, extended westward from the Delaware along both sides of the Brandywine. Because the banks were steep and densely covered with briers and woods, travelers were forced to cross at one of the breaks in the rough terrain. For this reason, Washington posted his army advantageously at several of these fording places.

The largest division of continentals guarded Chadd's Ford, where shallow water offered Howe the best crossing place. The remaining continentals formed the army's right flank, most of them near the next ford, named Brinton's. And three thousand Pennsylvania militia guarded a less likely ford a mile and a half downstream. Small detachments covered other fords for as far as three miles upstream to "the forks," where two creeks converged to form the Brandywine River. Washington was told that there were no more fords past these forks "for another twelve miles," and that the water upstream was "all but impassable." He would not find out until too late that both statements were false.

Despite being busy with battle preparations, George Washington had to entertain distinguished visitors - members of the Continental Congress - on September 10th, the day before what would be known as the Battle of Brandywine took place. The commander "showed the first gentlemen of Congress around," it was reported, and "was very pleased, *au moins il a fait semblant* [at least he made it appear so] that Howe should dare attack him in his strong and defensible positions."

Howe had intended to reach Kennett Square, six miles south of the Brandywine, by the evening of September 9th. He marched his army that day in two columns: the first, under Knyphausen, set out at 1 p.m.; the second, led by Cornwallis and accompanied by Howe, followed five hours later. Finding the road badly rutted by the first column, and with darkness approaching, Howe sent two adjutants forward with a guard of twelve dragoons to instruct Knyphausen not to go all the way to Kennett Square, but to halt at New Garden Meeting House. One of these two aides was Friedrich Munchhausen, who later expounded in his journal on the hazards of such duty:

> Although we twice came upon rebel dragoons who fired at us, we luckily got through. General Knyp-

hausen's vanguard was already at Kennett Square, and it was absolutely impossible for him to return to New Garden Meeting because of the loaded wagons and the ravined roads. We two aides rode back as quickly as possible to report this to our General. General Knyphausen permitted no fires, and was as quiet as possible so that Washington who was nearby would not discover his presence.

While we were away, the General [Howe] had sent forward with a few dragoons a Scottish Captain Campbell to get reliable information about Washington's position. Campbell, who had been told that Knyphausen was at New Garden Meeting, unfortunately ran into a patrol of the Knyphausen corps on the other side of Kennett Square. Since neither party supposed the other to be there, they fired at each other, and our poor Campbell was shot through the belly and will probably die.

On the 10th, Howe rested his army while he gathered intelligence and studied local maps. He decided to use the strategy that had worked so well for him at the Battle of Long Island the year before, when his Hessian division had "amused" the enemy at Flatbush Pass while he led a British flanking column on an all night march through an unguarded pass and pounced on the American rear. Captain John Andre explains Howe's battle plans for the next day, September 11th:

The army marched in two columns under Lord Cornwallis and General Knyphausen. Sir William Howe was with the former, and proceeded to the forks of Brandywine, crossed there and by a circuit of fifteen miles came upon the enemy's right flank, near Birmingham Meeting House. The latter took the straight road to Chadd's Ford, opposite to which the Rebel army lay.

The design, it seemed, was that General Knyphausen,

taking post at Chadd's Ford, should begin early to cannonade the enemy on the opposite side, thereby to take up his attention and make him presume an attack was then intended with the whole army, whilst the other column should be performing the detour. Lord Cornwallis's wing being engaged was to be the signal for the troops under General Knyphausen to cross the ford, when they were to push their advantage.

Knyphausen's column had not progressed very far when a Quaker lady, seeing the general approaching on his horse, ran out of her house and pleaded with him not to go to Chadd's Ford. "Dear man, George Washington is on the other side, and he has all the men in this world with him." Knyphausen smiled to himself, looked down at the frightened woman, and reassuringly replied, "Never mind, Madam. I have all the men in the other world with me."

A few American scouts were sent forward as far as Welch's Tavern, on the road leading to Chadd's Ford. They dismounted and went into the tavern for some refreshment. While inside, one of them, looking out the front window, observed uniformed men approaching. They were Knyphausen's vanguard. Realizing they were about to be surrounded, the American scouts fired a volley out the door, then fled on foot through a rear window. One of the Hessians' horses was killed, but but its rider gladly replaced his mount with one of the healthier American ones left tied up in front of the tavern.

Shortly after passing Welch's Tavern, Knyphausen's vanguard was in turn surprised by part of General William "Scotch Willie" Maxwell's light infantry. This was a special force of 700 men - 100 picked from each of the army's seven infantry brigades - Washington had formed a few weeks before to replace Morgan's rifle corps, which had gone north to assist Gates against Burgoyne. Maxwell's light infantry had been harassing the British intermittently ever since they landed at Head of Elk. Now they were doing it again, trying to retard the enemy's advance, before eventually falling back to the main American position on the north side of the Brandywine. Maxwell's battalion was augmented by 200 local militia who knew the terrain. A Hessian officer describes the ambush:

> General Knyphausen had hardly set out on his march when the Queen's Rangers and Ferguson's sharpshooters, which formed the advanced guard, fell into an enemy ambuscade concealed in a marshy wood on the right and left of the highway; nearly half were either killed or wounded.

Thomas Sullivan, a private in a British regiment farther back, later heard how the ambush took place:

> The Queen's Rangers and Riffle Corps at the head ... advancing to the foot of a hill, saw the enemy formed behind the fence, were deceived by the Rebels' telling them that they would deliver up their arms; but upon their advancing they fired a volley upon our men, and took to their heels, killed and wounded about thirty ...

The American detachment fell back a mile to a defensive position halfway between Welch's Tavern and Chadd's Ford. Here the road descended steeply in a defile, then leveled off in a wide marsh before climbing to the next rise. Except for a narrow strip along the road, the area was "an almost impenetrable morass." It was covered by American musketmen hiding in the surrounding woods. In addition, a battery of guns was posted on a ridge to Maxwell's right, guarding a side road leading to Brinton's Ford. The narrow pass would force Knyphausen's troops to bunch and form easy targets, so he needed to clear the hillsides of rebels before his column entered the defile. Major Carl Leopold Bauermeister provides an account of this action:

> The Queen's Rangers proceeded to the left and after a

short but very rapid musketry fire, supported by the 2nd English Regiment, which had filed out of the column to the left, quickly drove the rebels out of their woods and straight across the lowlands. The 28th English Regiment filed out of the column to the right and the rebels, who had been shouting "Hurrah" and firing briskly from a gorge in front of us, were quickly put to flight.

Now the marsh must be crossed and the far side cleared of rebels. "General Knyphausen ordered the Queen's Rangers to cross the marsh," and the Tories did, supported by Captain Patrick Ferguson's small party of British riflemen. The Rangers sloshed across the marsh and, facing a heavy rebel fire, "attacked the enemy with the bayonet so courageously without firing that [the rebel snipers] lost ground." Sergeant Stephen Jarvis of the Queen's Rangers recalled that final charge: "The enemy stood until we came near to bayonet points, then gave us a volley and retired across the Brandywine."

By now, Knyphausen had positioned "two heavy guns and two 3-pounders" on top of the hills leading to the marsh. His batteries pounded away at the retreating rebels while his infantry safely crossed the marsh in large numbers. But Maxwell's light infantry had done their job well, delaying the enemy's advance by keeping up "a running fire mixed with regular vollies for 5 miles ... untill they got almost within gun shot of the ford." About 10 o'clock, they waded the Brandywine to rejoin the main American position on the other side.

Knyphausen and Washington remained on their respective sides of Chadd's Ford for the next six hours, occasionally cannonading each other. Knyphausen marched his 6,800 troops back and forth around the hills to make Washington think he had the entire army with him. He would not attempt to cross the ford until he heard the signal indicating the British column of 8,200, under Howe and Cornwallis, had begun attacking the rebel army's right wing. In Howe's report to London the next day, he noted that Knyphausen "kept the enemy amused in the course of the day with cannon, and the appearance of forcing the ford, without intending to pass it, until the attack upon the enemy's right should take place."

Before noon, Washington received several messages apprizing him of the existence of a British flanking column. General John Sullivan, who commanded his right wing, west of Chadd's Ford, reported that Colonels James Ross and Moses Hazen had been scouting on the other side of the Brandywine as far as the Great Valley Road, below the river's forks. Just prior to 11:00 a.m., they had skirmished with advance parties of "a large body of the enemy, from every account five thousand, accompanied by General Howe." If it was true, Washington thought, Howe was making "a terrible blunder" by dividing his forces, leaving himself vulnerable to "defeat in detail."

Washington decided to take advantage of this opportunity. He would direct Generals Nathanael Greene and Anthony Wayne to cross Chadd's Ford and attack Knyphausen's division. Greene and Wayne would be supported by the Pennsylvania militia, which would cross at another ford downstream. Meanwhile, upstream, Sullivan would lead his division across Brinton's Ford and attack the rear of Howe's column on the Great Valley Road.

However, before this bold plan could be acted upon, another message arrived from Sullivan, stating that Major James Spear had been on the Great Valley Road and heard nothing of the enemy. Spear was "confident they are not in that quarter, so Colonel Hazen's information must be wrong." Why had this man not seen the enemy forces that Ross and Hazen saw? Perhaps it was bad timing, or the early morning "thick fog" that one British officer thought "contributed greatly to favour our march." Whatever the reason, General Washington chose to believe this latest report, although it contradicted the earlier ones. Major Spear's "reputation and knowledge of the country," Washington would later write, "gave him full claim to credit and attention." The American commander concluded that the earlier "movement of the enemy was but a feint, & that they were returning to reinforce Knyphausen at Chadd's Ford." So he called off both attacks, told Greene and Wayne to return to their defensive positions, and continued waiting for the big push at Chadd's Ford.

Just before two o'clock, a very large, dark complexioned man named Thomas Cheyney came riding hard into headquarters, shouting that the army must retreat or they will all be cut off. Though aides tried to quiet him, he kept shouting, demanding to speak to the commander in chief. Hearing the ruckus, the tall Virginian came out of the house and faced the man. He told Washington that he was a patriot, lived in the area, and had been out on his own doing some scouting all morning. The vanguard of a large British flanking column had seen him and fired at him, but he'd got away. They were a very large force and marching toward the right wing, from above the forks of the Brandywine.

Perhaps suspecting the man was a spy sent to deceive him, George Washington told him he must be wrong. Cheyney got down off his horse and quickly drew a rough map in the dirt, to illustrate where he had seen the enemy column, where they would cross, and the steep defile near it, where they could be ambushed. But the general still looked doubtful. Exasperated, Cheyney looked the big Virginian in the eye, and declared:

> You're mistaken, General. My life for it, you're mistaken. By hell! it's so. If you doubt my word, put me under guard till you can ask Anthony Wayne or Persie Frazer if I am a man to be believed. I would have you know that I have this day's work as much at heart as e'er a blood of you.

Just then, a rider reined in his horse and gave a note to Washington. It was from General John Sullivan again, this time informing him that an enemy column had been sighted west of Birmingham Meetinghouse. This information came from Theodorick Bland, who Washington had instructed late that morning to "send an intelligent, sensible officer ... to find out the truth." Sullivan's note:

> Two o'clock P.M.
> Dear General, Colonel Bland has this moment sent me word that the enemy are in the rear of my right about two miles, coming down. There are, he says, about two brigades of them. He also says he saw a dust back in the country for above an hour.

Convinced at last, Washington ordered Stirling and Stephen to march their brigades toward Birmingham Meetinghouse. There, they should take post on high ground, establish a defensive line, and hold off the enemy alone until Sullivan's arrival. He then ordered Sullivan to march to join Stirling and Stephen in their new dispositions.

Serving in the advance guard of Cornwallis's column, marching along the Great Valley Road, were some "pioneers" - axmen who would remove obstacles. But the elite fighting men were the Hessian *jagers* (sometimes called *chasseurs* by the British). They were led by their Captain, Johann Ewald. These were light troops, capable of fighting on foot or horseback, and carrying short German rifles rather than muskets. Thomas Sullivan commented on these foreign allies of his, while writing in his journal the previous summer:

> The chasseurs ... were always upon the flanks of the army, on the march; and in the front when they encamped. They hit a crown piece at 100 yards distance; and that for a dozen times together. They ... are so expert in shooting, that if an officer sees any of them miss the object he fires upon, they oblige them immediately to serve among the Hessian regiments, in the ranks, which they deem to be a very great punishment.
>
> The chasseurs in camp seldom drew any provisions except rum, they being always upon the flanks or in front, and having the plundering of every thing, which they do without scruple ... foraging for themselves.

After wading the three-foot deep second branch, two miles above the forks, Ewald halted his company. Here the road ascended up a long, winding, 35 degree slope before leveling off. Ewald explains:

> My guide asserted that if we did not meet with the enemy here, he must have been defeated by General Knyphausen, whose fire we had heard during the whole day. I was astonished when I had safely reached the end of this terrible defile which was over a thousand paces long, and could discover nothing of the enemy. Lord Cornwallis, who had followed me, was surprised himself and could not understand why the warning post with which I had fought [that] morning was not stationed here. The pass had been left wide open for us, where a hundred men could have held up either army the whole day.
>
> The advanced guard passed the defile and the entire army followed. A good quarter hour distant, or two thousand paces, Lord Cornwallis again came to me and ordered me to halt. The army then marched up, regiment behind regiment, and halted for about a half an hour, whereupon Adjutant General Ross brought me orders to proceed, and said to the jagers: "One more good hour's marching and you will eat Welsh hens. General Knyphausen has thoroughly beaten Washington."

Several curious Quakers, or as they preferred to be called, Friends, came out of their homes to see the spectacle: a European army filling up their fields. In their colorful uniforms, with their polished bayonets reflecting the bright sunlight "as bright as silver," they were so unlike the Whig army. Twenty-year-old Joseph Townsend later recalled:

> Admiring their appearance, we approached ... When a soldier under arms called out, "Where are you going?"

we replied "we wished to see the army, if there was no objection." Leave was readily obtained, and we found ourselves in the midst of a continual march of soldiers ...

The curious young Quaker spotted the mounted Lord Cornwallis, who "appeared tall, and sat very erect. His rich scarlet clothing loaded with gold lace epaulets occasioned a brilliant and martial appearance." But overall, Townsend thought the British officers were "rather short, portly men, well-dressed and of genteel appearance, and did not look as if they had ever been exposed to any hardship, their skins being as white and delicate as is customary for females."

Townsend and his companions came to a house and went in. The principal British officers, wanting to escape the hot sun, also entered the same house. They

were full of inquiries respecting the rebels. Brother William told them that, if they would have patience a short time, he expected they would meet with General Washington and his forces, who were not far distant. They inquired what sort of man Mr. Washington was. My brother replied that he was a stately, well proportioned, fine looking man of great ability, active, firm and resolute, of a social disposition, and was considered a good man ... to which one of them answered, "He might be a good man, but he was most damnably misled to take up arms against his sovereign."

My curiosity was increased; I invited James Johnson to accompany me, and we proceeded until we reached the advance guard who were of the German troops. Many of them wore their beards on their upper lips.

Cornwallis ordered the army to move out. The two Quakers found a spot with a good vantage point.

> We had a good view of the army as they advanced over Osburn's Hill. While we were amusing ourselves, to our great astonishment and surprise the firing of musketry took place. The advanced guard were fired upon by a company of the Americans ... [we] concluded it best to retire.

The initial firing these curious inhabitants had observed involved the Hessian jagers, led by their captain, Johann Ewald. Ewald continues his account:

> About half past three, I caught sight of some infantry and horsemen behind a village on a hill in the distance. I asked my guide what he thought about these guests, whereupon he replied [incorrectly] that this was surely a party covering the road to Chester, on which Washington was retreating. I said, "Good, we will attack the village," and rode over to Captain McPherson, whom I had to consult because he was the senior captain. I gave him my opinion, which he agreed with.
>
> I reached the first houses of the village with the flankers of the jagers, and Lieutenant Hagen followed me with the horsemen. But unfortunately for us, the time this took favored the enemy and I received extremely heavy small arms fire from the gardens and houses, through which however, only two jagers were wounded. Everyone ran back, and I formed them again behind the fences or walls at a distance of two hundred paces from the village. They shouted to me that the army was far behind, and I became not a little embarassed to find myself quite alone with the advanced guard. But now that the business had begun, I still wanted to obtain information about these people who had let me go so easily.
>
> I then took with me the mounted jager Hoffman, a

> very courageous fellow, and two Scots and tried to reach a hill which lay to the right of the village. I gazed in astonishment when I got up the hill, for I found behind it [on Birmingham Hill] - three to four hundred paces away - an entire line deployed in the best order, several of whom waved to me with their hats but did not shoot. I kept composed, examined them closely, rode back, and reported it at once to Lord Cornwallis by the jager Hoffman.

The long British column had, by now, advanced as far as Osburn's Hill, where they "formed in lines of brigades." As soon as each brigade formed, it sat down to eat the mid-day meal. Having by now marched 15 miles, they were tired. It was an unusually hot day for September, the thermometer already approaching 90 degrees. Captain William Scott noted that here the leader of the army joined the men.

> Sir Wm. Howe with the most cheerful countenance conversd with his officers and invited several to a light refreshment provided on the grass. The pleasing behavior of that great man on this occasion was to the satisfaction of all who beheld him. Every one that remembers the anxious moments before the engagement may conceive how animating the sight of the commander in chief [was], in whose looks nothing but security and confidence in his troops is painted.

When their half hour rest was over, orders went out to arrange the troops in battle formation. The British 1st Regiment's colonel gave a short, but effective speech to his men: "Grenadiers, put on your caps; for d----d fighting and drinking I'll match you against the world." From this hilltop, Howe would direct troop movements until he was satisfied with his dispositions, then he would ride down to be closer to the action. Cornwallis, observing the Americans on Birmingham Hill a mile and a half away, was heard to grudgingly remark, "The damn rebels form well." He was referring to the brigades of Stirling and Stephen, which had arrived and "formed two lines in good order." Howe gave the order to advance, and the musicians "played the *Grenadiers' March.*" Captain Muenchhausen provides an account of the initial action:

> At four in the afternoon our two battalions of light infantry and the Hessian jagers marched down the hill. They marched first in a column, but later, when they approached the enemy, in line formation, deploying to the left. Soon after this the English grenadiers did the same in the center, almost at the same time; just a little later, the English Guards formed the right wing.
>
> As soon as the third column had formed, the signal to march was drummed everywhere. When we got close to the rebels, they fired their cannon; they did not fire their small arms till we were within 40 paces of them, at which time they fired whole volleys and sustained a very heavy fire. The English, and especially the English grenadiers, advanced fearlessly and very quickly; fired a volley, and then ran furiously at the rebels with fixed bayonets.

The first contact involved Sullivan's division, while on the march to Birmingham Hill and still "half a mile" southwest of it. They were hard pressed by a regiment of Hessian grenadiers that Howe had thrown in to close up his lines when his right wing had gone too far toward the river. General Sullivan was not with his troops at this critical time, having ridden ahead to consult with Generals Stirling and Stephen atop Birmingham Hill. When fired upon, Sullivan's troops were in "a narrow lane" with no place to form, so they "countermarched through a gateway to the top of a hill, under a galling fire from the enemy - thus bringing their rear to the front." Within moments, 23 men from the regiment first hit lay dead in the lane. In this action, their colonel's horse threw him, leaving everything "in confusion," as one soldier put it, with "no person to reduce us to order."

Many of the men thought "a retreat had been ordered," because they saw some of their comrades take to their heels. The colonel had received no such order, and tried to make a stand. But he soon found himself with only a lieutenant and 30 men out of his original 220, so he "retired deliberately" in the direction his regiment had fled. Sullivan, observing all this from Birmingham Hill, sent four aides to help those officers trying to rally their men, but the men "could not be brought by their officers to do anything but fly." Stirling's and Stephen's troops, on the west slope of Birmingham Hill, opened their lines to let the fleeing men through, then closed the lines again to await the enemy. The panic had affected other regiments in Sullivan's division, too. Only 400 men, Hazen's "Canadian" regiment, stood firm and joined Stirling and Stephen on the hill. The other 800 from Sullivan's division didn't return to action that afternoon.

General Pruedhomme de Borre, acting as commander of the division in Sullivan's absence, could not stop the men from fleeing. Days after the battle, a member of Congress who had watched the battle called for de Borre to appear before a Congressional inquiry. The general resigned his commission and returned to France, offended that Congress would question his ability. The Congressman also called for Sullivan's resignation, but Washington wrote to Congress, supporting Sullivan and asking that they postpone indefinitely any investigation, because the army faced an imminent threat of another battle and would need Sullivan's services. Eventually he would be tried and exonerated.

The British now closed in on Birmingham Hill. To avoid the grapeshot coming from the American three- and four-pounders on the hill, some of the British regiments marched as close as they could to the American advanced party posted behind the compound of buildings around Birmingham Meetinghouse. At one point, British grenadiers, facing a "whole fire" from a line of rebel musketmen, quickly fell face down on the ground. They stayed down only long enough to fix bayonets, then stood up and charged.

One of the Americans, Captain Enoch Anderson, later recalled this part of the battle:

> Cannon balls flew thick and many from both sides, and small arms roared like the rolling of a drum for a considerable time, when the word was given again, "March, march to the right! The enemy wants to turn our right!"

Another American, Ebenezer Elmer, wrote that the action here was

> close and heavy for a long time, excessive severe [as] the enemy came on with fury. Our men stood firing upon them most amazingly, killing almost all before them for near an hour till they got within 6 rod of each other, when a column of the enemy came upon our right flank, which caused them to give way, which soon extended along ye whole line.

A British officer noted that they "pushed on with impetuosity" up Birmingham Hill, advancing against both American flanks.

> There was a most infernal fire of cannon and musketry; smoke; incessant shouting, "Incline to the right! Incline to the left! Halt! Charge!" The balls ploughing up the ground; the trees cracking over one's head, the branches riven by the artillery; the leaves falling as in autumn by grapeshot.

General Thomas Conway, an Irish-born veteran of the French Army now serving in the Continental Army, in all his years of combat "never saw so close and severe a fire." After an hour and three quarters of fighting, Sullivan was "obliged to abandon the hill we had so long contended for, but not till we had almost covered the ground between there and Birmingham meetinghouse with dead bodies of the enemy."

Forced from Birmingham Hill, Sullivan ordered new defensive positions be taken up on two hills not far behind it. Here the battle resumed "smart and hot, sometimes to the bayonet," recalled one American. "Five times did the enemy drive our troops from the hill, and as often was it regained, the summit often disputed almost muzzle to muzzle." They were standing firm - at least most of them. One who didn't, according to Enoch Anderson, was a surgeon "who had no business to fight" and should not have been on the battlefield:

> When the balls flew thickly [he] ran behind a tree and would then pop his head out and exclaim, "Thank God! I am safe yet!" He did this when he came, in succession, near several trees; until finally, thrusting out his head to look back as the army was retreating - a cannon ball took off his head. This settled all the Doctor's worldly concerns.

About 4:30 p.m., Howe ordered the signal guns be fired, "a sudden burst of cannon so loud that it was heard in Philadelphia," twenty-six miles away. Knyphausen heard it atop the hills overlooking Chadd's Ford and launched his assault across the river, against Washington's center. Nevertheless, by five o'clock Washington decided that his reserve - Greene's brigade - was needed more on the right wing than at Chadd's Ford. Soon after sending forth Greene, Washington decided to see for himself what was happening to his right wing. He did not have time to follow the roads, but sought a direct route through woods and pastures. A local resident named William Darlington explains:

> [Washington] was anxious to proceed thither by the shortest and speediest route. He found a resident of the neighborhood named Joseph Brown and asked him to go

as a guide. Brown was an elderly man and extremely loth to undertake that duty. He made many excuses, but the occasion was too urgent for ceremony. One of Washington's suite dismounted from a fine charger and told Brown if he did not instantly get on his horse and conduct the General by the nearest and best route to the place of action, he would run him through on the spot.

Brown thereupon mounted and steered his course towards Birmingham Meetinghouse with all speed - the General and his attendants being close at his heels. He said the horse leapt all the fences without difficulty, and was followed in like manner by the others. The head of General Washington's horse, he said, was constantly at the flank of the one on which he was mounted; and the General was continually repeating to him "Push along, old man. Push along, old man." When they reached the road, Brown said the bullets were flying so thick that he felt very uncomfortable; and as Washington now no longer required nor paid attention to his guide, the latter embraced the first opportunity to dismount and make his escape.

Washington took command and directed the placement of Greene's division in covering the retreat. With him was the recently arrived French volunteer, the Marquis de Lafayette, fighting in his first battle, five days after his 20th birthday. Earlier, at Birmingham Hill, riding back and forth to encourage Conway's men, the young Frenchman had been "favoured by a bullet" in his leg, but he kept on fighting.

Greene's reserves, covering "four miles in forty-five minutes," much of the time "at a trott," arrived too late to prevent the American retreat, but just in time to cover it. Opening their ranks, Greene's reserves let their exhausted comrades through to safety, then they closed ranks to oppose the oncoming regulars. They fell back to a heavily wooded defile, where they stood their ground for forty-five minutes, repeatedly turning back British and Hessian bayonet charges which, at times, reached the point of hand-to-hand combat. Here on Sandy Hill, a half mile from Dilworth, a New Jersey soldier was proud to see the retreat come to a halt and, "about sunset, we made a stand." Count Pulaski, a veteran of the Polish Army and another recently arrived volunteer in the cause, proposed that George Washington give him "command of his body guard, consisting of about 30 horsemen. Pulaski led them to the charge."

The sun went down as the fighting stopped, Greene finally forced from the pass by the increasing pressure of numbers. He turned now and hurried his troops down the road to Chester, to catch up with the rest of the fleeing army that they'd saved from annihilation.

During Greene's rear guard action, his subordinate, Colonel Peter Muhlenberg, was recognized by one of the Hessians as having once been their comrade in arms many years before in a previous war. As Muhlenberg led his regiment of continentals to the charge, his opponent joyfully alerted his fellow soldiers, "*Hier kommt Teufel Piet!* [Here comes Devil Pete!]"

Joseph Clark, who had quit the College of New Jersey in Princeton to fight for the cause, wrote that it was by Greene's "timely aid they made a safe retreat of the men, though we lost some pieces of artillery." Knyphausen's Hessians happily recaptured two guns the rebels had taken the previous December at Trenton. Not all was lost, though. Edward Hector, a Negro artillerist from Pennsylvania, saved a few wagonloads of ammunition and arms as the army withdrew.

Among the forces retreating was Anthony Wayne's brigade, falling back from Chadd's Ford to join the others. The British private, Thomas Sullivan, and his comrades, waded "up to our middle in the river" while "under a heavy fire of musquetry." They kept coming, though the rebels also "plaid upon us with four pieces of cannon." The British and Hessians under Knyphausen managed to ford the river, then force the defenders from their entrenchments with furious bayonet charges. Though outnumbered, Wayne's Pennsylvanians had provided Knyphausen with "obstinate resistance." According to a Hessian account,

Wayne's troops defended themselves "from wall to wall in the best way possible, constantly attacked from post to post by our gallant troops, and finally completely driven back over the hills toward Chester."

Sergeant Major John Hawkins of Congress's Own Regiment, like many a retreating soldier when pursued by the enemy, decided to increase his chances of survival by lightening his load.

> I lost my knapsack, which contained the following articles, viz: 1 uniform coat, brown faced with white; 1 shirt; 1 pair of stockings; 1 sergeant's sash; 1 pair knee buckles; 1/2 lb soap; 1 orderly book; 1 memo book of journal and state of my company; 1 quire paper; 2 vials ink; 1 brass inkhorn; 40 morning returns, printed blanks; 1 tin gill cup; a letter, and a book.
>
> The weather was very warm and though my knapsack was very light, [it] was very cumbersome, as it swung about when walking or running and in crossing fences was in the way, so I cast it away from me, and had I not done so would have been grabbed by one of the ill-looking Highlanders, a number of whom were firing and advancing very brisk towards our rear. The smoke was so very thick that about the close of the day I lost sight of our regiment and just at dark I fell in with the North Carolina troops and about two o'clock in the morning arrived at Chester.

When it was safe, the still curious Quaker, Joseph Townsend, came forward to view the carnage.

> When the engagement appeared to be nearly over and the day being on the decline, I proposed to some of my companions that we should go over to the field of battle and take a view of the dead and wounded, as we might never have such another opportunity. We hastened

thither, and awful was the scene to behold - such a number of fellow beings lying together severely wounded, and some mortally - a few dead, but a small proportion of them considering the immense quantity of powder and ball that had been discharged.

Some of the doors of the meeting house were torn off and the wounded carried thereon into the house to be occupied for an hospital. After assisting in carrying two of them into the house, I was disposed to see an operation performed by one of the surgeons, who was preparing to amputate a limb by having a brass clamp or screw fitted thereon, a little above the knee joint. He mentioned to his attendants to give [the patient] a little wine or brandy to keep up his spirits, to which he replied, "No, doctor ... my spirits are up enough without it." As I was listening to the conversation one of my companions caught me by the arm and mentioned that it was necessary to go out immediately, as they were fixing the picquet guards, and if we did not get away in a few minutes we should have to remain within the lines during the night. I instantly complied.

As the retreating Americans headed down the road toward Chester, General Howe called off the chase. His victorious troops were exhausted, and any further pursuit would be too risky because of the darkness. Once again, Howe had defeated Washington's army, but allowed it to escape. Captain Johann Ewald, who had seen this happen before at Long Island and Kip's Bay on Manhattan, confided to his journal a few days later, "I firmly believe that we still could have caught up with the greatest part of the enemy army ... if it had been the will of General Howe."

The retreating Joseph Clark saw "night coming on adding gloom to our misfortunes, amidst the noise of cannon, the hurry of people, and wagons driving in confusion from the field. I came off with a heart full of distress. In painful anxiety, I took with hasty step the gloomy path from the field, and traveled 15 miles to Chester, where I slept two hours upon a couple of chairs." By contrast, Timothy Pickering, a colonel from Massachusetts, thought it was "fortunate for us that the night came on, for under its cover the fatigued stragglers and some wounded made their escape." Enoch Anderson had a more positive reflection of the retreat, when he wrote about it years later:

> Here then we experienced another drubbing. But our army, wanting many things, also having a number of raw recruits, did, I think, as well as could be expected. We had our solacing words always ready for each other - "Come boys, we shall do better another time." Had any man suggested, merely hinted the idea of giving up - of relinquishing further opposition - he would have been knocked down, and if killed it would have been no murder!

The day's action almost saw an end to the life of the commander of the Continental Army, and perhaps with it the American cause. But, thanks to the honor of a British officer following the eighteenth century "rules of war," his life was spared. In the early morning, Washington and Lafayette had crossed Chadd's Ford to see firsthand the terrain where Maxwell's light infantry battalion would have to retard the enemy's advance. Captain Patrick Ferguson and his British sharpshooters were scouting ahead of Knyphausen's column. Ferguson explains the incident:

> We had not lain long when a rebel officer, remarkable by a hussar dress, passed towards our army within a hundred yards of my right flank, not perceiving us. He was followed by another dressed in dark green or blue, mounted on a bay horse, with a remarkably large cocked hat.

I ordered three good shots to steal near and fire at them. But the idea disgusted me. I recalled the order. The hussar in returning made a circuit, but the other passed again within a hundred yards of us, upon which I advanced from the woods towards him.

On my calling, he stopped, but after looking at me, proceeded. I again drew his attention and made signs to stop but he slowly continued his way. I could have lodged half-a-dozen balls in or about him before he was out of my reach. But it was not pleasant to fire at the back of an unoffending individual, who was acquitting himself very coolly of his duty, so I let him alone.

The day after, I had been telling this story to some wounded officers who lay in the same room with me, when one of my surgeons, who had been dressing the wounded rebel officers, came in and told us they had been informing him that General Washington was [in] the morning with the light troops and only attended by a French officer in a hussar dress, he himself dressed and mounted in every point as above described.

The Battle of Brandywine had been reminiscent of the Battle of Long Island in that, once again, the lack of a mobile communications force had resulted in the Americans being surprised by a British flanking column. But, this time, they proved that they could stand and fight on open ground against European regulars. Though outflanked and outnumbered, the Continental Army resisted the urge to panic, and troops were shifted from one position to another "with great speed and especially good order," according to Howe's Hessian adjutant, Captain Muenchhausen, who confided to his journal his own opinion that the "rebels fought very bravely."

Howe's army had suffered 543 killed, wounded and missing, while American casualties were twice that, including 315 deserters. But the American losses would be replaced within weeks by new recruits, something the British could not do. General Weedon, of Virginia, thought that one more such costly British "victory would establish the rights of America, and I wish them the honor of the field again on the same terms."

Howe had won the battle, but the rebel army had survived to fight another day. He had not captured Philadelphia yet. A battle-tested, more confident army would oppose him in his next battle for the rebel capital. After the Battle of Brandywine, General Nathanael Greene reflected on the resiliency of the Continental Army: "We fight, get beat, rise, and fight again."

CHAPTER THREE
MASSACRE AND LOSS OF A CAPITAL
SEPTEMBER 1777

"Before I came to the army, I entertained an exalted opinion of General Washington's military talents, but I have since seen nothing to enhance it."

- Colonel Timothy Pickering.

On September 13, 1777, two days after the Battle of Brandywine, the Continental Army stopped its retreat when it crossed over to the north bank of the Schuylkill River, near Philadelphia, and began entrenching at the most likely fording places. General Washington's General Orders that day:

HdQuars. German Town 13th Septr. 77
... The Hon'ble Congress, in consideration of the gallant behaviour of the troops on Thursday last, their fatigue since, & from a full conviction that on every future occasion they will manifest a bravery worthy the cause they have undertaken to defend, having been pleas'd to order 30 hogsheads of rum to be distributed among them in such a manner as the Commander in Chief shall direct, he orders the Commissary General to deliver to each officer & soldier one gill pr day while it lasts. ...

Washington wrote to his adversary, the British General William Howe, thanking him for his report on the condition of the American wounded left on the battlefield. And he gratefully accepted Howe's offer to have five American surgeons and their assistants come back and take over the care of their brethren.

Howe wanted to disemcumber himself of his own wounded, too, so he sent them along with the American wounded and doctors to nearby Wilmington. The day after the battle, his Hessian dragoons had taken that capital town, seizing rebel supplies and Delaware's rebel governor. Wilmington would now serve as a base for the British Navy in its mission to clear the river of rebel forts and other obstacles downriver from Philadelphia. Only then would General Howe be able to feed his army - assuming that his army could take the city. But first, he would probably have to do battle with Washington again.

Though the rebel army had lost more than one thousand men, between the casualties at the Brandywine and the inevitable desertions during the retreat afterward, reinforcements were slowly arriving. One of the recent arrivals in camp was a fourteen-year-old from North Carolina named Hugh McDonald. The son of Tory parents, Hugh had had no intention of joining the rebel party on that day, three months before, when they found him alone, plowing his father's field.

> Five men appeared on horseback at the fence, one of whom said, "Come, you must go with us to pilot us through the settlement, for we have a boy here who has come far enough. He is 6 miles from home and he is tired." I told [him] that I dare not go, for if I did, my father would kill me. ... Leading me by the hand, [he] put me on behind one of the company and discharged the other boy ... [Later] I was ordered to go home; I refused, and went with them, for I had told them the consequences of my going with them before they took me.

Hugh McDonald's party headed north to join Washington's main army. One day, the tedium of their march was interrupted by some humor at the expense of an obstreperous Tory.

> While we were passing through Richmond, a shoemaker stood in his door and cried, "Hurrah for King George!" No one took any notice. But after we halted in a wood a little distance beyond, where we cooked and ate our fish, the shoemaker came to us and began again to hurrah for King George. When the general and his aides mounted and started, he still followed them hurrahing for King George. Upon which the general ordered him to be taken back to the river and ducked. We brought him back and got a long rope, which we tied around his middle and seesawed him back and forth until we nearly had him drown; but every time he got his head above water he would cry for King George.
>
> The general having then ordered him to be tarred and feathered, a feather bed was taken from his own house, where were his wife and four likely daughters crying and beseeching their father to hold his tongue, but still he would not. We tore the bed open and knocked the head out of a tar barrel into which we plunged him headlong. He was drawn out by the heels and rolled in the feathers until he was a sight, but still he would hurrah for King George. The general now ordered him to be drummed out of the west end of town, and told him expressly that if he plagued him any more in that way he would have him shot. So we saw no more of the shoemaker.

They continued north, but stopped at Georgetown, Maryland, where they innoculated themselves with the smallpox. By the spring of 1777, Washington was insisting that this controversial practice be done by all new recruits before they reached camp. Innoculation involved cutting oneself - usually under a fingertip - then placing in the cut some smallpox germs taken from a pustule of an already infected sufferer. Hugh McDonald's party stayed there two weeks, waiting for the hopefully mild cases to develop and pass. He noticed that, in his whole brigade, only one soldier died during the quarantine period - a man "who, after he had got able to go about, imprudently went to swim in the Potomac, and next morning was dead."

Hugh McDonald reached the main army in time to see action at Brandywine. His company was among those posted at Chadd's Ford, where "our acute marksmen filled the ford with corpses and stained the pure stream of Brandywine crimson," before the company rereated with the rest of the army. They stopped, finally, at Chester.

> Some men had made their fires, got their kettles on, and drawn their provisions, others had not, when news came from the reconnoitering party that the British had left the battle ground and were marching toward Lancaster, where the Treasury and Congress had removed to. We were anxiously expecting our yesterday's breakfast, when the general came riding along, and in a mild and lovely manner, said to us, "Boys, we must fast today as well as yesterday. The British are going on to Lancaster where our all is, and we must try to head them, if we can, and frustrate their designs."
>
> We threw our kettles into the waggons, and by 4 o'clock in the evening we headed them at a place called White Horse Tavern. We ... drew our army in line across the road before the British. Then we took refreshments, the provision waggon coming to us that night about midnight.

At the White Horse Tavern, the army encamped for the night, three miles from the British camp. Howe had finally left the Brandywine early that morning, marching north to find his adversary. Just four days after his defeat, Washington was "determined to push the two columns forward and attack the enemy" the next morning, September

16th. His General Orders of the day before reflect his desire for the army to make a good showing in the coming battle:

> The Brigadiers or Officers commanding Reg'ts are also to post some good Officers in the rear to keep the men in order, & if in time of action any man who is not wounded, whether he has arms or not, turns his back on the enemy & attempts to run away or retreat before orders are given for it, those Officers are instantly to put him to death - the man does not deserve to live who basely flies, breaks his solemn engagements & betrays his country.

On the morning of the 16th, Howe's army advanced in two columns, as they had at Brandywine. That under Cornwallis set out at midnight, while Knyphausen's marched at dawn. Washington, informed of the enemy's advance about 9 a.m., ordered his own army to advance and meet them.

The vanguards started to skirmish, then a storm, which had been brewing for two days, finally broke above their heads with tremendous force. Hugh McDonald recalled, "In the morning, the advance guard fired two rounds, when there fell the heaviest rain that I ever saw before or since, which completely wet our ammunition." Major Bauermeister of the Hessians recorded that, "in a few minutes we were drenched and sank in mud up to our calves." His ally, Thomas Sullivan, noted, "We were all wet to our skin, and not able to fire a shot, our arms being very wet." Howe's regulars could not even press forward with their bayonets, because heavy winds were blowing the rain into their faces, so that they could not see for more than a few yards. Captain Muenchhausen noted the roads were "so bad that we simply had to stop." The artillery "remained three miles behind us."

Washington later explained to Congress why the attack had to be called off. "We had the mortification to find that our ammunition was entirely ruined." General Knox explained, in a letter to his wife, that

400,000 cartridges were damaged by the rain.

> This was a terrible stroke to us and owing entirely to the badness of the cartouche-boxes which had been provided for the army. This unfortunate event obliged us to retire, in order to get supplied with so essential an article as cartridges.

The boxes' lids were too narrow, allowing the rain to funnel into the interior of the boxes from both sides.

It was fortunate for Washington that the storm finally broke, curtailing the action. The British left wing, one of three columns marching to meet his own advance, had already scattered his own right wing, composed of militia who did not stand their ground. Behind the Continental Army was a steep embankment, and then very soft ground led to a river, so his army might have been routed or even captured if forced to retreat. If it came to hand-to-hand combat, the British, much better supplied with bayonets, would have had a decisive edge. Elias Dayton "much feared the ruen of the army ... [if] G. Howe advanced upon us in this situation. But fortunately for us he never mooved towerds us."

As it was, whether Washington knew he was in danger of being flanked or not, he ordered the army to fall back. So the Americans turned around, slid down the embankment, trudged through the quagmire leading to the river, waded across, and kept marching on (or through) the roads to Reading, where they would be able to replenish their ammunition. Lieutenant James McMichael, of Pennsylvania:

> At 3 o'clock we received marching orders and halted at 2 a.m., but remained under arms until daybreak. The rain fell in torrents for eighteen hours. This march, for excessive fatigue, surpassed all I ever experienced.

North Carolina's Hugh McDonald also noted the wearisome retreat:

After marching all day in the rain, we came late at night to a creek at the foot of a high hill. The front making a halt, I very well remember that the platoon in which I was, halted in the creek. Resting my head on the butt end of my musket, I fell asleep. The first thing I knew, I was punched by some one behind me, and my file leader had gone a hundred yards. This caused a trot in the whole line to fill the gap which my weariness had occasioned.

Here, at Reading, the men "stay'd all night on the brow of a hill without tents." The next morning, "We got paper and our wet powder, and drawing from the magazine one pound of fresh powder to every two damaged, we made our cartridges all anew." Washington took new measures to save what powder the men had. General Orders now included such particulars as "not one gun is to be fir'd in order to clean it," and "tin canteens serv'd out for the purpose of carrying ammunition."

They resumed their march, onward to Warwick and the north bank of the Schuylkill River, to again place themselves at likely fording places. In the three days since the aborted battle near White Horse Tavern, which was now being called the Battle of the Clouds, they had slogged 29 miles over muddy roads.

Howe, though, rested his army, moving it only eight miles east to Tredyffrin, just south of Valley Forge and west of the Schuylkill River. With the Continental Army away, an unprotected supply depot at Valley Forge was stumbled upon by a Hessian foraging party. They returned triumphantly to camp with "3800 barrels of flour, soap and candles, 25 barrels of horse shoes, several thousand tomahawks and kettles and intrenching tools."

Before crossing the Schuylkill a few miles north of Valley Forge, Washington had detached General Anthony Wayne's division - 1,500 men and four field pieces - to secret themselves in the wooded country in Howe's rear, with the aim of "cutting of[f] the enemy baggage" as soon as Howe moved forward to cross the Schuylkill. Unfortunately, a Tory informed General Howe of Wayne's bivouac, about two miles southwest of Paoli Tavern. Howe assigned General Charles Grey - soon to be known as "No Flint" Grey - to make a night attack on Wayne's camp. Grey's light infantry and dragoons set out on the evening of September 20th. Grey knew that, though the rebels had a reputation as good marksmen, they were vulnerable to hand-to-hand combat. Grey's aide, Captain John Andre, provides this account:

> No soldier was suffered to load. They took out the flints. We knew nearly the spot where the Rebel corps lay, but nothing of the disposition of their camp. It was represented to the men that firing discovered us to the enemy, hid them from us, killed our friends and produced a confusion favorable to the escape of the Rebels and perhaps productive of disgrace to ourselves. On the other hand, by not firing we knew the foe to be wherever fire appeared and a charge ensured his destruction: that amongst the enemy those in the rear would direct their fire against whoever fired in front, and they would destroy each other.
>
> Grey's detachment marched by the road leading to the White Horse [tavern] and took every inhabitant with them as they passed along. About three miles from camp they turned to the left and proceeded to the Admiral Warren [tavern] where, having forced intelligence from a blacksmith, they came in upon the out sentries, pickets and camp of the Rebels. The sentries fired and ran off.

Until they reached the American picquets, the British had moved as silently as possible through the dark forest, searching for Wayne's camp. They had been told the vicinity, but not the exact location.

Now that the Americans had fired on them, they charged at full speed, using the retreating sentries as guides. General Grey rode to the head of his column shouting, "Dash on, Light Infantry! Dash on!"

With the British still half a mile from camp, General Wayne quickly ordered the artillery to the rear, the light infantry to the front, and Colonel Humpton to form the main body on high ground to the left of camp. Wayne then rode forward to the front, where, looking back, he soon realized that the main body was not moving as directed. He sent back the order to Humpton twice more, but to no avail. The troops were moving in front of the campfires to the right and, in the process, silhouetting themselves for the charging British, who were closing now with their bayonets. Captain John Andre continues his account:

> On approaching the right of the camp we perceived the line of fires, and the light infantry being ordered to form to the front, rushed along the line putting to the bayonet all they came up with and, overtaking the main herd of the fugitives, stabbed great numbers and pressed on their rear till it was thought prudent to order them to desist.

Another British soldier reflected on the nighttime attack:

> We saw their wigwams or huts, partly by the almost extinguished light of their fires and partly by the light of a few stars, & the frightened, wretched rebels endeavoring to form. We then charged. For two miles we drove them, now and then firing scatteringly from behind trees, fences, &c. The flashes of their pieces had a fine effect in the night - then followed a dreadful scene of havoc. The light dragoons came on, sword in hand. The shrieks, groans, shouting, imprecations, the clashing of swords and bayonets, &c., &c. were more expressive of horror than the thunder of artillery on the day of action.

Wayne led a rear guard action to cover the retreat and managed to withdraw with his horses, cannons, ammunition wagons and the majority of his men. Although successful, the "Paoli Massacre" had not been the complete surprise that Grey had hoped for, because Wayne had ordered his men to be ready "to march at two o'clock in the morning. Thus most of his men were awake and dressed." Nevertheless, the Americans suffered heavy casualties. Though Wayne never reported his exact losses, estimates ranged from 167 to 380 killed, wounded and missing. Grey reported four killed and five wounded. According to Major Bauermeister's journal:

> The wounded were taken to nearby houses. General Washington was advised of this by a flag of truce, and given permission to send surgeons to dress their wounds.

The next day, the British went over the ground and picked up one thousand muskets left behind by the fleeing Americans. Months later, to stop negative talk in camp, Anthony Wayne would insist on being tried for his conduct at Paoli. At the court-martial, held in May 1778, Wayne would be acquitted "with the highest honors."

Because Wayne's defeat at Paoli relieved Howe of worry about his rear, he immediately set his army in motion again. Howe contrived a successful ruse to lure Washington away from the Schuylkill, so he could cross it unopposed. He did this by first heading north from Tredyffrin, toward the rebel depot at Warwick, instead of going south toward the easier fords closer to Philadelphia. To Washington, this seemed a "perplexing manoeuvre."

> This induced me to believe that they had two objects in view, one to get round the right of the army, the other, perhaps, to detach parties to Reading, where we had considerable quantities of military stores. To frus-

trate those intentions, I moved the army up the river, determined to keep pace with them; but early this morning I received intelligence that they had crossed the [lower] fords [behind us].

George Washington marched his Continental Army a total of fifteen miles before discovering that he had been tricked. William Howe had kept marching his men all night and, in a retrograde, returned to cross the river at one of the lower fords, scattering the defensive forces posted on the far side. After resting his army at Norristown on September 24th, he marched it to Germantown on the 25th. They made a lasting impression on one twelve-year-old resident, who many years later recalled the British troops marching into the village:

> Like a vast machine in perfect order, the army moved in silence, there was no display of colours, not a sound of music. There was no violence and no offense. Men occasionally dropped out of line, asked for milk or cider.

The next day, Howe gave Cornwallis the honor of taking one quarter of the army for a triumphant march into Philadelphia, his musicians playing *God Save the King* "amidst the acclamation of some thousands of the inhabitants, mostly women and children." One Philadelphian could not help but stare at the fearsome Hessians, adorned with "terrific mustachios," while the British troops exhibited a "tranquil look" of "dignified experience."

As to the whereabouts of the city's rebels, Captain John Andre guessed that "a great many desperadoes have withdrawn" to the countryside, perhaps to join the rebel army. With the British Army's arrival in town, a Tory newspaper declared an end to Whig tyranny. "Numbers who have been obliged to hide themselves, to avoid being forced into measures against their conscience, have reappeared to share the general satisfaction and to welcome the dawn of returning liberty."

But not everyone welcomed the British and Hessian regulars. Captain Ewald of the jagers was not pleased by the reception he received as he rode through Germantown on his way to Philadelphia.

> The inhabitants are mostly Germans but are against us ... [and] could hardly conceal their anger and hostile sentiments. One old lady, sitting on a bench before her front door, answered me in pure Palatine German when I rode up to her and asked for a glass of water. "Water I will give you, but I must also ask you: What harm have our people done to you, that you Germans come over here to suck us dry and drive us out of house and home? We have heard enough here of your murderous burning. Will you do the same here as in New York and in the Jerseys? You shall get your pay yet!"

The New England delegates in Congress tended to blame the loss of the capital on its being in "the very regions of passive obedience." John Adams explained, in a letter to his wife, Abigail, that, "The whole country through which [Howe's] army passed is inhabited by Quakers." Elbridge Gerry, also from Massachusetts, agreed, in a letter to Connecticut's governor: "The loss of Philadelphia was unexpected, and had it been in any other state than Pennsylvania, Delaware or Maryland, I question whether it would have happened."

At Bethlehem, where the Marquis de Lafayette was recuperating from his Brandywine leg wound (the doctor being personally ordered by George Washington to "treat him as if he were my own son"), he wrote a reassuring letter to his teenage wife, Adrienne, in Paris:

> I must give you a lesson, as the wife of an American officer. ... [Your friends] will say to you, "They have been beaten." You will answer, "That's true, but ... they had the pleasure of killing very many more of the enemy than they lost themselves."

After that they will add, "That's all right, but Philadelphia is taken, the capital of America, the rampart of liberty." You will reply politely, "You are fools. Philadelphia is a sorry city ... which the residence of Congress has somehow or other made famous ... which, by the way, we shall make them return sooner or later."

If they continue to press you with questions, you will send them on their way.

Washington rested his exhausted army thirty miles upriver from Philadelphia, at Pennypacker's Mill. They had marched 140 miles in the last eleven days. Thousands of them had no tent or blanket at night, having left these on the Brandywine battlefield. Nearly a thousand men also had completely worn out their shoes and were now wearing rags wrapped around their feet.

Congress, before departing the city, had given Washington emergency powers for 60 days, "to take, wherever he may be, all such provisions and other articles as may be necessary for the subsistence of the army ... paying or giving certificates for the same." He was loathe to obtain supplies in this way, but Congress could not provide enough for his army, and the chilly nights were already foretelling a harsh winter ahead. So, prior to Howe reaching Philadelphia, Washington had sent his aide, Alexander Hamilton, there to "produce from the inhabitants contributions of blankets and clothing, with as much delicacy and discretion as the nature of the business demands." But Hamilton discovered the Whigs had already "parted with all they could spare," and the Tories and neutral Quakers "hid their goods the moment the thing took wind." Hamilton's foragers then tried the countryside, but with no better luck.

On September 28th, news arrived of Gates's victory at the first battle of Saratoga. This provided a shocking contrast to Washington's results at Brandywine and along the Schuylkill. Timothy Pickering, his adjutant from Salem, Massachusetts, discussed it with Rhode Island's Nathanael Greene, one of Washington's most trusted generals.

"Before I came to the army," Pickering commented, "I entertained an exalted opinion of General Washington's military talents, but I have since seen nothing to enhance it." Greene agreed that "the General does want decision." Baron de Kalb, recently arrived from Europe, wrote home about this time: "In my opinion, whatever success he may have will be owing to good luck and to the blunders of his adversaries. I may even say that he does not know how to improve upon the grossest blunders of the enemy."

These were honest opinions, no doubt, but probably unfair. Washington proved at Trenton and Princeton his ability to take advantage of his opponent's mistakes. He now learned, from intercepted letters, that Howe was once again dividing his forces: 3,000 were sent south to escort supplies overland from Head of Elk; 3,000 more had gone east, across the Delaware River to New Jersey, to commence operations against rebel forts downriver from the city; and another 3,000 were billeted within Philadelphia. The remaining 9,000 troops were sent six miles north, to the village of Germantown, where they would establish camp between the city and the rebel army.

Captain John Andre was pleased with the capture of the rebel capital, but knew that his British Army fared better when it was actively campaigning, not in a stationary camp.

> Moving and pushing distracts and demolishes these people. When we lay still, their treacherous engines go to work; they get intelligence; they harass us and retrieve their own losses.

Indeed, since James Allen was noting that "women are suffered to go in and out of the city without inquiry," a very active rebel spy ring was supplying George Washington with good intelligence about the British Army's dispositions in and around the city. Enough to encourage the rebel commander in chief to plan a surprise attack.

CHAPTER FOUR
WASHINGTON COUNTERATTACKS:
GERMANTOWN, OCTOBER 1777

"By this time General Howe had come up, and seeing the battalion retreating, all broken, he got into a passion and exclaimed, 'For shame, Light Infantry! I never saw you retreat before. Form! Form! It's only a scouting party.' However, he was soon convinced it was more than a scouting party, as the heads of the enemy columns soon appeared. ... three pieces of cannon in their front immediately fired at the crowd that was standing with General Howe under a large chestnut tree. ... we really all felt pleased to see the enemy make ... the grape rattle about the commander in chief's ears, after he had accused the battalion of having run away from a scouting party. He rode off immediately full speed."

- British Lieutenant Martin Hunter.

Just as Colonel Rall had failed to entrench at Trenton the previous December, Howe did not adequately dig in at Germantown, lest his enemy view it as a sign of weakness. By October 2nd, bolstered by the arrival of 4,000 militia from Virginia and the Jerseys the day before, George Washington advanced his army to within 15 miles of Germantown, and called another council of war. Now he renewed his proposal of five days before, to attempt another Trenton. This time, his generals, more confident, gave him their unanimous approval.

The plan of attack for what would become known as the Battle of Germantown was patterned after Cannae, Hannibal's victory over the Romans in 216 B.C. It entailed a great pincers movement by four converging columns - two in a frontal attack, and two others that would get in the enemy's flanks and rear. Washington anticipated a "decisive and glorious" victory here, which, coupled with Gates's recent success against Burgoyne, might end the war.

It certainly was an ambitious plan, probably too much so for a relatively inexperienced army. Success would require all four American columns to reach their objective at about the same time, so Washington uncharacteristically gave each of his division leaders very detailed written instructions.

Early on the morning of October 3rd, the troops were issued "two days cooked provisions and forty rounds of ammunition" per man, and at noon, "the sick were sent to Bethlehem." Lt. James McMichael, writing in his journal, concluded it all "indicates that a sudden attack is intended."

The commander in chief's General Orders, read to the troops that same day, included an inspirational preamble which appealed to each soldier's pride, heroism and honor:

> ... This army, the main American Army, will certainly not suffer itself to be outdone by their northern brethren ...Covet! my countrymen and fellow soldiers! Covet! a share of the glory due to heroic deeds! Let it never be said, that in a day of action, you turned your backs on the foe. Let the enemy no longer triumph.
>
> ... [Your enemies] brand you with ignominious epithets. Will you patiently endure that reproach? Will you resign your parents, wives, children and friends to be the wretched vassals of a proud, insulting foe? And your own necks to the halter?

Setting out at 8 o'clock, the evening of October 3rd, each soldier marched with "a piece of white paper in his hatt." After marching ten miles or more, the columns were "to get within two miles of the enemy's picquets on their respective routs by 2 oclock and there halt till four." Then, covering the remaining two miles in an hour, each column was "to attack the picquets in their respective routs precisely at 5 oclock with charg'd bayonets without fireing, and the column to move on to attack as soon as possible." To ensure all this critical coordination of movements, the columns were "to communicate with each other from time to time by light horse."

As events would turn out, the extreme flanking columns would not be significantly engaged. Their objectives depended on the enemy outposts in their path either being overwhelmed or drawn off to help Howe in the center; and neither of those scenarios materialized.

The American center was composed of two large columns - the "left wing" under Greene, and a "right wing" under Sullivan. Greene, with nearly half the army, arrived a half hour later than Sullivan, because Greene's guide "mistook the way, so that although the right wing halted a considerable time, yet it attacked first, though later than intended."

Greene's division, marching a less direct route than Sullivan's, was perhaps also slowed by the poor visibility caused by the cloudy sky and an early morning dense fog. One of the men in his vanguard was Joseph Plumb Martin, a private from Connecticut.

> When I arrived at camp it was just dark, the troops were all preparing for a march. Their provisions (what they had) were all cooked, and their arms and ammunition strictly inspected and all deficiencies supplied. Early in the evening we marched in the direction of Philadelphia. We naturally concluded there was something serious in the wind. We marched slowly all night. In the morning there was a low vapor lying on the land which made it very difficult to distinguish objects at any considerable distance. About daybreak our advanced guard and the British outpost came in contact.

It was dawn now, and gunfire could be heard two miles to the west, where Sullivan's van was already in contact with other British picquets. So Greene's van did not catch anyone by surprise as they advanced down the Limekiln Road. Joseph Plumb Martin continues his account:

> The curs [muskets] began to bark first and then the bulldogs [artillery]. Our brigade moved off to the right into the fields. We saw a body of the enemy drawn up behind a rail fence on our right flank; we immediately formed in line and advanced upon them. Our orders were not to fire till we could see the buttons on their clothes, but they were so coy that they would not give us an opportunity to be so curious, for they hid their clothes in fire and smoke before we had time to examine their buttons.
>
> They soon fell back and we advanced ... They left their kettles, in which they were cooking their breakfasts, on the fires, and some of their garments were lying on the ground which the owners had not time to put on.

Before Greene's contact on the Limekiln Road, Sullivan's division, coming straight down the Skippack Road which led into the heart of Germantown and the British camp, made contact with British picquets first on Chestnut Hill and then at Beggarstown (Mount Airy). Anthony Wayne was in the center, and his Pennsylvanians were eager to avenge the Paoli Massacre. He had written to his wife in the morning, predicting that before darkness fell he would be "entering Philadelphia at the head of troops covered with laurels." Wayne encountered stiff resistance at Mt. Airy, closer to town, because Howe had recently placed a regiment of light infantry there. Howe had warned them that an attack was imminent, having himself been alerted just the day before, by Captain Johann Ewald. A citizen had told Ewald to "be on your guard to-night and to-morrow." Lieutenant Sir Martin Hunter describes the early action at Mount Airy:

> General Wayne commanded the advance, and expected to be fully revenged for the surprise that we had given him. When the first shots were fired at our pickets, so much had we all Wayne's affair in remembrance, that the battalion was out and under arms in a minute. At this time the day was just broke; but it was a very foggy morning, and so dark that we could not see a hundred yards before us. Just as the battalion had formed, the pickets came in and said that the enemy were advancing in force.
>
> They had hardly joined the battalion when we heard a loud cry of "Have at the bloodhounds; revenge Wayne's affair!" and they immediately fired a volley. We gave them one in return, cheered, and charged. ... On our charging they gave way on all sides, but again and again renewed the attack with fresh troops and greater force. We charged them twice, till the battalion was so reduced by killed and wounded that the bugle was sounded to retreat; indeed, had we not retreated at the very time we did, we should have all been taken or killed, as the enemy nearly got around our flanks. But this was the first time we had retreated before the Americans, and it was with great difficulty we could get our men to obey our orders.

Delaware's Captain Enoch Anderson also remembers the action at Mount Airy:

> We pushed down all fences in our front and marched to the battle. It was a very foggy morning. Bullets began to fly on both sides. Some were killed, some wounded, but the order was to advance. We advanced in line of the division. The firing on both sides increased and, what with the thickness of the air and the firing of

> guns, we could see but a little way before us.
> My position in the line brought me and my party opposite the British infantry behind a small breastwork, and here began the hardest battle I was ever in, at thirty feet distance. Firing from both sides was kept up for some time, all in darkness. My men were falling very fast. I now took off my hat and shouted as loud as I could, "Charge bayonets and advance!" They did so, to a man. The British heard me and run for it.

Wayne's men rushed upon their enemy, eager to show that they, too, knew how to wield deadly bayonets. In a letter to his wife two days after the battle, Wayne described this charge on Mt. Airy: "Our officers exerted themselves to save many of the poor wretches who were crying for mercy, but to little purpose. The rag'd fury of the soldiers was not to be restrained for some time - at least until a great number of the enemy fell by our bayonet." Howe's Hessian adjutant, Freidrich Muenchhausen, "arrived just at that time, and was astounded to see something I had never seen before, namely the English in full flight."

By now, General Howe, whose headquarters was in Germantown, had sent forward two brigades of infantry up the Skippack Road to reinforce the light infantry who had fought so well at Mount Airy. Sir Martin Hunter continues his account:

> The enemy were kept so long in check that the two brigades ... [advancing nearly to Mt. Airy] met our battalion retreating. By this time General Howe had come up, and seeing the battalion retreating, all broken, he got into a passion and exclaimed, "For shame, Light Infantry! I never saw you retreat before. Form! Form! It's only a scouting party." However, he was soon convinced it was more than a scouting party, as the heads of the enemy columns soon appeared.

One, coming with three pieces of cannon in their front, immediately fired at the crowd that was standing with General Howe under a large chestnut tree. I think I never saw people enjoy a discharge of grape before, but we really all felt pleased to see the enemy make such an appearance, and to hear the grape rattle about the commander in chief's ears, after he had accused the battalion of having run away from a scouting party. He rode off immediately full speed.

They retreated to Germantown. Shouting "repeated huzzahs," the Americans drove the British light infantry back "two full miles." The "Light infantry ammunition being almost expended, Lt. Colonel Thomas Musgrave, who had been sparing of his ammunition, told the light infantry that he would cover their retreat, which he did in a most masterly manner till he arrived at his old encampment," Benjamin Chew's estate. The Light Infantry escaped, but Musgrave, finding himself surrounded, ordered his men to take refuge inside Chew's large stone house. Sullivan's division moved past Musgrave's men, who fired at them from the second story windows, but without effect due to the fog.

General Howe formed his various brigades along Schoolhouse Lane to oppose the advance of Sullivan's division. He also sent word to Philadelphia to have Cornwallis come forward with his 3,000 men, including a large force of cavalry. Now was the time for the American reserve, which had been marching behind Sullivan on the Skippack Road, to come up and join the battle. The same was true of Greene's division, which was not making swift enough progress coming down the Limekiln Road. The two flanking parties had so far not been heard from: Armstrong, with 1,500 militia, was being stopped by 300 Hessians near the Schuylkill; and Smallwood, on the extreme left, was doing battle with a regiment of Tories, the Queen's Rangers.

Soon the American reserve arrived at the Chew house. Seeing the action there, General Stirling halted to await instructions from Washington. At this critical moment, General Henry Knox, Washington's well-read chief of artillery, convinced him that the reserve must stay and reduce the Chew mansion. "Never leave an enemy castle in the rear," he declared in his great stentorian voice.

An adjutant's assistant was sent forward carrying a white flag and a summons to surrender. Before reaching the house he received a fatal wound from an upper floor window. So, as the jager, Johann Ewald, later remarked, "the usually so-called 'Clever Washington' immediately attacked the house with several brigades and artillery ... [when] he should have used a battalion for it and continued his advance." Major Benjamin Tallmadge, who later wrote that Musgrave's holed up forces "would have been harmless if we had passed them by," was disgusted by "the importunity of General Knox," which resulted in 300 American casualties for no purpose.

An anonymous British officer describes Musgrave's defense of the Chew house with just 120 infantry against Knox's artillery, Maxwell's sharpshooters, and a host of other foes:

> Colonel Musgrave found himself entirely surrounded, and all means of retreating cut off. ... The rebels pressed so close upon their heels that they must inevitably have entered the house at the same time if he had not faced the regiment about and given them a fire which checked them enough for him to have time to get his regiment into the house and shut the door.
>
> Musgrave ordered all the window shutters of the ground floor to be shut, as the enemy's fire would otherwise have been too heavy there. He placed, however, a certain number of men at each window, and at the hall doors, with orders to bayonet everyone who should attempt to come in. He disposed of the rest in the two upper stories, and instructed them to cover themselves, and direct their fire out of the windows.
>
> He then told them "their only safety was in the de-

fence of that house; that if they let the enemy get into it, they would undoubtedly every man be put to death; that it would be an absurdity for anyone to think of giving himself up with hopes of quarter; that their situation was nevertheless by no means a bad one, as there had been instances of only a few men defending a house against numbers; that he had no doubt of their being supported and delivered by our army; but that at all events they must sell themselves as dear as possible to the enemy."

By this time the rebels had brought up four pieces of cannon (three-pounders) against the house, and with the first shot they burst open the hall doors, and wounded some men with the pieces of stone that flew from the wall. Captain Hains, a brave intelligent officer, who commanded on the ground floor, reported to Colonel Musgrave what had happened, and that he had thrown chairs, tables and any little impediments he could before the door, and that he would endeavor to keep the enemy out as long as he had a single man left. He was very soon put to the test, for the rebels directed their cannon (sometimes loaded with round, sometimes with grape shot) entirely against the upper stories, and sent some of the most daring fellows from the best troops they had, to force their way into the house under cover of their artillery. To do them justice, they attacked with great intrepidity, but were received with no less firmness. The fire from the upper windows was well directed and continued. The rebels, nevertheless, advanced and several of them were killed with bayonets getting in at the windows and upon the steps, attempting to force their way at the door.

The thick stone walls "proved too strong for the metal of our field pieces," an American officer later admitted, and the attempts to force entry were also futile. After the battle, a witness inspected the house and found that the inside "looked like a slaughter house because of the blood scattered around." He "counted seventy-five dead Americans, some of whom lay stretched in the doorways, under the tables and chairs, and under the windows." Washington had wasted not only many American lives here, but also "upwards of an hour," needlessly giving Howe time to compose his army and prepare a counterattack.

Hugh McDonald was in Francis Nash's North Carolina brigade, part of Stirling's reserve division that halted at the Chew house. Here he saw General Nash (for whom Nashville is named) killed. Hugh also saw a captain named Armstrong hit by a split musket ball that lodged in his shin bone. "We afterwards called him 'Hickory Shins,' making out that the shin had cut the ball." Hugh also recalled that during the investiture of the Chew house, Washington and his aides

> were riding in front of us, when an illbred soldier by the name of John Brantly, a native of Deep River, N.C., who had picked up a jug of wine in the course of the day, seeing General Washington coming by, dropt his musket and went to meet him, saying, "Won't you drink some wine with a soldier?"
>
> The General said, "My God, boy, there is no time for drinking wine."
>
> "God Almighty d--n your proud soul," says the soldier, "You are above drinking with soldiers." On hearing which, the general put his chestnut sorrel about suddenly, saying, "Come, I will drink with you."
>
> Brantly then gave him the jug, which he put to his mouth and handed back.
>
> "Give it to your servants," says the soldier, meaning his aides. They all applied it to their lips and returned it. "Now," says the soldier, "I'll be d----d if I don't spend the last drop of my heart's blood for you," and the general proceeded on his way.

Greene's division, the American center's left wing, finally arrived, having forced their way through the British outpost at Luken's Mill on the Limekiln Road. They encountered stiff resistance from General Grant, the right-most brigade of Howe's line of defense, strung out along Schoolhouse Lane. But Greene's men were too much for them and forced them back nearly to the crossroads at the center of Germantown. Though an hour late, Greene was finally about to connect with Sullivan. Despite the non-appearance of the flanking columns of Armstrong and Smallwood, the Americans were now in position to overwhelm Howe's center. Washington, about this time, was finally deciding to stop the futile assault on the Chew house and push on with the reserve, which he ordered Stirling to form for the march into Germantown.

Suddenly, everything fell apart and the "glorious victory, fought for and eight tenths won, was shamefully but mysteriously lost." There were several developments at this time that caused the sudden American retreat. Adam Stephen, general from Virginia, marching down the Limekiln Road in Greene's division, had heard the artillery and musket fire to the west, near the Chew house, and, without orders from Greene, diverted his troops to the right instead of continuing to follow Greene. Wayne, near the center of Germantown, had also heard the firing in his rear and, not knowing that the reserve was firing on the Chew house, thought Sullivan was being attacked from behind. So he faced his brigade about and marched to the rear to support Sullivan.

The early morning mist had turned into what Elias Dayton termed "the thickest fog known in the memory of man, which together with the smoke brought on allmost midnight darkness." There was no wind to carry away the smoke, and by this point in the battle, it "was not possible to distinguish friend from foe for five yards distance." Washington later reported that not until after the battle was over did anyone know "how near we were to gaining a complete victory." Howe's best ally was indeed the fog. Washington saw it as an extreme annoyance on many counts:

> This circumstance, by concealing from us the true situation of the enemy, obliged us to act with more caution and less expedition, and gave the enemy time to recover from the effects of our first impression; and, which was still more unfortunate, it served to keep our different parties in ignorance of each other's movements, and hinder their acting in concert. It also occasioned them to mistake one another for the enemy.

Not surprisingly, Stephen's troops and Wayne's closed, and each mistook the other for the enemy. Stephen's men fired first. Wayne's returned fire. Within minutes, both forces started retreating away from Germantown, despite their officers' efforts to stop them.

Their departure gave the officers in the center of the British line time to collect and form their troops. And, because neither flank had yet been harassed by Armstrong or Smallwood, Howe was free to deploy his forces in a counteroffensive. He sent part of Grant's brigade to attack Sullivan's left, while Grey's brigade moved against his right. With Wayne gone off to the rear, Sullivan's men were left unsupported, and Greene's front was still several hundred yards away. One soldier recalled that, by now, Sullivan's troops "had expended their ammunition. Some of the men unadvisedly calling out that their ammunition was spent, the enemy were so near that they overheard them" and took advantage with a bayonet charge.

An officer called out, "We are surrounded! We are surrounded!" and the flight was on. They turned and ran "with as much precipitation as they had before advanced." Washington tried to halt them, in the process "exposing himself to the hottest fire," as he had at Kip's Bay a year earlier, but to no avail. The British did not at first pursue Sullivan, but turned and converged on Greene. Without support, he too was forced to retreat. Soon after, Smallwood's flanking column arrived, but, seeing the rout, they turned back, too.

Perhaps because of chafing, or just because the day was "very warm," Hugh McDonald noticed that some men "pulled off their pantaloons in order to run the better." Though the retreat at first was rapid, it slowed and "everybody marched at his own pace" once they realized that the British were not seriously pursuing them. Cornwallis's cavalry arrived from Philadelphia and gave chase but, after a brief skirmish with Pulaski's dragoons, they kept at a comfortable distance, and eventually turned back. The Americans stopped to rest on Chestnut Hill, then kept on until they reached their former campground at Pennypacker's Mill. They were exhausted. James McMichael, suffering "unspeakable fatigue," felt like dropping. "I should have remained on the road all night, had it not been for the fear of being taken prisoner." Enoch Anderson noted that, coupled with the previous night's 16 mile march, this 24 mile retreat meant "we old soldiers had marched forty miles. We eat nothing and drank nothing but water on the tour."

Howe's army suffered 535 killed and wounded. American losses were 673 killed and wounded, with an additional 438 captured. And one must add to these, Muenchhausen wrote, the numbers "who normally run away into the country when their forces take a whipping." General Adam Stephen, who had left the intended route and fired on Wayne's brigade, was court-martialled and cashiered from the army. According to Hugh McDonald, Stephen was "sentenced to go home to his plantation with a wooden sword, for his drunkenness and disobedience." McDonald also noted the misdeed of a future Governor of North Carolina, Alexander Martin:

> [Colonel] Alexander Martin ... seeing a soldier slip into a hollow gum tree ... ordered him to come out or be run through with his sword. The soldier obeyed, and our gallant colonel took shelter from danger in his place, which was proved on him the next day in court martial, and he was sent home to Hillsboro with a wooden sword. ...
>
> These officers who were dismissed proved very useful

in North Carolina ... taking Tory companies who were in gangs through the state. These gentlemen proved more useful to their own state than they could have been to their country, had they been retained in the army.

Two days after the battle, George Washington returned one of the British missing in action, with a personal note to the British commander:

> General Washington's compliments to General Howe. He does himself the pleasure to return his dog, which accidentally fell into his hands, and by the inscription on the collar, appears to belong to General Howe.

Captain Johann Ewald credited Colonel Musgrave's "courage and decision" at the Chew house with saving the army and Howe's career. "For had the English army been defeated here ... all honor truly would have been lost, through the negligence of the Commanding General." But the American Colonel William Heth thought that the fog was the decisive factor:

> The heavy smoke, added to a thick fog, was of vast injury to us. It undoubtedly increased the fear of some to fancy themselves flanked and surrounded, wh[ich] like an electrical shock seized some thousands, who fled in confusion, without the appearance of an enemy.
>
> What makes this inglorious retreat more grating is that we now know the enemy had orders to retreat and rendezvous at Chester; that upwards of 2000 Hessians had actually crossed the Schuylkill for that purpose; that the Torys were in the utmost distress and moveing out of the city; that our friends confined in the New-Gaol made it ring with shouts of joy; that we passed in pursuing them [into Germantown] upwards of twenty pieces

of cannon, their tents standing filled with the choicest baggage.

Washington wrote Congress that the results of the mixed up battle were "unfortunate rather than injurious. Our troops, who are not in the least dispirited by it, have gained what all young troops gain by being in actions." Thomas Paine agreed with Virginia's General Weedon, who wrote, "Though the enterprise miscarried, it was worth the undertaking." Paine felt that men must learn fighting "by practice and by degrees." The soldiers in his regiment "seemed to feel themselves more important after, than before, as it was the first general attack they had ever made." A few days later, Anthony Wayne informed Washington:

> The men are convinced that the enemy may be driven. Our people have gained confidence, and have raised some doubts in the minds of the enemy, which will facilitate their total defeat in the next trial.

Colonel William Heth spoke for many, when he wrote:

> Tho we gave away a victory, we have learned this valuable truth: to beat them with vigorous exertion, and that we are far superior in point of swiftness.
>
> We are in high spirits. Every action gives our troops fresh vigor and a greater opinion of their own strength. Another bout or two must make [Howe's] situation very disagreeable.

CHAPTER FIVE
FIGHT FOR THE DELAWARE
OCTOBER - NOVEMBER 1777

"Tell your general that Germans are not afraid to face death."

- Colonel Carl von Donop, arguing for the honor of leading the attack against Fort Mercer.

Indeed, William Howe would find his situation very disagreeable if he could not feed his army or replenish other critical supplies. Though his army had taken possession of Philadelphia, his navy and its supply ships could not yet reach the city, because of rebel forts and other obstacles downriver. George Washington knew that his adversary must open the Delaware River to shipping before winter. Otherwise, Howe would have to evacuate the city and return to New York. As George Washington put it, for General Howe, "the acquisition of Philadelphia may, instead of his good fortune, prove his ruin." Such humiliation, coupled with Burgoyne's failure on the Hudson, might be enough to dissuade Parliament from further support of this costly war.

Part of the American defenses consisted of the Pennsylvania Navy: a half dozen lightly armed ships, plus a dozen row galleys of one 18-pounder each, a couple floating batteries, and some fire ships. The whole was under the command of Commodore John Hazelwood, a longtime resident of Philadelphia who was appointed to the post because of his "knowledge of the river," having spent years piloting merchant vessels through the dangerous shoals of the Delaware.

The sole Continental Navy warship on the river, the frigate *Delaware*, which was the Americans' most powerful ship, had already been lost to the enemy on September 27th, the day after the British occupied Philadelphia by land. Its Continental Navy captain had sailed upriver and approached the city's shoreline, under orders from Hazelwood to warn the British establishing batteries there to depart, or else risk the burning of the city. But, against orders, instead of delivering the message, he started firing broadsides at the British. Equal to the task, they fired back with vigor. The cook of the *Delaware* "had his head taken off by a cannon ball," and the frigate caught fire in three places. "The people were thrown into great disorder, neglected the management of the sails, and she ran aground" directly opposite the British batteries. Her crew soon struck her colors and abandoned ship.

Acting quickly, a handful of grenadiers rowed over to the *Delaware* to douse the flames and save the ship. When high tide came, they managed to free the frigate from the sandbar. Now the British had their own armed frigate to use in controlling the upper Delaware in the vicinity of the city. This would allow Howe's army freedom of movement across the river, a key factor when it would come time to attack rebel positions on the New Jersey side.

All the American defenses were downriver from Philadelphia. Besides the Pennsylvania Navy, there were three forts and two sets of underwater obstacles known as *chevaux-de-frise*. These were large wooden cratelike structures. After construction, they were towed out to the river's channel and weighted down with stone until they sank to the bottom. Strong beams projected upward from them at a 45 degree angle, so that their tips were about four feet below the water at low tide. Forged iron spikes were securely fastened to these tips. If a wooden-hulled warship came sailing upstream, it would run right into these obstacles, the iron spikes gashing the hull.

Therefore, before British provision ships could reach the city with supplies for the army, the navy must first locate and then "weigh" - that is, raise - these sunken devices. To prevent that, the Americans placed their forts within a cannon shot on the Pennsylvania and New Jersey shores. This meant the British would have to reduce the rebel forts before any supply ships could reach the army at Philadelphia.

The lower set of chevaux-de-frise, several miles below the city, was protected on the Jersey side by Fort Billingsport. On September 30th, the fort's commandant, hearing the unmistakable sound of bagpipes, held up his spyglass to observe a long column of kilted men marching north, toward his little fort. They were the dreaded "Black Watch," Britain's 42nd Regiment of Foot. These Scottish Highlanders were famed for their courage in battle, when they would wield their fearsome broadswords in close, hand-to-hand combat. The isolated fort's 300 man militia garrison listened to the ominous skirl of the Highlanders' bagpipes, and watched them make preparations to assault the fort by land. Because the fort was "open in the rear" - having been built to withstand attack from the water side only - the commandant "concluded it was better to evacuate than resist." He ordered the garrison to quickly spike the guns, set fire to the barracks, and march north to safety.

So the British Navy began the time-consuming process of raising the lower set of chevaux-de-frise. It would take them three weeks to clear a wide enough path for their frigates to warp through the remaining obstacles and move upriver to attack the rebel forts three miles below Philadelphia: Forts Mercer and Mifflin.

With the fall of Fort Billingsport, George Washington was becoming anxious. He knew he had a golden opportunity; Howe was in a vulnerable position, with his back to the river and no naval support yet. Washington wanted to beat Howe in battle before Howe could regain communications with the British Navy. Despite his recent failure at Germantown, Washington considered launching another attack. But this time, Howe would be prepared. On October 19th, he pulled all his forces out of Germantown and concentrated them in Philadelphia. Having learned his lesson, Howe put them to work fortifying the city's outskirts with a ring of earthworks, anchored at intervals by nine redoubts along the high ground, "framed, planked and of great thickness, and surrounded by a deep ditch inclosed and fraised."

General Washington was not sure the garrisons of the river forts could hold out by themselves. So he put the idea of an attack to his subordinate generals at a council of war. He asked them

> whether, in case the enemy should make an attack upon the forts upon the Delaware, it would be proper with our present force to fall down and attack the enemy in their lines near Philadelphia? Ansr. In the negative, unanimously.

They told him that he needed a superiority of numbers to attempt it. Numerically, the two armies were about even because part of Howe's army was still away at Wilmington and elsewhere. But Washington's forces were a mixture of continentals and less dependable militia. He needed the seasoned continentals he'd loaned to his subordinate on the Hudson River, Major General Horatio Gates, head of the northern army. Washington had first requested them back in September.

But Gates was taking his time about returning them. The "Hero of Saratoga" did not hold a high opinion of Washington, whose "grand army" had achieved so little compared to his own. To show his contempt, Gates had recently taken to submitting his reports to the Congress instead of to his superior, the commander in chief. Even the momentous news of Burgoyne's surrender Washington had to learn of indirectly, by inquiring to Congress. Gates insultingly alluded to it in a letter to Washington weeks afterward: "I am confident your Excellency has long ago received all the good news from this quarter."

The delay in the return of the troops lent to Gates was also partly due to George Washington's willingness to accomodate a meddling Congress. They had instructed him to "consult" with Gates - rather than issue direct orders - concerning any extractions he wished to make from the northern army. Some Congressmen, such as John Adams, even voted for a resolution (it failed) that would put a numerical limit on the troops Washington could take away from Gates. Compounding the problem was the commander in chief's management style, in which he usually took a democratic approach to decision making. He had a decidedly ungeneral-like habit of deferring to his subordinates' judgment, and his orders to his generals were often worded more like requests than firm directives.

But by October 30th, a very frustrated Washington was despairing over the non-arrival of the troops. So he decided to dispatch his aide, Alexander Hamilton, to ride north and inform Horatio Gates of "the many happy consequences that will accrue" if he releases the troops immediately, so they could be used in another attack against Howe. He told Hamilton to use his own discretion about how to persuade the former British officer, but to be sure to relate a sense of urgency.

> What you are chiefly to attend to, is to point out, in the clearest and fullest manner to General Gates, the absolute necessity that there is for his detaching a very considerable part of his army at present under his command to the reinforcement of this.

By the time Alexander Hamilton arrived in Albany, the northern army's commander had actually released the particular troops requested. But the brash, twenty-year-old Alexander Hamilton insisted that Gates release even more. Ignoring Washington's orders not to interfere with Gates's plans for other brigades, Hamilton pretended that it was the commander in chief's expressed desire that Gates release additional brigades, beyond those originally requested. "I am under necessity of requiring," he lied, "by virtue of my orders from him, that one of the other ... [brigades be sent] and that you will be pleased to give immediate orders for its embarkation." Hamilton managed to extract the additional brigade.

It would take them until nearly the end of November to reach the main army outside Philadelphia. By then, the matter of the Delaware forts would already have been resolved, and the army, instead of attacking Howe, would soon be heading for its winter encampment at Valley Forge.

Three miles below Philadelphia, beneath the water's surface, lay the upper set of thirty chevaux-de-frise, sunk in three parallel rows. They were guarded on the New Jersey side by Fort Mercer, at a place called Red Bank because of the color of the soil, and on the Pennsylvania side by Fort Mifflin, which was on Mud Island.

Between the island and the Pennsylvania shore ran a side current, which was too shallow for large ships. However, the British, desperate for supplies, had been sneaking a small fraction of their needs up this narrow channel in low draught flatboats. They did it in broad daylight because they could not be observed by the fort's garrison. "The shade of the trees" overhanging the western bank camouflaged the tiny boats. As of October 21st, according to Captain John Andre, "The flat boats bringing them [provisions] past the fort had never yet been insulted."

But the commander of Fort Mifflin, Lt. Colonel Samuel Smith, was not ignorant of what was happening. Smith could tell, "by the noise of oars," that flatboats were passing, though he could not see them. Frustrated, he realized that "firing at sounds would be wasting precious ammunition." Smith therefore asked Commodore Hazelwood to use his small vessels to sail downriver to a point where he could prevent this illicit traffic from entering the narrow channel. Hazelwood objected, pointing out that such an effort would place his vessels within range of the large British warships, which were anchored downstream, just below the chevaux-de-frise; a single shell from them would wreck one of his little ships. Annoyed by Hazelwood's answer, Colonel Smith retorted, "Yes, and one falling on your head or mine will kill, but for what else are we employed or paid?"

So the trickle of supplies continued, but Howe knew this would not be enough for his army. So he sought the destruction of both forts - Mifflin, on Mud Island, and Mercer across the river at Red Bank. He had earlier instructed his engineer, Captain John Montresor (who, ironically, had built Fort Mifflin back in 1772), to establish batteries on the Pennsylvania shore and force the rebel garrison to quit the island fort. By October 16th, Howe was complaining to Montresor that "three weeks were elapsed" since that order, yet the rebels were still obstinately holding out. Montresor explained that he was not able to procure sufficient ordnance to bring the necessary "weight of metal" against the enemy.

Howe now realized that the extreme shortages necessitated a bolder approach. He therefore devised a three-prong attack. He would have Montresor better equipped to step up his shelling of Fort Mifflin from the Pennsylvania shore. At the same time, two of the ships of the line would venture as close to the chevaux-de-frise as possible and bombard the island's fort from the river. The ships would also provide a covering fire for a land assault against Fort Mercer, across the river at Red Bank.

For this dangerous assignment against the New Jersey fort, Howe chose a tall, thin, forty-year-old Hessian nobleman, Colonel Carl von Donop. He had been second in command during the disaster at Trenton the previous December, and was anxious to remove that stain against his reputation. Lately, Donop had been openly critical of the British leadership. He also resented criticism of his grenadiers' part in the recent Battle of Brandywine - such opinions as the following, written by Lieutenant Hale of the 45th Regiment of Foot:

> The Hessians, who are allowed to be the best of the German troops, are by no means equal to the British in any respect. I believe them steady, but their slowness is of the greatest disadvantage in a country almost covered with woods, and against an enemy whose chief qualification is agility in running from fence to fence, and thence keeping up an irregular but galling fire on troops who advance with the same pace as at their exercise.
>
> At Brandywine when the first line formed, the Hessian grenadiers were close in on our rear, and began beating their march at the same time with us; from that moment we saw them no more till the action was over, and only one man of them was wounded by a random shot which came over us.

Donop, tired of being outdone by his arrogant allies, was itching for a chance to show what his troops could do. So he volunteered to go against Fort Mercer, arguing that "the Hessians had done nothing of consequence this campaign."

Dispensations were made for the expedition. After studying them, Donop felt he would definitely need heavier ordnance than the measly 3-pounders allotted. So he sent a written request to General Howe. An aide returned with the commander in chief's answer, which unreasonably denied Donop's request, and added the insulting remark that, if Donop's men were "not up to it, the English will take the fort." Donop bristled and, controlling his emotions, grimly informed the aide, "Tell your general that Germans are not afraid to die." Afterward, Donop told his officers, "Either the fort will soon be named Fort Donop, or I shall have fallen."

One of Donop's men recorded in his journal entry for October 21st, "We marched early and passed through Philadelphia before daylight. Close to the city we were loaded in flatboats, and at daybreak landed on the other side ... At seven o'clock in the evening we arrived" at Haddonfield. One of their guides, a slave named "Dick Ellis, who deserted from his master," was "a negroe, the property of Colo. [Joseph] Ellis who commanded a regiment of militia." Haddonfield's leading loyalists eagerly came forward to advise Donop which were the houses of active rebels and rebel sympathizers. The Hessian colonel thought it wise to oblige them, for he wanted no one to warn the fort's garrison. Therefore, he detached small parties of grenadiers to find and seize the rebel families. They were forced to spend the night outdoors, by a campfire in the middle of a street, surrounded by a strong guard.

However, the next morning, after the Hessians left town, one of these men, Jonas Cattell, ran off into the woods. Circling around the Hessian columns' flankers, he managed to reach and warn the garrison by noon. The fort's commandant was not sure, though, whether this enemy force intended to attack his fort, or was simply foraging; he had heard that Howe's army was becoming desperate for food supplies. So he dispatched a few men to reconnoiter, and sent others to a nearby farm, where Job Whitall recorded in his journal that day, "They drove away 21 heads of cattle. The people of the fort drove away from Father and me 47 sheep into the fort."

The 1,200 man attacking force, with its little train of artillery, left Haddonfield at four o'clock in the morning. It was October 22nd, a day that "will certainly remain in our thoughts forever," wrote one Hessian diarist. They approached the fort by a roundabout route, because of a bridge's planks having been taken up by the local militia. Nearing the fort, Donop halted the column at noon to allow his men to sit down, rest, and eat their mid-day meal. Some of the veterans did not eat, knowing from experience that a musket ball would go through one's midsection more easily if the intestines were empty.

But, for the most part, they were supremely confident. Ensign Carl Rueffer recorded in his journal his "great sorrow" that his sick captain had to remain in Philadelphia, and would miss the "opportunities" for glory.

A captured American, Captain Oliver Clark, taken three miles from Fort Mercer while reconnoitering the enemy, lied to Donop, telling him that "the garrison had no idea of the enemy's presence." The Hessian colonel believed the rebel was telling the truth. After all, he had just used his own spyglass to observe the fort, and had seen men atop the parapet "hanging out their wash to dry." Donop did not know that this was just a ruse to deceive him. He expected that his force's mere appearance might scare the enemy into capitulating without a fight. If not, he was confident his men could take it by storm.

The fearsome reputation of the Hessians, King George III's hired mercenaries so willingly leased to him by greedy German princes, was well known to the rebels. Gruesome stories about them had been circulating widely in the army ever since the Battle of Long Island, when some rebels had been impaled by Hessian bayonets to the trees at Brooklyn's Flatbush Pass.

The Hessians were professional soldiers, and they took pride in performing their trade expertly. Sir George Osborne, a British colonel, was impressed with his Hessian allies.

> [When advancing] in battle ... they watch steadily the arms of the enemy. If they see them moved & waving much about in the ranks, they are sure the men who bear them are dismayed & without courage, and that a vigorous attack will break them. ... When the rebels were drawn up to oppose our troops both on Long Island & Fort Washington, I well remember to have seen this tremulation of the arms among them, and that they did not hold them steadily. The consequence was, they ran as soon as they were attacked.

Ensign Carl Rueffer: "After Colonel von Donop appraised the situation, at three-thirty in the afternoon he permitted the fort, through the English Major [Alexander] Stuart, the opportunity to surrender." Stuart and a few others went forward under a white flag. They were accompanied by a drummer, beating *Parley*. Captain Johann Ewald was returning from scouting, when he passed the flag party going toward the fort. He thought they were obviously full of confidence and "regarded the affair with levity." However, when they returned a few minutes later, they "brought back a spiteful refusal." This, according to Captain Ewald, was "news the colonel did not expect."

The flag party had halted "about 12 rods from the fort" and awaited the commandant's representative, Lt. Colonel Jeremiah Olney. When Olney arrived, they treated him with disdain; even "the drummer boy was as insolent as his officer." In his contemptuous English accent, Major Stuart delivered Colonel Donop's message: "The King of England orders his rebellious subjects to lay down their arms, and they are warned that, if they stand the battle, no quarter whatever will be given." This threat was one to be taken seriously. According to the journal of Thomas Sullivan, after the debacle at Trenton, Donop had

> resolved to be revenged; he therefore went thro' the ranks and declared openly to his men, that any of them

who would take a rebel prisoner would receive 50 stripes; signifying to them they were to kill all the rebels they could without mercy.

Lieutenant Colonel Jeremiah Olney's reply to Donop's demand for the surrender of Fort Mercer:

We shall not ask for - nor expect - any quarter, and mean to defend the fort to the last extremity. Colonel Greene, who commands the fort, sends his compliments and he shall await Colonel Donop.

Fort Mercer's garrison - two Rhode Island regiments totaling 425 men and officers - was led by Colonel Christopher Greene. Greene had been taken by the British in Benedict Arnold's unsuccessful attack on Quebec, and spent more than a year as a prisoner of war, before being released in an exchange. Like Donop, he was itching for a fight.

Washington had recently sent to Greene a young volunteer engineer from France, the Chevalier de Mauduit du Plessis, with orders to strengthen the fort to withstand a land attack. The French engineer found that the Americans, "little practised in the art of fortification," had overbuilt the works "beyond their strength" to defend it. So he put them to work making a fort within a fort. He left unaltered the outside wall and its surrounding ditch and *abatis* (sharpened tree branches sticking out toward the enemy). Leaving a space of open ground inside the north wall, he had the garrison construct a new inner wall, protected by an abatis and a ditch "15 feet across and 12 feet deep." These interior improvements were not visible to Donop.

Donop's attack was supposed to be covered by the British ships, which were to engage the rebel vessels to prevent them from bombarding the advancing columns. "But," as Captain Muenchhausen recorded, "a completely contrary wind prevented the warships from coming upriver. Consequently, General Howe requested Donop not to attack this afternoon." The journals of several of Colonel Donop's officers confirm that he received the order to postpone the assault a day. One account states that he asked his ally, Major Stuart, to advise him what to do, but the Englishman would have no part in such an important decision. Major Stuart declined, saying he was "too young" - that is, junior in rank - to advise the colonel what to do; the colonel would have to make the decision himself.

Donop decided to ignore Howe's order and launch the attack immediately. Perhaps he thought the garrison was being evacuated, and the rebels would all escape capture if he waited any longer. His scouts probably had seen, earlier that afternoon, two large parties leaving the fort. The first to leave was the New Jersey militia, who Greene had found were extremely reluctant troops, and "expected to be relieved every three days." Greene did not want to depend on "militia, who undertake to judge for themselves," rather than submit to the will of Continental Army officers. So he told them to "secure their persons" by marching for home. The other party was a regiment of Virginians who had been ordered to Fort Mifflin, but had come over to Fort Mercer by mistake. Greene insisted they row across to the other fort. This left him with only the two regiments of continentals from his home state of Rhode Island, men he knew he could trust.

Donop gathered his forces and had them throw down their "knapsacks into a pile and put on their [iron-banded] grenadier caps." He gave them a short speech, telling them to act with valor. Then, following Donop's lead, each of his officers, "with sword in hand," stepped to the front to lead the charge. Captain Ewald, of the jagers:

> A hundred *fascines* [bundles of sticks] were made at once by the battalions and a battery of six regimental pieces [3-pounders], two 6-pounders and the howitzers were mounted in the wood at rifle-shot distance from the fort. ... One hundred men ["sappers"] from each battalion were to carry the fascines and march in a line at a distance of two hundred paces in front of the battalion. With these the ditch was to be filled, crossed, and the

fort scaled with sword in hand.

I placed sixteen good marksmen at the edge of the wood in the vicinity of the battery, who were to shoot at those men who showed themselves on the parapet. ... The three battalions advanced against the fort with indescribable courage.

Evidently, either Ewald's snipers had not yet taken their positions, or they held their fire when they saw the rebel commandant, for Colonel Greene had clambored up on top of the parapet. To inspire his men with courage, he calmly walked its length, in plain view of his foe. Now and then, he stopped to raise his spyglass and observe the enemy. Finally, he jumped down into the fort and said, "Fire low men. They have a broad belt just above their hips - aim at that."

At 4:45 p.m., the attack began with fifteen minutes of shelling from the two howitzers at the edge of the woods. The three-pounder "regimental guns advanced more than 100 steps ... to shell the fort from a very short distance." Captain Stephen Olney:

The enemy field pieces made the gravel and dust fly from the top of our fort, and took off all the heads that happened to be in the way. ... [Their] artillery intimidated some of the men so much they were afraid to show their heads above the breastworks, [they] raised their guns and fired by guess work.

To make these timid men face the enemy, an officer "was busily employed thrashing them with his hanger," which was a leather strap connecting belt to sword. The three grenadier battalions advanced "at the doublequick" in three columns - north, east and south of the fort - while the jager companies "covered both flanks to the water to prevent a landing from the ships, which nevertheless did the force much damage with their cannons." The Pennsylvania Navy's row galleys, each sporting one 18-pounder, had, according to Johann Ewald, "moved into position during the summons" for the fort's surrender. Now they kept "a galling fire" of grapeshot and ball pouring into the Hessians' northern column. The galleys also communicated the enemy's movements to the fort's garrison "by means of speaking tubes."

While the northern column was hindered by a raking fire from the rebel row galleys, the southern column's approach was easier, as they only had to put up with musketry and artillery fire from the fort. So they were the first to reach the fort. Unlike the northern half of the fort, which had been strengthened by the new inner works, the southern half had only the original wall as a barrier, along with its external ditch and abatis.

One company of American musketmen, on a salient that projected from the east wall so it could overlook both north and south ditches, helped out by firing over the heads of their comrades defending the south wall. In this way, Asa Potter died when accidentally shot from behind by a fellow American. The next day, "twelve bullets were found here, where the Hessians could not possibly have placed them."

None of the Hessians attacking the south wall had been provided "axes and saws" with which to cut down the abatis. So they desperately hacked away with their swords at the sharpened branches outside the south wall, all the while under fire from the rebel musketmen. Despite suffering heavy casualties, the Hessians made a couple openings and began to climb over the abatis and up the berm to the parapet. But they were repulsed by a withering fire of musketry at point blank range. One defender recalled that "two officers were killed on the brim of the breastwork," before the Hessian southern column fell back and retreated out of musket range.

This left the eastern and northern columns, which merged and, led by Donop himself, aimed for the fort's north wall. Greene had evacuated the original north wall when the attack began, "except for a few sentinels to deceive the enemy" who he posted on the *banquette*, or musketry ledge, inside this outer wall. Even these decoys Greene now pulled back to the inner fort as the enemy neared.

In the attack against the north wall, Lt. Colonel Minnigerode noted that "a few faint-hearted ones showed signs of wishing to run away," but they were prevailed upon to push on. The large column soon "took the outer defenses with little effort." The sappers carrying the fascines, far out in front of the grenadiers, had taken too much hostile fire for their liking. When they reached the outer ditch, they "merely threw the fascines in the ditch," turned, and ran, letting the soldiers do the rest. The grenadiers came up and jumped in the ditch, then stacked the fascines and used them, and sometimes each other's shoulders, to climb up and over the north wall.

They were elated over their apparent easy victory. The next day, the *New Jersey Gazette* printed an anonymous letter, stating that when the Hessians "got into the old part of the works, they thought it was all their own, and gave three cheers." Greene's men watched some of them shout, *"Vittoria!"* and throw their hats over their heads. Another defender remembered that they "huzzaed and came on."

Having already entered the fort, they must have been surprised to see another set of abatis blocking their path. But they overcame it, hacking their way through with their swords. At this point, there was an eery silence from the defenders behind the breastworks, as they held their fire and intently watched their enemy come closer. Sweaty palms, and nervous fingers on musket triggers, waited for Colonel Greene's command to fire.

Pushing past the abatis, Donop's men could now see that beyond it was another ditch - inside the fort! They had not expected this, just as they had not expected the second set of abatis. Nevertheless, driven by adrenaline and duty, they entered the ditch. But they found it too deep; they could not get up its far wall to reach their enemy. They had left their fascines in the outside ditch, and they had no scaling ladders. This "moat" became a death trap.

When the Hessians were nearly all in the wide ditch, Greene finally gave the command to fire. His chief artillery officer, Du Plessis, "lashed them with 4 pieces of cannon loaded with canister shot, which created great havoc among them." A "canister shot" was a tin can, filled with many lead balls slightly bigger than musket balls; after leaving the cannon's muzzle, the can would burst open, spreading the balls over a wide area, inflicting many casualties when fired at close range.

Captain Stephen Olney's musketmen, in the salient that overlooked both ditches, turned their attention away from the no longer active south wall and focused on these new victims. They raked the grenadiers, crowded together in the ditch, with a deadly crossfire. Olney:

> My company was stationed in a salient angle, connected within the curtain of the breastwork, to rake the ditches on each side. When fighting, I thought my company quite secure, as the enemy looked to the bastions on each side; therefore my men were deliberate, except one little Irishman, who was frightened out of his senses, but a few strokes with the but-end of my gun brought him to his duty.
>
> While the enemy were in confusion, not more than 20 paces off, a man by the name of Sweetzer insisted that I should see him kill when he fired. I indulged him four or five times, and his object fell. I then directed him to fire at an officer, and he only made him stagger a little.

The dead and dying bodies began piling up on top of each other, the air filled up now with German screams of the wounded and terrified. Colonel Donop and several other "officers persisted in pushing forward the men." But, unable to scale the wall, they resorted to just firing back at any exposed heads above them. Eventually, wrote Captain Olney, "our fire proved so destructive that they gave it up and retreated, leaving their dead and wounded." Colonel Donop, himself, was struck by "thirteen balls" of canister and musketry while rallying his men for the last time. His officers started to carry him out, but he told them no, he "did not desire to go with them." He ordered them to leave him in the fort, and waste no time in securing their own retreat.

The jagers covered the grenadiers' retreat. It was dark now. The shattered and stunned remains of the expeditionary force proceeded by a "forced march" six miles before stopping for the night at Haddonfield. The next morning, they would continue on and meet some British troops that Howe sent over to cover their crossing to Philadelphia. Many years later, Captain Johann Ewald recalled the retreat:

> Since we had flattered ourselves in advance with a successful surrender, no retreat was thought of, and no wagons brought to transport the wounded. The seriously wounded officers were carried on the guns and horses, and all the privates who could not drag themselves away on their wounded limbs fell into enemy hands. ...
> This day was especially sad for me. I lost five of my oldest friends, among whom was a relative, and four of my best friends were severely wounded. As long as I have served, I have not yet left a battlefield in such deep sorrow.

The assault had failed miserably, though the Hessian grenadiers had given their American foes an awesome display of courage. The battle had lasted just 45 minutes, during which time the Hessians had lost to death, wounds, and capture or desertion one third of their total force of 1,207 men. American casualties were only 14 killed, 23 wounded.

General Howe had relied on intelligence that was three weeks old, when Fort Mercer was still incomplete. That was when Colonel Sterling, after having taken Fort Billingsport with his Highlanders, had requested permission to press on and also take Fort Mercer. Howe had denied the request, saying it "would have been very precarious" to supply and defend "a post so detached" from the rest of the army. If Howe had consented to Sterling's request back then, when Fort Mercer was far from complete, the result might have been much different. Colonel William Harcourt wrote to his father, after Donop's demise, "Unfortunately, our intelligence was bad, and what was represented as a battery, erected entirely against the ships and open behind, proved a very strong fort with a deep ditch."

Colonel Greene feared another attack during the night, so he dared not send any detachments out to either harass the enemy's retreat or reconnoiter their location. He "placed sentries round the whole fort." One of them later wrote that, "the groans and cries of the wounded and dying was dreadful music to my ears," as they lay unattended on the cold ground all night.

As for what happened to the wounded Colonel Donop, we can rely on the account of Greene's artillery officer, the Chevalier de Mauduit du Plessis. Three years after the battle, he related to his friend, the Marquis de Chastellux, an anecdote about that night, and the marquis recorded it for posterity:

> M de Mauduit [du Plessis] wanted to replace some of the [abatis] stakes which had been torn out; he sallied forth with a few men, and was surprised to find about twenty Hessians ... [half-crazed with fear] glued against the face of the parapet. ...
>
> A voice rose from the midst of the corpses, and said in English, "Whoever you are, take me out of here." It was the voice of Colonel Donop. M de Mauduit had the soldiers lift him up and carry him into the fort, where he was soon recognized.

An American soldier with a bayonet threatened Donop, "Well, is it settled, that no quarter is to be given?" Others joined in, baiting the defeated leader who had earlier promised that no quarter would be given to the Americans. Donop answered his tormentors, "I am in your hands. You can avenge yourselves." But an indignant Du Plessis intervened, rebuking the scoundrels. Donop, hearing the accent, asked, "Sir, you appear to be a stranger; who are you?" "A French officer," Du Plessis answered. To this, a relieved Colonel Donop sighed and said, in French, "I am content. I die in the arms of honor itself."

Several days later, two captive Hessian officers were paroled and released, after swearing "not to take up arms again until such time as they were exchanged." After they reached Philadelphia, they talked to Ensign Rueffer, who recorded their comments:

> Colonel Donop died yesterday and was buried with military honors. Two hundred men marched out for his burial, of whom half fired three times. Also, three cannons were fired. ... They gave high praise for the care and treatment provided by the enemy, not alone to Colonel von Donop, but to all the prisoners and wounded.

Eventually, a spot of ground between the fort and the neighboring Whitall farmhouse would be marked with a plaque, stating, "Here lies the dead body of Colonel Donop." Captain Johann Ewald concluded his memoir of the battle by reflecting on his fellow officer, who, he felt, had been sacrificed by General Howe. "In a word, Colonel Donop was a man of action." He had been outspoken in his criticism and "offended the pride of the English. They led him into danger and he fell; whereby so many men - indeed, so many really brave men - had to bite the dust."

The assault against Red Bank's Fort Mercer was an astonishing defeat for the British. Joseph Plumb Martin, who would see action during virtually the whole war, judged it to be "as brilliant an action as was fought during the Revolutionary War, considering the numbers engaged, Bunker Hill to the contrary notwithstanding." One newspaper, alluding to the Hessians' having shown no quarter in an earlier battle, termed it "revenge for Long Island."

Even more so than Trenton, Red Bank killed the Hessians' enthusiasm for the war. In Philadelphia, Major Bauermeister learned of the terrible casualties, including his nephew, whose arm had to be amputated. Disillusioned, he wrote, "It is truly to be desired that this miserable war will end soon." Three months later, another Hessian officer wrote home, "For some time we have lost our desire to serve the English."

A rumor circulated that the allies might pull out of their agreement with King George III. But, on January 13, 1778, Sir Joseph Yorke would write to Admiral Howe from London, reassuring him and his brother that, "There is not a word of truth about the states of Hesse. Those countries are only afraid you should send back their troops." He was referring to the greedy German princes, who received bonuses for each man killed or wounded. No, the Hessians would stay for the duration of the war, though by some estimates as many as 12,000 of the by war's end 30,000 mercenaries would elect to settle in America rather than return to their fatherland.

What exactly had happened to Donop's naval support? During the action at Red Bank, several British warships, despite the "continuing contrary winds" from the north, had tried to warp upriver within range to help in the attack. The ship captains were under orders from their Admiral, Lord Richard Howe, to be ready to "give every assistance to the Hessians" in their attack on the rebel fort, said to be planned for either October 22nd or 23rd, as soon as naval support was in place.

At 4 p.m. on the 22nd, the *Augusta*, carrying 64 guns, finally made it through the narrow opening made in the lower set of chevaux-de-frise near Billingsport. Coming upriver, her captain was surprised to observe rebel row galleys "flanking a party of Hessians going to assault Red Bank" - apparently, Donop had not waited for his naval support. Determined to do whatever he could to help, the captain at 5 p.m. ordered all nearby ships to move in and draw the rebels' fire.

The *Augusta* ran aground on a shoal, and the other British ships, trying likewise to tack against the wind in too narrow confines for such difficult maneuvers, began congregating around the stricken ship. Two more grounded. Here was an opportunity for the Pennsylvania Navy. "At 1/2 past five," Commodore Hazelwood ordered his nearest row galleys to commence firing. By 7 p.m., he was sending four fire rafts floating downriver on the outgoing tide. But the enemy acted quickly, sending out longboats full of sailors with grappling hooks to intercept the fire rafts and tow them through the congestion to open water downriver.

The action between the opposing naval forces ceased at 9 p.m. Throughout the night, the British ships struggled to haul the *Augusta* off the sandbar. Unfortunately, the high tide that night was "a foot below normal," and they were unsuccessful. Shortly after daybreak of the 23rd, Commodore Hazelwood, seeing the *Augusta* still aground, resumed the attack with "12 galleys and two floating batteries." The British ships fought back and also bombarded Fort Mifflin, on nearby Mud Island, a mile southwest of Red Bank.

The American vessels "all performed well" - in fact, well enough to set the *Augusta* on fire. By 11 a.m., "the sides and all the after part of the ship was ablaze." British longboats from the other ships came over to help evacuate the 500 sailors, some of whom dove off the burning ship into the river. Then the squadron withdrew safely out of range, knowing that eventually the fire would spread to the *Augusta*'s huge powder magazine. "At 10 minutes past 12, a violent shock shook the earth," one soldier wrote from the American camp west of Philadelphia, as the *Augusta*'s powder magazine exploded, causing broken windows for miles around. Thomas Paine, writing to Benjamin Franklin, described it as "a report as loud as a peal of a hundred cannon at once ... a thick smoke rising like a pillar and spreading from the top like a tree."

The end of this "most furious" naval engagement is described by Colonel William Bradford:

> The fire was so incessant that by all accounts the elements seemed to be in flames. ... [Before] the *Augusta* blew up ... she lay broadside-to aground, and the flames issuing thro every port she had. The action still continued with the other ships and at three o'clock the *Merlin* took fire and blew up also, being aground, and then the fire soon ceased. Thus ended two glorious days.

Three days later, the good news reached York, Pennsylvania, where the Congress was temporarily seated while the British occupied Philadelphia. An elated John Adams wrote to his wife, Abigail:

> I have seized a moment, to congratulate you on the great and glorious success of our arms at the northward [Burgoyne's surrender], and in Delaware River. The forts have been defended with a magnanimity which will give our country a reputation in Europe. Colonel Greene repulsed the enemy from Red Bank, and took Count Donop and his aide prisoners. Colonel Smith repulsed a bold attack upon Fort Mifflin, and our gallies disabled two men of war, a 64 and 20 gun ship, in such a manner that the enemy blew them up. This comes confirmed this evening, in letters from General Washington inclosing original letters from officers in the forts.
>
> Congress will appoint a [day of] thanksgiving, and one cause of it ought to be that the glory of turning the tide of arms is not immediately due to the commander in chief, nor to southern troops. If it had been, idolatry and adulation would have been unbounded, so excessive as to endanger our liberties ... Now we can allow a certain citizen to be wise, virtuous and good, without thinking him a deity or a saviour.

John Adams was not simply jealous of George Washington's popularity; he feared for the fate of American republicanism, should the Virginian succomb to the temptations of a military dictatorship. Soon, though, Adams would be out of the picture, having just been appointed by Congress to replace Silas Deane in Paris as one of America's three plenipotentiaries to the court of King Louis XVI. On December 15th, when John again wrote to Abigail - this time from Portsmouth, New Hampshire - he was able to describe a different beneficiary of adulation:

> One morning, I asked my landlady what I had to pay?

> Nothing, she said - "I was welcome, and she hoped I would always make her house my home, and she should be happy to entertain all those gentlemen who had been raised up by Providence to be the saviours of their country." This was flattering enough to my vain heart. But it made a greater impression on me as a proof how deeply this Cause has sunk into the minds and hearts of the people.

By the end of October, the British Captain Montresor was writing in his journal that the army was "somewhat dejected" by recent events, whereas the Americans were in great spirits. Their camp was alive with "shaves," or rumors, that Burgoyne had surrendered somewhere south of Ticonderoga, a place called Saratoga. Howe's adjutant, Captain Muenchhausen, first learned this disconcerting news while visiting the wounded Hessians at Red Bank. Annoyed with the Americans' impudent good spirits, he refused Colonel Greene's invitation to dinner, "because Greene, though he was very courteous, nevertheless showed a great pride, partly on account of the news they had, that Burgoyne was captured with his entire force."

Since Horatio Gates had not informed him, the exasperated General Washington had to ask Congress to confirm or deny the rumors about Burgoyne. Several days later, he finally received confirmation, and the Virginian decided to schedule a *feu de joie*, or celebratory firing, to honor the occasion. Hugh McDonald provides an account of the camp celebration, held November 9, 1777:

> We rejoiced with great shouting and firing all day, our officers being more joyous than the common soldiers and, I think, more so than was necessary - prancing and capering about on their horses ... which were scared by the thundering of the artillery from Carolina as we discharged our cannon. At the same time, General Stirling was riding near our artillery on a likely bay mare, which,

springing sideways from under him, gave him a very bad fall. After lying for some time, he got up and shook himself like a great water dog, acknowledged himself not hurt, but walked away directly to his quarters and left off his folly for that night.

Although General Howe had provided insufficient artillery for the Red Bank expedition, he would not make the same mistake in his assault against the other rebel stronghold, Mud Island's Fort Mifflin. This time, he readied a force of British infantry to storm the fort, but he decided to hold them back until he could soften the rebel garrison with an overwhelming artillery barrage.

By November 10th, his engineer, Captain Montresor, had constructed five platforms for batteries on the swampy Pennsylvania shore, giving the British a total of fifteen cannons and mortars to harass the island fort, just 600 yards away. According to Captain John Andre, "The batteries played with very little interruption day and night upon the fort" and its garrison of 450 unfortunate continentals. But the Americans obstinately held out, thanks to the leadership of their commandant, Lt. Colonel Samuel Smith, and his young French volunteer engineer, Lt. Colonel Francois Louis Teissedre de Fleury, who drove the garrison hard to keep the works in a constant state of repair.

After the successful defense of Fort Mercer, many patriots thought Howe must surely quit Philadelphia. Colonel Greene noted this on November 4th, when he wrote that, "It is the general opinion of the best of citizens that the enemy will evacuate the city if the Fort [Mifflin] holds out until the middle of next week." James Allen reported that John Adams had recently spoken of the evacuation

> as a certain event, & said the struggle was past & that independence was now unalterably settled; the crisis was over. ... Even the Tories believe Genl Howe, thus circumstanced, must quit the city.

Howe's army was desperately short of food and other critical supplies. He insisted that his troops not plunder the inhabitants, that they pay for produce and other foodstuffs. But, his soldiers bitterly complained, "The inhabitants bring us nothing." On their faces their malice and hatred toward us can be seen. We have to be more careful of the farmers than of the enemy soldiers." Lieutenant Feilitzsch echoed the same sentiments, writing on the first day of November: "We still have no provisions. If the Delaware River were open, everything would be different." Back in September, Washington had ordered the removal of grinding stones from all gristmills in the vicinity of Philadelphia. This caused a hardship to the citizens of Philadelphia, as Howe pointed out in a letter to his adversary, but Washington felt that the citizens must temporarily suffer, too, until the British were forced from the city.

As October came to a close, the gloomy situation caused by the diminishing food supplies was worsened by those rumors still circulating in the British camp. Burgoyne's surrender at Saratoga was officially confirmed on November 3rd, according to Feilitzsch:

> The very sad news was received that General Burgoyne had been captured ... Good night peace! Without God's help, we will not be able to enjoy the sweet hope this year. ... Would to God I were in my fatherland and no longer had to worry about it.

Even General Howe's Hessian adjutant, Friedrich Muenchhausen, noted the despondency, confiding to his own journal, "Many of us hope that England will give in."

With winter fast approaching, George Washington was more determined than ever that the forts must hold out. He sent reinforcements into Fort Mifflin, among them sixteen-year-old Joseph Plumb Martin. Many years later, in his memoirs titled *A Narrative of Some of the Adventures, Dangers and Sufferings of a Revolutionary Soldier*, the private recalled his time at Fort Mifflin:

Here I endured hardships sufficient to kill half a dozen horses. ... In the cold month of November, without provisions, without shoes or stockings ...

Neither the [officers'] house nor the barracks were of much use at this time, for it was as much as a man's life was worth to enter them, the enemy often directing their shot at them in particular. ...

Between the stone wall and the palisadoes was a kind of yard or pen ... the only place in the fort that anyone could be in any degree of safety. Into this place we used to gather the splinters broken off the palisadoes by the enemy's shot and make a little fire, just enough to keep from suffering. We would watch an opportunity to escape from the vigilance of Colonel Fleury, and run into this place for a minute or two's respite from fatigue and cold. When the engineer found that the workmen began to grow scarce, he would come to the entrance and call us out. He had always his cane in his hand, and woe betided him he could get a stroke at. At his approach I always jumped over the ditch and ran ...

It was utterly impossible to lie down to get any rest or sleep on account of the mud, if the enemy's shot would have suffered us to do so. Sometimes some of the men, when overcome with fatigue and want of sleep, would slip away into the barracks to catch a nap of sleep, but it seldom happened that they all came out again alive. I was in this place a fortnight and can say in sincerity that I never lay down to sleep a minute in all that time.

The 450 Americans, mostly Pennsylvania and Connecticut continentals, were holding out the best way they could. When an enemy cannon's muzzle flashed, a sentry would shout "A shot!" and everyone would hunker down behind the walls. Each night, the wounded and dead were rowed over to Fort Mercer under cover of darkness. The rowers returned shortly after with new construction materials, including beams of oak, with which the worn out but determined defenders would, before dawn, repair the previous day's damage to the walls. They also brought over food cooked at Fort Mercer, transporting it "in old flour barrels, mostly corned beef and hard bread."

When the British fired exploding shells, they usually landed in the soft mud inside the fort, at times sinking so deep "their report could not be heard when they burst ... only a tremulous motion of the earth" was felt by the garrison. At other times, a shell lodging nearer the surface would "throw the mud fifty feet in the air." Eventually, the British artillerists realized what was happening, and made an adjustment. They "cut the fuses of the bombs such a length as to make the shells burst in the air, over the heads of the garrison, so the shells fell in pieces among the soldiers." Private Martin describes other hazards:

> As their point-blank shot would not reach us behind the wall, they would throw elevated grapeshot from their mortar, and when sentries had cried, "a shot," and the soldiers, seeing no shot arrive, had become careless, the grapeshot would come down like a shower of hail about our ears. ...
>
> We had a thirty-two-pound cannon in the fort, but had not a single shot for it. The British also had one ... so fixed as to rake the parade in front of the barracks. ... The artillery officers offered a gill of rum for each shot fired from that piece, which the soldiers would procure. ... The shot would often be seized before its motion had fully ceased, and conveyed off to our gun, to be sent back again to its former owners. When the lucky fellow who had caught it had swallowed his rum, he would return to wait for another, exulting that he had been more lucky or more dexterous than his fellows.

By now, the chevaux-de-frise had diverted enough of the Delaware's tidal current away from the main channel to cause a deepening of the shallow current that ran between Mud Island and the Pennsylvania shore. So, in the pre-dawn hours of November 14th, the British moved some guns into the channel, but, by noon, Lt. Colonel Fleury was recording that his garrison had "silenced the enemy's floating battery." John Andre wrote that the rebel sniper "fire from the blockhouses was so hot that the crew jumped overboard and waded ashore after firing very few shots."

The garrison's success in the channel was short-lived, for, the next morning, the floating battery would return to action. This time, it would be supported by the Pennsylvania shore batteries and the arrival of several British warships, bringing dozens more guns to bear, increasing the magnitude of the bombardment to a level that would not be seen in America again until the Civil War, eighty-five years later. One soldier thought the noise was like "a constant thunderstorm." Muenchhausen describes the action in the river:

> November 15. About eight o'clock in the morning, the *Vigilant* luckily worked herself through and anchored about 200 paces from the fort. With her, a small sloop arrived, aboard which Admiral Howe had a battery of three 18-pounders mounted. At the same time, five large warships moved as close as possible to the chevaux de frise and covered the battery ship with a continuous strong fire, for the rebel ships that were near Red Bank tried to come around [the southern tip of Mud Island] to ruin the *Vigilant* and the sloop with their much heavier fire.
>
> At this time the fire from our land batteries started again, with new vigor. The fire of our ships stopped the rebel ships from coming around, after which our ships turned their fire on the fort. The rebel floating batteries,

galleys, sloops and frigate answered our fire well, and the *Isis* was badly damaged, having taken 34 shells that went right through her. Their fort on the island fired only a few shots.

The British ships had managed to come up within striking distance of the fort, after seemingly sailing right through the chevaux-de-frise! How could that have happened? Robert Whyte, the man who had been in charge of planting the chevaux months before, evidently was a secret Tory at heart, for he had recently defected. He reportedly persuaded a very discouraged General Howe to persevere and make one final push against Fort Mifflin. Whyte piloted the British ships through a narrow gap that only he and a few others knew about. Now the British ships were dangerously close to Fort Mifflin, which lay at the southern tip of Mud Island, just north of the chevaux.

The end would come soon, though the fort's engineer, the young Frenchman, Lieutenant Colonel Fleury, could not see it coming. The day before, he had noted in his journal:

> The fire of the enemy will never take the fort. It may kill us men, but this is the fortune of war. And all their bullets will never render them masters of the island if we have courage enough to remain on it.

Captain Muenchhausen continues his account of November 15th:

> Everyone expected that they would surrender because their parapets and log houses had suffered so much from our continuous fire since the 10th of the month that one could see through them, and because they now receive the strongest fire from all sides. On the *Vigilant*, English riflemen were posted on the masts; they fire from up there, quite accurately, into the fort.
> General Howe as well as Lord Howe, who had come

up by boat early this morning, were in the mortar battery till seven o'clock in the evening. ... Everyone believed and wished that the General would give the command to storm any moment. But he did not do so, for he maintained that the enemy could not stand our dreadful fire much longer, and would leave the fort voluntarily.

Nevertheless, the landing force had their orders. Ensign Rueffer recorded in his journal on November 15th that, "In case the ships can not compel the fort to surrender today, the troops are to storm the fort tomorrow at four o'clock." Private Joseph Plumb Martin describes the action of November 15th:

> At the dawn, we discovered [the enemy's ships] ... We immediately opened our batteries upon them, but they appeared to take very little notice of us. We heated some shot, but by some mistake twenty-four pound shot were heated instead of eighteen ... The enemy soon began their firing upon us and there was music indeed.
>
> The soldiers were all ordered to take their posts at the palisadoes, which they were ordered to defend to the last extremity, as it was expected the British would land under the fire of their cannon and attempt to storm the fort. ...
>
> In the height of the cannonade it was desirable to hoist a signal flag for some of our galleys to come to our assistance. The officers inquired who would undertake it. As none appeared willing for some time, I was about to offer my services. I considered it no more exposure of my life than it was to remain where I was. While I was hesitating, a sergeant of the artillery offered himself.
>
> He accordingly ascended to the round top, pulled down the flag to affix the signal flag to the halyard; upon which the enemy, thinking we had struck [our colors],

ceased firing in every direction and cheered.

"Up with the flag!" was the cry of our officers in every part of the fort. The flags were accordingly hoisted, and the firing was immediately renewed. The sergeant then came down and had not gone half a rod from the foot of the staff when he was cut in two by a cannon shot. This caused me some serious reflection at the time. ...

As soon as it was dark we began to make preparations for evacuating the fort and endeavoring to escape to the Jersey shore. ... They were so nigh that I could hear distinctly what they said on board the sloop. "We will give it to the d----d rebels in the morning." The thought that then occupied my mind I as well remember, "The d----d rebels will show you a trick which the devil never will; they will go off and leave you."

November 16th was a very cold day, with snow that began falling at noon. It was also noteworthy for other reasons. Ensign Rueffer:

> This morning, about two o'clock, the rebels evacuated Mud Island, after having set their barracks on fire. The damage ... is indescribable. There is no place a foot in length where one can walk which has not been hit by a cannonball. ... Noteworthy is the fact that, one year ago today, Fort Knyphausen [formerly Fort Washington, on New York Island] fell into our hands.

Private Joseph Plumb Martin evacuated with the other survivors to Red Bank. Outside the fort, he saw one of his messmates on the ground, "lying in a long line of dead men who had been brought out of the fort to be conveyed to the main." He was "the most intimate associate I had in the army." Martin concludes his account:

> Here ends the account of as hard and fatiguing a job as occurred during the Revolutionary War. But there has been but little notice taken of it, the reason of which is there was no Washington, Putnam or Wayne there. Great men get great praise; little men, nothing. ...
>
> The second day of our march we met two regiments advancing to relieve us. When asked where they were going, they said to relieve the garrison in the fort. We informed them that the British had done that already. ...
>
> We continued our march until we arrived in the vicinity of the main army. We again turned into a wood for the night. The leaves and ground were as wet as water could make them. It was then foggy and the water dropping from the trees was like a shower. We endeavored to get fire by flashing powder on the leaves, but this failing, we were forced by our old master, Necessity, to lay down and sleep if we could, with three others of our constant companions, Fatigue, Hunger and Cold.

With the British capture of Fort Mifflin, Red Bank was now vulnerable. Howe sent General Lord Cornwallis over to New Jersey with a large British force, to prepare a second land attack against Fort Mercer. Washington reacted by sending General Nathanael Greene with several thousand men to cross over the river, too. And, in keeping with his long-standing philosophy of attacking the enemy only when its forces were divided, Washington instructed Greene to look for an opportunity to attack Cornwallis.

However, though Greene had been given authority to act independently, he suspected that any action he initiated must result in a victory, or else not be undertaken at all. Greene feared that another defeat might cause Congress to supplant Washington with Gates. (Even the enemy, apparently, knew of the precarious position the American commander was in. Major Bauermeister, about this time, noted, "All the deserters tell us that he has fallen out with Congress and that General

Gates is now esteemed much more.") Therefore, Greene hesitated to engage Lord Cornwallis, who reportedly had superior numbers. Nathanael Greene wrote to George Washington on November 24th:

> Your Excellency observes in your last, you must leave the propriety of attacking the enemy to me. Would you advise me to fight them with very unequal numbers? ... For your sake, for my own sake, & for my country's sake, I wish to attempt every thing which will meet with your Excellency's approbation. I will run any risque, or engage under any disadvantages, if I can only have your countenance if unfortunate. With the publick I know success sanctifies every thing, and that only.

While Greene hesitated, Washington received, on November 25th, "accounts from the city [which] say Lord Cornwallis was expected back today or tomorrow." This made Washington fear that "they mean to collect their whole force while ours is divided, and make an attack on the army on this side." Therefore, he wrote to Greene, "I desire (except you have a plan or prospect of doing some thing to advantage) that you will rejoin me with your whole force as quick as possible." Greene evacuated Red Bank's Fort Mercer, and returned with his command to the main army on the west side of the river.

With the evacuation of Forts Mifflin and Mercer, Commodore Hazelwood ordered his entire fleet be set afire, rather than have it fall into the enemy's hands. A Philadelphian named Robert Morton walked down to the river's edge to see the moving spectacle.

> The American Navy on fire coming up with a flood tide, and burning with the greatest fury. Some of them drifted within 2 miles of the town and were carried back by the ebb tide. They burnt nearly 5 hours; four of them blew up.

Muenchhausen also enjoyed the show, "caused by 15 burning ships during the dark night ... [moving] up and down with the tide. It was the most spectacular sight I have ever seen."

Thus ended the Americans' commendable efforts to hold the Delaware River and force the British to evacuate Philadelphia. Sir William Howe could relax now, and settle in with his mistress for a comfortable, relatively peaceful winter, one filled with plays, balls and other diversions, almost as if to deny the very existence of a state of war. Howe's adversary, though, would not have it so easy. George Washington would struggle with all his might to keep his army intact through another hard winter, this time at a place called the Valley Forge.

CHAPTER SIX
VALLEY FORGE
DECEMBER 1777 - JUNE 1778

"No meat! No coat! No blanket! No soldier!"

- *Popular chant at Valley Forge.*

December 3, 1777, Passy, France. The three American plenipotentiaries to the court of King Louis XVI are at Benjamin Franklin's residence in this suburb of Paris. A carriage rolls to a stop on the gravel courtyard in front of the house, the horses much lathered from their ride. Jonathan Austin, a courier from Boston, has arrived with news for Franklin, Silas Deane and Arthur Lee, who are just now coming out of the house as Austin steps from the carriage. Lee's secretary, who is secretly in the employ of the British government, provides us with the following account:

> When Mr. Austin's chaise was heard in the court, they all went out to meet him. Before he had time to alight, Dr. Franklin cried out, "Sir, is Philadelphia taken?"
> "Yes, sir," replied Austin.
> Upon hearing this, Dr. Franklin clasped his hands and turned as if to go back into the house. "But sir," said Austin, "I have greater news than that. General Burgoyne and his whole army are prisoners of war."

Many historians have been quick to point to Burgoyne's defeat at Saratoga as the turning point in the war, claiming it convinced the French to finally agree to a military alliance. But Washington's aggressiveness in attacking Howe's camp at Germantown may deserve as much credit. The Viscount de Noailles, French ambassador in London, had forwarded to Paris a glowing report of George Washington's performance at Germantown, and described Howe's situation at Philadelphia as desperate - not "establishing a free communication with his navy ... [and] encircled on all sides." No less a critic of George Washington than Congressman John Adams would write home from Paris on July 23, 1778:

> General Gates was the ablest negotiator you had in Europe; next to him, General Washington's attack on the enemy at Germantown. I do not know, indeed, whether this last affair had not more influence on the European mind than that of Saratoga. Although the attempt was unsuccessful, the military gentlemen of Europe considered it as the most decisive proof that America would finally succeed.

Now, Franklin decided, the time had finally come to pressure the French to commit themselves. King Louis had been holding back, waiting for his uncle, King Charles of Spain, to give him advice and to join him in such an alliance. However, the Spanish King, ruler of the largest colonial empire in the world, was reluctant to support a colonial uprising. Would the French King be willing to venture into the alliance without his Bourbon ally?

The Comte de Vergennes, French Prime Minister, had been informed by Noailles that the British Parliament was about to convene a new session, and that British Prime Minister Lord North was preparing to introduce a new conciliatory offer to end the war on peaceful terms, keeping America within the British Empire. Benjamin Franklin, also aware of these reports, used them to his advantage, knowing what the French desired most. He told Vergennes, "There is not a moment to be lost ... [if King Louis] wishes to secure the friendship of America, and detach her entirely from the mother country."

Vergennes agreed, and pressed the king to stop waiting for a reply from his uncle in Madrid. The prevailing line of reasoning supporting a Franco-American alliance held that here was an opportunity, not to be missed, to humiliate England. As the Frenchman, Louis DuPortail, chief engineer in Washington's army, had recently written to the French minister of war, "True, it will cost millions," but it will be worth it to break the "power of England, which, when bereft of her colonies [and] without [her American] commerce, will lose her consequence in the world and leave France without a rival." This, King Louis was finally persuaded, should overrule his passion for balancing the budget. On December 6th, a courier from the palace at Versailles arrived at Passy to verbally deliver a message to Benjamin Franklin:

> His Majesty has resolved to recognize the independence of, and enter into a treaty of commerce and alliance with, the United States of America; and he will not only acknowledge their independence, but actually support it with all the means in his power.

The formal signing of the treaty of alliance would come two months later, in February, 1778. Looking optimistically to the end of the war, the treaty's terms called for the United States to give up any claims on the British Sugar Islands, while France would forego all claims on Bermuda and British Canada. Neither France nor the U.S. would be allowed to make a truce or sign a treaty of peace with Britain without first obtaining the formal consent of her ally. The treaty also stipulated, at France's insistence, that neither party would cease hostilities against Britain until America's independence was assured. France was in this war to break up the British Empire. Spain would eventually join the alliance in 1779, followed by the Netherlands in 1780, both looking for the spoils of war without contributing much militarily.

* * * * *

The alliance had finally come, but it would be several months before any warships or troops arrived from France. In the meantime, back in Pennsylvania, life went on as usual for the opposing armies.

Private Joseph Plumb Martin had reached his seventeenth birthday five days after he and his comrades evacuated Mud Island's Fort Mifflin. Now, three weeks later, he and the rest of the army were celebrating a "Continental Thanksgiving, ordered by Congress." Martin had to stand at attention and listen to the chaplain's thanksgiving sermon, after receiving his entire rations for that day: "half a gill of rice and a tablespoonful of vinegar," the rice to provide sustenance and the vinegar to ward off intestinal diseases.

In those same General Orders for December 17th, in which George Washington announced the thanksgiving, he had made it a point to thank his army for its dedication in the long campaign just concluded:

> The commander in chief with the highest satisfaction expresses his thanks to the officers and soldiers for the fortitude and patience with which they have sustained the fatigues of the campaign. Altho' in some instances we unfortunately failed, upon the whole, Heaven has smiled on our arms and, by a spirited continuance of the measures necessary for our defence, we shall finally obtain the end of our War for Independence, Liberty and Peace. ...

The next day, having already sent General Smallwood's Maryland brigade to Wilmington, Delware, to protect points south of Philadelphia, and Count Casimir Pulaski and his dragoons to New Jersey, Washington marched the rest of the army to a wooded hillside 22 miles northwest of the city. This rural hamlet, called "the Valley Forge," was chosen at the suggestion of General Anthony Wayne. His homestead being just five miles away, he was familiar with the natural strengths of this area of gently rolling low hills. In the words of General Washington's aide-de-camp, Lieutenant Colonel John Laurens, it was "far enough from the enemy not to be reached in a days march, and properly interposed between the enemy and the most valuable part of the country."

Some of Washington's generals had wanted the army to winter in a populated area, for the ease of transporting food supplies and a ready supply of housing. Rhode Island's James Varnum thought it was horrible "to establish winter quarters in a country wasted" already by both armies, and "without a single magazine." Johann Kalb, who was the son of a German peasant but styled himself Baron Johann de Kalb, objected to "wintering in this desert," and was disappointed that his own advice to winter at Wilmington had been disregarded by the commander in chief. He wrote to his friend and patron, Count Charles-Francis de Broglie:

> [Where to encamp] was discussed in all its length and breadth - a bad practice to which they are addicted here - and good advice was not taken. ... It is unfortunate that Washington is so easily led. He is the bravest and truest of men, has the best intentions and a sound judgment ... It is a pity he is so weak and has the worst of advisers in the men who enjoy his confidence. If they are not traitors, they are certainly gross ignoramuses.

Chaplain Ebenezer David, though, disagreed with Kalb. He wrote home to Rhode Island on December 22nd:

> I believe the measures to be the best possible in present circumstances. ... Had we retired to any of the towns, we should have found them crowded with refugees. ... We ruin the country for miles around, wherever we lay.

Reverend David, signed on as a chaplain in 1776, would serve in the medical department at Valley Forge, and die there in March, 1778, a victim of "an epidemic disease."

Private Joseph Plumb Martin relates the army's difficult march to Valley Forge:

> The army was now not only starved, but ... [much of it] shirtless, barefoot, and destitute of blankets. I procured a small piece of raw cowhide and made myself a pair of moccasins, which kept my feet from the frozen ground, although the hard edges so galled my ankles while on a march that it was with much difficulty and pain that I could wear them afterwards. But the only alternative I had was to endure this or go barefoot, as hundreds of my companions had to, till they might be tracked by their blood upon the rough frozen ground.
>
> ... We arrived at the Valley Forge in the evening [December 19, 1777]. It was dark; there was no water to be found and I was perishing with thirst. I searched for water till I was weary and came to my tent without finding any. I felt at that instant that I would have taken victuals or drink from the best friend I had on earth by force. ... Two soldiers, whom I did not know, passed by. They had some water in their canteens ... I tried to beg a draught of water from them, but they were rigid. At length, I persuaded them to sell me a drink for three pence, Pennsylvania currency, which was every cent of property I could then call my own.
>
> I lay here two nights and one day and had not a morsel of anything to eat all the time, save half of a small pumpkin, which I cooked by placing it upon a rock, the skin side uppermost, and making a fire upon it. By the time it was heat through, I devoured it with as keen an appetite as I should a pie made of it at some other time.

Joseph Plumb Martin was one of the lucky ones, for he was ordered "on command," that is, on an expedition. Instead of staying in camp and having to help chop down trees and build a cabin to live in, he was assigned to be part of a foraging detail. Before they left, an emaciated steer was butchered so that the party of 21 could have some food to sustain them. They were ordered to march into the countryside, find food, persuade the farmers or merchants to sell, and leave receipts for what was taken.

> We marched till night, when we halted and took up our quarters at a large farmhouse. The lieutenant took up his quarters for the night with the people of the house. We were put into the kitchen. We had a snug room and a comfortable fire, and we began to think about cooking our *fat* beef. One of the men proposed to the landlady to sell her a shirt for some sauce [vegetables]. She readily took the shirt, which was worth a dollar at least. After we had received the sauce, we went to work to cook our supper.
>
> By the time it was eatable, the family had gone to rest. We saw where the woman went into the cellar [to fetch the vegetables], and, she having left us a candle, we took it into our heads that a little good cider would not make our supper relish any the worse. So some of the men took the water pail and drew it full of excellent cider, which did not fail to raise our spirits considerably.
>
> Before we lay down, the man who sold the shirt, having observed that the landlady had flung it into a closet, took a notion to repossess it. We marched off early in the morning before the people of the house were stirring, consequently did not know or see the woman's chagrin at having been overreached by the soldiers.

While Private Martin and his foraging detail were having their adventures, most of the other 10,000 soldiers were busy constructing huts for the winter. A few days after they reached Valley Forge, General Washington, who had promised the soldiers he would "share in your hardships," left his own canvas marquee and moved into one of the first completed huts. In late January, when the majority of the more than one thousand huts were complete, he would finally take up residence, with his slave, Billy Lee, and his nine aides, crowding into one of the eleven farmhouses that composed the hamlet of Valley Forge.

The house was a medium-sized one, built of stone, and owned by a Quaker named Isaac Potts. The Potts family, to make room, moved into an attic above the kitchen. As he had done during previous winters at Cambridge, Massachusetts, and Morristown, New Jersey, the commander in chief sent for his wife. On February 10th, Martha Washington arrived and immediately persuaded her husband to have his soldiers build a log dining room, off the kitchen, since she would be hosting innumerable meals during the six months the house served as headquarters. Martha would be an indispensable source of comfort and encouragement to George during perhaps the most trying time of his life. Martha would write home to Virginia, confiding to a friend, "The General is well, but much worn with fatigue and anxiety. I never knew him to be so anxious as now."

"Valley Forge." There was no forge now, since the British, passing through the area in September, had destroyed it while on their march to Philadelphia. And there was no valley, just a broad slope overlooking Valley Creek near its confluence with the Schuylkill River. Ironically, the slope's highest point, near its western end, was named Mount Joy; here Henry Knox would establish his artillery park, and the French engineer, General Louis le Begue de Presle Duportail, would oversee the digging of entrenchments along the slope. Combined with the natural protection of nearby Schuylkill River and Valley Creek, the camp soon offered a seemingly impregnable defensive posture. When a British officer, coming out to reconnoiter, returned to Philadelphia, he would advise William Howe that an attack on the rebel camp would be "unjustifiable."

Streets were laid out, with row upon row of log huts, each built and occupied by twelve privates or non-commissioned officers, "each mess to build their own" hut. Behind these was a street of officers' huts, each to house from one to six officers, depending on rank. Each brigade also had several huts for the women and children camp followers, though some women undoubtedly shared bunks with their men. General Orders for December 18th included instructions for the huts:

> Plan for the construction of hutts. Dimensions 14 by 16 foot, sides, ends & roof made of logs, the roof made light with split slabs, the sides made tight with clay; the fire places made of wood & secured with clay in the inside 18 inches thick, this fire place to be in the rear of the hutt, the door to be in the end next the street ... Side walls 6 1/2 feet high.

To encourage the men, Washington promised "to reward the party in each regiment which finishes their hut in the quickest, and most workmanlike manner with twelve dollars." In many of the huts, before building them the men would dig down a foot or two, so the earth would provide some insulation from the cold. Although the orders specified that each hut should be 14 feet wide and 16 feet long, recent archaeological digs have discovered huts of various dimensions, some as small as eight by ten feet.

Shortages of every kind of necessary tool accounted for the construction dragging on well into January. A surgeon's mate, Jonathan Todd, wrote home to his father in Connecticut:

> Dec. 25 - We have but one dull ax to build a logg hutt. When it will be done knows not. ...
> Jan. 19 - I will give you a description of our hutt which is built nearly after the same model of the others. It is 18 feet long & 16 broad, two rooms and two chimneys at opposite corners of the house. The floor is made

of split loggs, as is the partition & door. The whole of it was made with one poor ax & not another tool ... the roof is not the best in wet weather, oak slabs cover'd with turf & earth. Our inards work is not yet completed.

Though the huts finally gave the suffering army some shelter, life inside was primitive. The roofs leaked terribly whenever it rained, and, despite their best efforts to chink mud between the logs, the wind found its way through the walls. With a severe scarcity of blankets and even straw, the bunks were uncomfortable, and the only furniture was typically a couple of thick logs to sit upon in front of the fireplace, which was nearly always smoky from burning green wood.

Weakened by exposure to the weather and a lack of sustenance, the men could not progress very fast at building the huts. But they struggled on, anxious to leave their campfires for the shelter the completed huts would provide. Dr. Albigence Waldo, a highly educated and well liked surgeon of the Connecticut Line:

> December 21. ... Heartily wish myself at home. My skin and eyes are almost spoiled with continual smoke. A general cry thro' the camp this evening among the soldiers, "No meat! No meat!" The distant vales echoed back the melancholy sound - "No meat! No meat!" Immitating the noise of crows and owls, also, made a part of the confused musick.
>
> What have you for your dinners, boys? "Nothing but fire cake [flour mixed with water, then heated] and water, Sir." At night: "Gentlemen, the supper is ready." What is your supper, lads? "Fire cake and water, Sir."
>
> December 22. Lay excessive cold and uncomfortable last night. My eyes are started out from their orbits like a rabbit's eyes, occasioned by a great cold and smoke.
>
> What have you got for breakfast, lads? "Fire cake and water, Sir." The Lord send that our Commissary of

> Purchases may live [on] fire cake and water till their glutted guts are turned to pasteboard. ...
>
> December 23. This evening an excellent player on the violin ... in the next tent to mine, [playing] soft airs immediately called up in remembrance all the endearing expressions, the tender sentiments ... from the first time I gained the heart & affections of the tenderest of the fair. ... [It] forced out the sympathetic tear. I wish'd to have the musick cease, and yet dreading its ceasing, lest I should lose sight of these dear ideas which gave me pain and pleasure at the same instant. ...
>
> December 24. Huts go on slowly. Cold and smoke make us fret. But mankind are always fretting ... we are never easy, allways repining at the providence of an all-wise & benevolent being, blaming our country or faulting our friends. But I don't know of anything that vexes a man's soul more than hot smoke continually blowing into his eyes, & when he attempts to avoid it, is met by a cold and piercing wind.

When most of the huts had been completed, General Orders specified that the tents should be turned in for repairs and storage. But instead, "the General was pained ... [to learn] that some tents have already been cut up by the soldiers" to wrap around their feet. The men felt that, if there was going to be an army to need tents next spring, that army must first survive the winter.

From recent archaeological research, we know that the occupants, after eating, typically discarded their meat bones into a corner of the hut. This must have only added to the vermin and stench that gradually increased during the winter and spring. In April, General Orders directed that the chinks between the logs be removed "and every other method be taken to render them as airy as possible ... [and] the powder of a musquet cartridge burnt in each hutt daily to purify the air."

The air was not much better outside the huts. Fifteen hundred horses died at Valley Forge, and lay above hard frozen ground until spring. Any extended period of stationary camping always produced unhealthful conditions, as hygiene tended to be lax. A review of General Orders for the six months the army was at Valley Forge shows frequent admonishments relating to the necessity of using and maintaining the latrines, or "vaults." The standard punishment for not using them was five lashes, though one brigade had a guard of three "sentinals to fire on any man who shall be found easing himself elsewhere than in ye valts." By June 10th, conditions were so unhealthy that the army brought the tents and moved one mile away, due to "unwholesome exhalations from the ground, arising from a deposit of filth accumulated during six months."

Early in the encampment, another problem was addressed: soldiers whose enlistments had expired were taking their blankets home with them. On January 21st, "Commanding officers of regts [were] directed to stop all the blankets" leaving camp; "men who are going home" must leave their blankets behind to "afford more comfort to their brother soldiers who keep the field."

Lack of proper food and clothing meant low resistance to disease. About 2,000 men would die of various causes at Valley Forge, some from hypothermia, influenza or pneumonia, others from "putrid fever" (typhoid, typhus), or the "bloody flux" (dysentery). Their stiff, frozen bodies were stripped naked and stacked, like firewood, in back of the hospital until spring could thaw the rock-hard ground sufficiently to allow graves to be dug.

One universal health problem was "the itch" (scabies). Johann Kalb observed many "poor fellows covered over and over with scabs" from it. On January 8th, all regimental surgeons were directed to see to it that those with the itch be "anointed." Joseph Plumb Martin describes how the soldiers in his hut administered the cure to themselves:

> I had it to such a degree that by the time I got into winter quarters I could scarcely lift my hands to my head. Some of our foraging party had acquaintances in

> the artillery and by their means we procured sulphur ... [and] made preparations for a general attack upon it.

The cure was a gooey salve made by heating a mixture of sulfur and tallow to the boiling point, then applying it to the skin, where it would burn and blister, and give off an overpowering stench. First, the patients stripped themselves naked and laid down on ox hides they'd spread upon the dirt floor in front of a blazing fireplace.

> We began the operation by plying each other's outsides with brimstone and tallow, and the inside with hot whiskey sling. Had the animalcule of the itch been endowed with reason, they would have quit their entrenchments and taken care of themselves when we had made such a formidable attack upon them ...
> We obtained a complete victory, though it had like to have cost some of us our lives. Two were so overcome, not by the enemy, but by their too great exertions in the action, that they [ran outside and] lay all night naked upon the field. The rest of us got to our berths somehow, as well as we could; but we killed the itch and we were satisfied, for it had almost killed us. This was a decisive victory, the only one we had achieved lately.

The first few days at Valley Forge had been notable as a period of famine, an occurrence to be repeated two more times during that winter. Eventually, the chorus of "No meat!" would take on additional verses of "No coat! No blanket! No soldier!" as the men threatened to desert. Many did desert that winter, and headed for home. Others, watching their hutmates die one by one, and agonizing over the decision to leave, decided to stay, fearing most the terrible cold and distance to travel to their homes. In Philadelphia, the British reported more than 1,000 rebel deserters coming in to their lines, though Lieutenant Feilitzsch suspected that some of "the rebels only wish to get uniforms from us," then desert and return to their comrades.

Deserters who were caught, often by the foraging parties, were brought back to camp, court-martialled, and executed in front of a sampling of the army. In one condemned man's case, on January 10, 1778, forty men from each brigade had to stand at attention and witness his hanging. Some, though, escaped the death sentence when a general would occasionally show compassion. While at Valley Forge, General Anthony Wayne resided at the house of his cousin, a widow named Sarah Walker, known as "grandmother" to all in the village. When Mrs. Walker learned that Anthony Wayne had presided over a court-martial that sentenced five deserters to death, she had the general summoned to her room.

> Cousin Wayne! I hear five deserters have been taken and are sentenced to be shot. This must not be. Poor fellows - hungry, cold and almost naked. If I were a soldier, I would do so, too.

General Wayne was moved enough to commute their sentences. Nevertheless, there were plenty of executions. Fifteen-year-old Hugh McDonald was forced to witness one. William McKay, a spy, was "the first man I ever saw hung. It so affected me that I could not bear the sight, nor did I eat anything for two days afterward."

It was not just the privates and non-commissioned corporals and sergeants who were leaving. Though not technically deserting, hundreds of officers resigned their commissions and went home, ninety from Virginia alone. Dr. Waldo, alluding to the common practice back home of a village providing support for the families of soldiers and sailors who were away, reflected on the seriousness of the problem:

> December 28. The present circumstances of the soldier is better by far than the officer's, for the soldier's family is provided for at the public expence, but the officer [himself is] obliged to pay for the officer's family. ...

> Many cannot procure half the material comforts that are wanted in a family - this produces continual letters of complaint from home. When the officer has been fatiguing thro' wet & cold and returns to his tent where he finds a letter directed to him from his wife, fill'd with the most heart aching tender complaints a woman is capable of writing, acquainting him with the incredible difficulty with which she procures a little bread for herself & children ... she begs of him to consider that charity begins at home, and not suffer his family to perish with want. ... What man is there who would not be disheartened from persevering in the best of causes, the cause of his country?
>
> December 29. So much talk about discharges among the officers ... his Excellency lately expressed his fears of being left alone with the soldiers only. ...

The next day, Doctor Waldo noted that the Americans were not the only ones tired of war:

> December 30. Eleven deserters came in to-day, some Hessians & some English. One of the Hessians took an ax in his hand & cut away the ice of the Schuylkill ... and waded through to our camp - he was 1/2 hour in the water. They had a promise when they engag'd that the war would be ended in one year; they were now tired of the service.

To stop the wholesale resignations by officers, General Washington persuaded Congress to pass a resolution guaranteeing pensions to all commissioned officers who committed to stay in the army for the duration of the war.

Lack of food and clothing were the most frustrating problems, and these were due to a myriad of causes, but often the blame was placed on the Continental Congress. Private Dennis Kennedy spent most of his time "threatening to desert as soon as he got shoes, and cursing Congress." On January 19th, a soldier named Joseph Clark noted in his journal that, "The cry against Congress still continued as high as ever ... with the greatest contempt and detestation."

A common expression in camp that winter, for a man freezing to death, was to say he was "dying of meases." The reference was to the Congress-appointed clothier general, James Meases. Before winter's end, General Steuben would be observing coatless officers, dressed "in a sort of dressing gown made of an old blanket or woolen bed cover."

Barefoot sentries were seen standing on their hats, to protect their feet from the cold ground. Sometimes they did not return to their huts, too frozen or frostbitten to make it back. They would fall asleep, or fall down from exhaustion, too weak from lack of food to fight off the packs of wolves that nightly surrounded the camp. At other times, their hutmates, worried at their not returning, would go in search of them, and bring them in, their "feet and legs," in Lafayette's words, "froze till they became black, and it was necessary to amputate them."

The Commissary Department, the organization for feeding the army, was taken over by Congress in the summer of 1777, in order to keep a closer eye on expenses and abuses. Congress split the Commissary Department into a Bureau of Supply and a Bureau of Issue, which actually made it more inefficient. Congressional committees now oversaw the operation, appointed all deputy commissioners, approved contracts, etc. No longer would the commissaries and their deputies be awarded commissions on purchases; instead, they would now receive a flat salary. This disincentive to work hard, coupled with all the other frustrations caused by Congressional interference, led to the resignations of capable, experienced personnel.

Their replacements, while learning their jobs, had to cope with overwhelming obstacles. Suppliers and teamsters balked at price ceilings set by Congress. This being a time of rampant inflation, fixed prices were doomed to fail. Farmers and wagonmasters could readily find someone else to contract with who would pay two or three times the army's fixed rate. New York flour ended up being shipped to New England markets. New Jersey pork, destined for the army at Valley Forge, instead, spoiled for lack of transport. Civilians, able to pay higher prices, competed successfully for supplies with the agents of the army's commissary and quartermaster departments. A writer for the *Independent Chronicle* asked, on March 26, 1778, "How can it be that any and every individual can purchase shirts, stockings, shoes, etc. the vulture-eyed agents [are] unable to purchase for the soldiery?" William Ellery, Congressman from Rhode Island, despaired over the situation:

> The love of country and public virtue are annihilated. If Diogenes were alive and were to search America with candles, would he find an honest man?

The soldiers and officers bitterly resented being forced to endure starvation amidst plenty. Colonel John Brooks wrote to a friend in Massachusetts:

> I know of no reason why one part of the community should sacrifice their all for the good of it, while the rest are filling their coffers. The states of Pennsylvania and Maryland do not seem to have any more idea of liberty than a savage has of civilization.

Some farmers held onto their grain and cattle, waiting for prices to rise. Or they sold it to the British Army, which offered hard sterling, not rapidly depreciating paper Continental dollars. A common derisive expression of the time was, "Not worth a Continental!" In vain, Washington appealed to Congress for help, but they merely passed the problem back to him, authorizing him to "subsist his army" by seizing whatever it needed from "such parts of the country as are in its vicinity." This, Washington wrote back, he was unwilling to do. Congress then reproved him for his "delicacy in exerting military authority." But Washington knew that the consequences of commandeering what his army needed from citizens would be a serious loss of popular support for the cause.

So the supply problems continued, and by February, during another period of famine, Washington was fearing "a melancholy and alarming catastrophe," the mutiny and dispersion of his army, for lack of provisions. But they stayed, and the aristocratic Virginian, who at times had been critical of his rank and file, found himself praising them in a private letter: "Naked and starving as they are, we cannot enough admire the incomparable patience and fidelity of the soldiery."

Finally, changes were made in critical departments. Jeremiah Wadsworth filled the vacant position of commissary general, and Major General Nathanael Greene was asked to take on the duties of quartermaster general, a position last filled so ineffectually by Thomas Mifflin who had resigned in the fall. At first, Greene was reluctant, thinking he would have to give up his field command. "Who," he asked his commander, "ever heard of a quartermaster in history?" So George Washington told him he could retain command of his division of the army, while also handling these new duties. Greene agreed.

Washington directed Greene to sweep the countryside for cattle, horses, sheep, oxen, and "every kind of forage that may be found." Greene would take what was reasonable, and leave certificates of valuation for the stock and "provender" taken. Greene instructed his officers, on February 14th: "Harden your hearts, ... we are in the midst of a damn nest of Tories." He also took firm control over the administration of the distribution channels, so that by late winter the army at last started to have, with some regularity, enough to eat.

Troops assigned to foraging details were envied and hated by those left behind to starve in camp, because the foragers were the only ones who consistently had enough to eat. One such fortunate soldier was Joseph Plumb Martin.

> We fared much better than I had ever done in the army before, or ever did afterwards. We had very good provisions all winter and generally enough of them.

Some of us were constantly in the country with the wagons; we went out by turns and had no one to control us.

The foragers found it easier to take food than other, more essential, property from the Pennsylvania farmers. Private Martin:

> When we had got possession of a horse we were sure to have half a dozen or more women pressing upon us, until, by some means or other, they would slip the bridle from the horse's head, and then we could catch him again if we could. It would answer no purpose to threaten to kill them with the bayonet or musket; they knew as well as we did that we would not put our threats in execution, and when they had thus liberated a horse, they would laugh at us and ask us why we did not do as we threatened, kill them, and then they would generally ask us into their houses and treat us with as much kindness as though nothing had happened.
> The women of Pennsylvania, taken in general, are certainly very worthy characters. I was always well treated both by them and the men, especially the Friends or Quakers ... [These] southern ladies had a queer idea of the Yankees (as they always called the New Englanders); they seemed to think that they were a people quite different from themselves. ... We stopped at a house, the mistress of which and the wagoner were acquainted. She had a pretty female child about four years old. The teamster was praising the child, extolling its gentleness and quietness, when the mother observed that it had been quite cross and crying all day. "I have been threatening," said she, "to give her to the Yankees."
> "Take care," said the wagoner, "how you speak of the Yankees, I have one of them here with me."
> "La!" said the woman. "Is he a Yankee? I thought he

was a Pennsylvanian. I don't see any difference between him and other people."

Some of the Pennsylvania troops, familiar with the Schuylkill's annual April shad run, led their comrades in a four week long flurry of net fishing. Also that month, so many cattle were making it into camp, from places as far away as Connecticut and Virginia, that General Washington had to request only "well-fatted" ones be sent.

Though clothing was hard to procure through official channels, it filtered into camp in other ways, including donations by patriotic civilians, and booty from captured British supply ships. The "greatest prize ever taken from them" was the frigate *Symmetry* which, while sailing from New York to Philadelphia, went aground in the lower Delaware and was taken by General Smallwood's Marylanders. They sent on the cargo, which included cloth and epaulets for officers' uniforms, 1,000 Brown Bess muskets, and General Howe's "silver plate and kitchen furniture." The ship also had a supernumerary cargo, according to Lafayette, who gleefully wrote to his wife about the "chaste officers' wives, who had come to rejoin their husbands; they were in great fear of being kept for the American army," but were sent under escort to Philadelphia.

In April, a shipment of shoes arrived from France, though Washington noted they were of such poor quality that they "afforded little more than a day's wear." By mid-June, when the army would finally leave Valley Forge, less than 100 soldiers would be without shoes, down from over 2,000 in December.

* * * * *

Life at Valley Forge that winter was a constant struggle to survive, a far cry from the pleasant times that a few officers had experienced just a few months before. An entertaining series of letters by a sixteen-year-old girl, Sarah ("Sally") Wister, shows the effects contact with army officers had on impressionable young ladies. Back in October, Sally and her friends, refugees from British-occupied Philadelphia, were living in a village west of Germantown when, one day, they heard the Continental Army passing by.

> October 19. As I lay in bed, Liddy came running into the room and said there was the greatest drumming, fifing and rattling of waggons that she had ever heard. We dressed and down stairs in a hurry. ... We returned with excellent appetites for our breakfast.
>
> Several officers called to get some refreshment, but none of consequence till afternoon. Cousin Prissa and myself were sitting at the door; I in a green skirt, dark short gown. Two genteel men of the military order rode up to the door. "Your servant, ladies," &c.; asked if they could have quarters for General Smallwood. Aunt Foulke thought she could accomodate them as well as most of her neighbors could. One of the officers dismounted and wrote "SMALLWOOD'S QUARTERS" over the door, which secured us from straggling soldiers. After this he mounted his steed and rode away.
>
> When we were alone, our dress and lips were put in order for conquest, and the hopes of adventures gave brightness to each countenance.

The general and his aides departed on November 3rd, which left Sally and the other girls of the house "very sober and immured in solitude." But Sally's favorite, a Major Stoddert, returned in December to recuperate there from a fever. Other guests in the house at that time included a Mister Tilly, who was "bashful when with girls," though "a very great laugher." He "talks so excessively fast that he often begins sentences without finishing the last, which confuses him very much, and then he blushes and laughs; in short, he keeps me in a perpetual good humour," wrote Sally Wister.

On December 12th, Major Stoddert, knowing that the Wister family was in possession of a life-size wooden caricature of a British grenadier, painted by Captain John Andre for one of their past plays, suggested a scheme to use the wooden dummy for some fun, at Mister Tilly's expense. That evening, the plan was put into execution, with the girls and a slave as co-conspirators. Sally relates:

> The gentlemen were very merry, and chatting on public affairs, when Seaton's negro opened the door, candle in hand, and said, "There's somebody at the door that wishes to see you."
> "Who? All of us?" said Tilly.
> "Yes, sir," answered the boy. They all rose and walked into the entry, Tilly first. The first object that struck his view was a British soldier. In a moment his ears were saluted with, "Is there any rebel officers here?" in a thundering voice.
> Not waiting for a second word, he darted like lightning out of the front door, through the yard, bolted o'er the fence, swamps, fences, thorn-hedges, and ploughed fields. ... The woods echoed with, "Which way did he go? Stop him! Surround the house!" ...
> "Major Stoddert," said I, "go call Tilly back. He will lose himself - indeed he will." ...
> After a while, we being in rather more composure, and our bursts of laughter less frequent, yet by no means subsided, Tilly entered, all splashed with mud. ... "Where have you been, Mr. Tilly?" asked one officer. (We girls were silent.) "I really imagined," said Major Stoddert, "that you were gone for your pistols. Pray, where were your pistols, Tilly?" ...
> He broke the silence by the following expression: "You may all go to the Devil."
> Stoddert caught hold of his coat, "Come back and see what you ran from," and dragged him to the door.

He gave it a look, said it was very natural, and his expressions gave fresh cause for diversion. We all retired to our different parlours, for to rest our faces, if I may say so. ...

December 20. General Washington's army have gone into winter quarters at the Valley Forge. We shall not see many of the military now. We shall be intimate with solitude. I am afraid stupidity will be a frequent guest.

* * * * *

Sally Wister and her girlfriends did not venture over to the camp at Valley Forge, nor would they be welcome there. On February 4th, General Orders included the following warning to the army:

The most pernicious consequences having arisen from suffering persons, women in particular, to pass and repass from Philadelphia to camp under pretence of coming out to visit friends in the army ... but really with an intent to intice soldiers to desert. All officers are desird to exert their utmost endeavors to prevent such interviews in future by forbiding the soldiers, under the severest penalties, from having any communication with such persons, and by ordering them when found in camp to be immediately turned out of it.

Two weeks before, a woman named Mary Johnson had been "charged with laying a plot to desert to the enemy." Six soldiers in the case were sentenced to 100 lashes, another was reprimanded, and Mary received 100 lashes and a drumming out of camp. As usual, the army had to be assembled to watch. In a typical "drumming out" ceremony, the offending party was "mounted on a horse back foremost without a saddle, coat turned wrong side out, hands tied behind - the fifes to play and the drums to roll till [the offender] be out of the lines of the Army - never more to return."

Besides the hardships endured there, we remember Valley Forge as the place where the ragtag army gained the discipline and confidence of a professional army. One man, a new arrival from Europe, was responsible for this metamorphosis: Friedrich Steuben. After stopping at York to present himself to the Congress, he showed up at Valley Forge on February 23rd. Forty-seven years old, of medium height and stocky build, a large nose and slightly balding pate, the man was magnificently uniformed, and trailed by a retinue of one secretary, a servant and two aides. He announced himself as Baron Friedrich von Steuben. He had added the "Baron" and the "n" to Steube, his born surname, just as his father had earlier added the "von," though the claim to nobility was spurious.

George Washington and a delegation of his top officers rode out from camp to welcome this former Prussian officer, and usher him to the encampment. The next day, the army mustered for his review. One curious soldier was suitably impressed, recalling his first impression of Steuben many years later:

> Never before or since have I had such an impression of the ancient fabled God of War as hen I looked on the baron: he seemed to me a perfect personification of Mars. The trappings of his horse, the enormous holsters of his pistols, his large size, and his strikingly martial aspect, all seemed to favor the idea.

Earlier, upon landing at Portsmouth, New Hampshire, Steuben had forwarded to Congress and General Washington copies of his letter of introduction, written by Benjamin Franklin in Paris. He described Steuben as a former "Lieutenant General in the King of Prussia's service," the most disciplined army in the western world.

Actually, his highest rank had been captain, and his most recent military position, in 1763, was deputy to the quartermaster general, which, translated into French, was *lieutenant general quartier maitre*.

So, Franklin introduced this "lieutenant general" in his letter to Congress, saying that Steuben (though he was really unemployed and penniless) had "given up an honorable and lucrative rank" to volunteer for the cause. Years after the war's conclusion, while living on his farm near Utica, New York, Steuben would write to his friend, Alexander Hamilton, and admit to "having made use of illicit stratagems to gain admission into the service of the United States." So who hadn't?

Steuben made a better initial impression than most of the army's other Europeans had, with their pompous airs, their condescension toward American officers, and their constant demands for promotion. In his covering letter, again in Benjamin Franklin's hand, Steuben informed George Washington:

> My greatest ambition is to render your country all the services in my power and to deserve the title of a citizen of America by fighting for the cause of your liberty.
>
> If the distinguished ranks in which I have served in Europe should be an obstacle, I had rather serve under your Excellency as a volunteer than to be a subject of discontent to such deserving officers as have already distinguished themselves amongst you.

Though Steuben spoke not a word of English, he impressed Washington as "a man of military knowledge" and a gentleman. Alexander Hamilton and another of Washington's aides, John Laurens (son of the new Congressional President, Henry Laurens), knew French, as did Steuben, so they served as his first translators. After a few days, John Laurens suggested that this rotund, likeable fellow was the "properest man" for the neglected post of inspector general (Thomas Conway was away at Albany). Washington asked Steuben to perform some of Conway's duties, despite having neither the title nor yet a commission. Steuben agreed and, ten days later, his results were already proving to be so astounding that Washington instructed the army to consider him Inspector General of the Army "till the pleasure of Congress shall be known."

After observing the army's deplorable state, and talking - through his two young interpreters - with most of its officers, Steuben realized the magnitude of his assignment. He found that there was not one standard procedure for the manual of arms, reloading, etc., but several. Individual soldiers favored whatever had first been taught to them, the various methods being either original or patterned after the French, English or Prussian standards. For the crash course in military discipline that he was developing, Steuben devised uniform and simple maneuvers, rather than try to teach "the entire [Prussian] system ... and inevitably fail."

Steuben decided to start with a model company, General Washington's Life Guard. Once trained, they would split up and go forth, with newly appointed brigade inspectors, to train the rest of the army. On March 17th, General Orders included this paragraph:

> One hundred chosen men are to be annexed to the Guard of the Commander in Chief for the purpose of forming a corps to be instructed in the maneuvers to be introduced into the army, and serve as a model for the execution of them.

Steuben trained them, spending from 6 a.m. to 6 p.m., with one meal break, every day on the muddy parade ground. Each evening he spent writing the next day's lesson in German, to be translated into French, then English, and finally copied by secretaries so that each brigade inspector could have his own copy. Steuben's "blue book" of *Regulations* would become the army's standard for decades.

Not knowing the language, Steuben often became frustrated with the awkwardness and ignorance of the men he was trying to teach. Then he would burst into violent fits of cussing, sometimes in German, sometimes in French, but always interlaced with several "Goddamns." Exasperated, he would ask his translator, Captain Benjamin Walker, to take over for him in English. *"Viens,* Walker, *mon ami, mon bon ami!*

sacre! Goddam de *gaucheries* of dese *badauts. Je ne puis plus.* I can curse them no more." His seventeen-year-old secretary, Pierre Duponceau, would years later recall that Steuben's "fits of passion were comical, and rather amused than offended the soldiers."

Before long, the men were able to keep step by watching the officer at the head of their column, instead of listening to a drummer. Steuben made the standard pace of the march 24 inches; the cadence he changed to 75 per minute for the "common step," 120 per minute for the "quick step." Steuben's new common step was a more satisfactory medium speed, between the former slow and quick steps.

At Brandywine, the old militia tradition of marching in one long "Indian file" had resulted in the rear of the line reaching the scene of action too late to be of use. Now, on a march, the army would no longer be strung out in long, unmanageable files, but stay in compact column formations four men across and double ranked. Steuben introduced platoon columns as the most compact and maneuverable. The men learned to wheel left or right, and quickly deploy from marching column into a battle line, facing either front or rear. Regardless of what the day's lesson was, time was found each day to practice using the bayonet. This was intended to build confidence for future engagements, when they would face British and Hessian bayonet charges. A New Jersey private wrote home in the spring, describing the changes in the army:

> It was almost impossible [before] to advance or retire in the presence of an enemy without disordering the line and falling into confusion; that misfortune, I believe, will seldom happen again - for the troops are instructed in a new and so happy a method of marching that they soon will be able to advance with the utmost regularity, even without musick.

Though he had been trained in the extreme discipline of Frederick the Great's Prussian Army, Steuben was now forced to accept a much different type of soldier. This he confided in a letter to a former comrade in Prussia:

> The genius of this nation is not in the least to be compared with that of the Prussians, Austrians or French. You say to your soldier, "Do this," and he doeth it, but I am obliged to say, "This is the reason why you ought to do that," and then he does it.

Company grade officers (captain or lieutenant) would now personally speak their orders to their men, abandoning "the miserable British sergeant system," in which orders had to be relayed through the non-commisioned sergeants (British officers did not lower themselves to speak to mere soldiers).

This did not please the French officers, who, Steuben informed his Prussian friend, "liked me as little in the forests of America as they did on the plains of Rossbach" in the previous war. Those American officers who were from the more aristocratic states of Pennsylvania and Virginia were also only gradually and reluctantly won over, though the New Englanders, "social levelers," were receptive to this new system of directly speaking to their men. Steuben later recalled:

> To remove that English prejudice which some officers entertained, namely, that to drill a recruit was a serjeant's duty and beneath the station of an officer, I often took the musket myself to show the men the manual exercise.

This impressed Colonel Alexander Scammel, adjutant general of the army:

> To see a gentleman, dignified with a lieutenant general's commission from the great Prussian monarch, condescend with a grace peculiar to himself to take under his direction a squad of ten or twelve men in the

capacity of a drill sergeant, commands the admiration of both officers and men.

Steuben's new *Regulations* also called for "patience and mildness" in training recruits, and stressed that officers should be attentive to their own duties, as well as the well-being and grievances of the privates. An officer should strive "to gain the love of his men; respect and obedience would naturally follow." At inspections, Steuben "inquired into the conduct of the officers towards their men ... and even visited some of the sick in their cabins," setting an example for the officers.

Friedrich Steuben was a lover of food and hated to eat alone. Unlike the other senior officers, he invited captains and lieutenants to his dinners, further endearing himself to the men, particularly the Yankees, who felt comfortable with this "leveling general." Sympathetic to the plight of these ragged Americans, he hosted one dinner "to which no one who had a whole pair of breeches was admitted." Steuben fondly recalled it, many years later, as his *sans culottes* dinner.

A second lieutenant from New Jersey, George Ewing, was very pleased with the new style of marching, as well as the greatly reduced number of steps in the manual of arms:

> This forenoon the brigade went through the maneuvers, under the direction of Baron Steuben. The step is about halfway betwixt slow and quick time, an easy and natural step, and I think much better than the former. The Manual also is altered by his direction. There are but ten words of command, which are as follows: 1. Poise Firelock. 2. Shoulder Firelock. 3. Present Arms. 4. Fix Bayonet. 5. Unfix Bayonet. 6. Load Firelock. 7. Make Ready. 8. Present. 9. Fire. 10. Order Firelock.

Before Steuben's *Regulations* was published in 1779, the eighth step in the manual of arms, "Present," was changed to "Take Sight," to emphasize the need to aim before firing.

Freidrich Steuben, himself, recognized his progress:

> My enterprise succeeded better than I had dared to expect, and I had the satisfaction, in a month's time, to see not only a regular step introduced into the army, but I also made maneuvers with ten and twelve battalions with as much precision as the evolution of a single company.

On April 1, 1778, John Laurens proudly wrote to his father, "If Mr. Howe opens the campaign with his usual deliberation, and our recruits or drafts come in tolerably well, we shall be infinitely better prepared to meet him than ever we have been."

Those who survived the terrible winter in reasonably good health broke up the monotony of camp life with various kinds of recreation. A few officers recorded a habit of taking long walks with each other. One officer from New York, a dance master before the war, gave dance lessons. Officers looked forward to hosting or being guests at each other's modest dinners. Some even put on amateur theatricals. Officers and soldiers alike enjoyed sharing spiritous liquors, when available. While at Valley Forge, as he did throughout the war, General Washington tried in vain to curb gambling at cards and dice. Albigence Waldo noted their love of singing, recording that many a barefoot soldier "labours thro' the mud and cold with a song in his mouth extolling *War & Washington*."

With the arrival of spring, the sport of "wicket," or cricket, was popular; even General Washington took up the bat and joined a match with the artillery officers. The enlisted men played a sport called "base," a form of rounders, precursor to baseball. "Long bullets" was a form of bowls, and here it was played with cannon balls.

Practical jokes, of course, were another form of amusement. One day, the quartermaster discovered that someone had tied straw to his horse's tail, then set it on fire. In another incident, a captain of artillery was nearly court-martialled after he put the words "SMALL POX" on the doors of some new recruits.

In March, while some newly arrived Irish soldiers from Maryland were celebrating St. Patrick's Day, someone in a Pennsylvania regiment forged a trap, shaped like a four leaf clover, from an old harrow with spiked teeth, then put potatoes in it as bait. While he and his comrades from Pennsylvania hid and watched, the Irish Marylanders cautiously looked it over and, without touching it, concluded aloud that it was "A trap to catch the Irish." They were not amused, and regarded it as a serious insult. Discovering the laughing Pennsylvanians, they charged and commenced a bloody brawl, as soldiers from the two states poured forth from their huts and joined in the fray. Finally, a horseman came riding toward them from Mount Joy, racing down the steep slope at breakneck speed. One soldier recalled it as "a marvelous exhibition of horsemanship." It was the commander in chief, himself, who reined in his chestnut sorrel in the middle of the melee and angrily gave all concerned a tongue-lashing. The rioters meekly returned to their huts.

Pierre Duponceau, Steuben's secretary, noted other forms of entertainment, at least for some of the officers:

> In the midst of all our distress, there were some bright sides to Valley Forge. Mrs. Washington had the courage to follow her husband in that dismal abode ... the lady of General Greene [etc.] ... They often met at each other's quarters and the evening was spent in conversation over a dish of tea or coffee. There were no formal soirees, no dancing, cardplaying or amusements of any kind, except singing. Every gentleman or lady who could sing was called upon, in turn, for a song. I soon learned the favourite English songs, and contributed my share to the pleasures of the company.
>
> Thus the time passed until the beginning of May, when the news of the French alliance burst suddenly

upon us. Then the public distress was forgotten amidst the universal joy. Rejoicings took place throughout the army, dinners, toasts, songs ... I thought I should be devoured by the caresses which the American officers lavished upon me as one of their new allies. Whenever a French officer appeared he was met with congratulations and with smiles. O, that was a delightful time!

George Washington, himself, would reflect, "I believe no event was ever received with more heartfelt joy." He informed the army officially on May 5th, and planned a celebration for the next morning in the natural amphitheater that formed the center of the campground. His General Orders announced that, "It becomes us to set apart a day for gratefully acknowledging the Divine goodness & celebrating the important event which we owe to His benign interposition."

George Washington was moved by the occasion to be compassionate. From his General Orders for May 6, 1778:

> The commander in chief, being more desirous to reclaim than punish offenders, and willing to show mercy to those who have been misled by designing traitors, and that as many as can may participate [in] the pleasures of this truely joyfull day - is pleased to pardon William McGrath of the artillery & John Marrel of Col. Jackson's regiment, now under sentence of death, & orders their immediate relief from confinement; hoping that gratitude to his clemency will induce them in future to behave like good soldiers.

At 9 a.m., a single cannon shot called the army to assemble, without arms, and stand to listen to each brigade chaplain deliver prayers "of thanksgiving and a discourse suitable to the occasion." Next, the commander in chief's words - "most eloquent and very touching" praise for the King of France - were read aloud.

A second cannon, at 11:30, signaled the brigades to go to their huts, fetch their muskets, and return. Washington and the other generals slowly walked their horses, reviewing the troops, and noticed the "remarkable animation with which they performed the necessary salute as the general passed along." Many of the soldiers struggled "to express their feelings in a way more agreeable to nature."

Then the "grand maneuvers" started, orchestrated by Steuben. The brigades paraded with confident precision, wheeling from marching column into line of battle, etc., just as the drillmaster had taught them. Steuben had also instilled in them a sense of pride in their personal attire and equipment, and now it showed; one observer noted "the cleanliness of their dress, the brilliancy and good order of their arms." Observing all this was a British spy from Philadelphia, who was caught later that day. But, rather than hang the man, they released him, on condition that he "go back and tell his employers what he has seen."

The grand maneuvers were followed by the firing of a third cannon, signaling commencement of a feu de joie. Thirteen cannons were fired in consecutive order, then each soldier fired his own musket immediately after the man on his left, all up and down the double-ranked army, the whole running fire having "a beautiful effect." An anonymous letter, printed in the *New York Journal*, reported:

> It was conducted with great judgment and regularity. The gradual progression of the sound from the discharge of cannon and musketry, swelling and rebounding from the neighboring hills, with ... huzzas to "Long live the King of France," "Long live the friendly European Powers," and "Long live the American States," composed a military music more agreeable to a soldier's ear than the most finished pieces of your favorite Handel.

Afterwards, the commander in chief took the opportunity to announce, to thunderous cheers, that the Congress had authorized the appointment of Baron von Steuben as a major general and the official

Inspector General of the Army. When it was over, General Washington stood to take his leave.

> There was a universal clap, with loud huzzas, which continued till he had proceeded a quarter of a mile, during which there were a thousand hats tossed in the air. His Excellency turned round with his retinue and huzzaed several times.

Spring had come, and with it, a revitalized and larger army. Back in January, a soldier named Jeremiah Greenman had noted in his journal, "All ye spayr officers sent home to recrute a nother regiment." Now those new recruits were pouring into camp, swelling the ranks to nearly the size of the opposing army in Philadelphia. Soon George Washington would be leading the army away from this camp, onward to the field of battle, and he was more optimistic than ever before. During the dark days prior to Trenton, he had written despairingly, "The game is pretty nearly up." Now he was writing, "The game ... seems now to be verging fast to a favourable issue."

Ready for a new campaign, this army, hardened and more confident after their ordeal of the last six months, was not the same one that had faced Sir William Howe the previous year. Like many another continental soldier, Pierre Duponceau would spend his last remaining days at Valley Forge "amidst the dreams and hopes of future triumphs."

James McMichael sent his "superfluous baggage and some of my books," including his journal, away for safe keeping. His last entry:

> Farewell my Journal, we must part
>   Which contains some nature but no art --
> The companion of my sore fatigues
>   Throughout the war, but not intrigues,
> Therefore adieu my ambiguous book,
>   May you be pleasing to those who in you look.

CHAPTER SEVEN
THE CONWAY CABAL

"The Board of War ... will throw such obstacles and difficulties in your way as to force you to resign."

- *Dr. James Craik, warning his friend, George Washington.*

As if George Washington did not have enough problems on his mind during the trying winter of 1777-1778, he became convinced that there was a "cabal," or conspiracy, of officers and Congressmen working to have Horatio Gates supplant him as commander in chief.

Washington was certainly aware that, since the victory at Saratoga, the commander of the Northern Department, Major General Horatio Gates, was the darling of Congress. Since Gates, in his report to Congress, had given Benedict Arnold no credit for his battlefield heroics, Congress was unaware that Gates, who stayed in his quarters during the action, was not deserving of the title "Hero of Saratoga." Nevertheless, comparisons between his success at Saratoga and Washington's recent failures in the Philadelphia campaign were inevitable. While at Valley Forge, Lieutenant Nathaniel Chipman heard

> that it is a common topic of conversation in Connecticut and, indeed, throughout New England, that General Washington will not fight. "Let Gates," say they, "take the command, and we shall see an end of the war."

On January 26th, an anonymous diatribe blasting the commander in chief's faults, titled *The Thoughts of a Freeman*, was left on the steps outside the meeting hall of Congress. Among the charges were:

> The proper method of attacking, beating and conquering the enemy has never yet been adopted by the commander in chief. ...
>
> The late success to the northward was owing to a change of commanders ... the southern army would have been alike successful, had a similar change taken place ...
>
> The people of America have been guilty of idolatry, by making a man their god; and the God of heaven and earth will convince them by woeful experience, that he is only a man; that no good may be expected from the standing army until Baal and his worshipers are banished from the camp. ...

President Henry Laurens was handed the paper and, after perusing it a moment, forwarded it to George Washington, who immediately recognized the handwriting as that of Dr. Benjamin Rush, head of the army's medical department. Rush soon afterward found an excuse to resign. Earlier in January, Virginia's Governor Patrick Henry also received an anonymous letter, and sent it on to Washington. An excerpt:

> The northern army has shown us what Americans are capable of doing with a GENERAL at their head. The spirit of the southern army is no ways inferior to the spirit of the northern. A Gates, a Lee, or a Conway would in a few weeks render them an irresistible body of men.

Jonathan Sergeant, Attorney General of Pennsylvania, declared:

> We want a general; thousands of lives and millions of property are yearly sacrificed to the insufficiency of our commander in chief. Two battles he has lost for us by

> two such blunders as might have disgraced a soldier of three month's standing, and yet [we] are so attached to this man that I fear we shall rather sink with him than throw him off our shoulders.

Sergeant was one of several prominent politicians in Pennsylvania and New Jersey who were voicing their displeasure over General Washington's inability to prevent the British capture of Philadelphia. They also were upset with his decision to settle into winter quarters, instead of making another attack against Howe. Such attitudes were typified by the journal of a Philadelphia apothecary, Christopher Marshall, residing as a refugee in Lancaster. On December 28th, he recorded his thoughts about British depredations upon the inhabitants, concluding:

> All this is done in the view of our generals and our army, who are careless of us, but go to spend the winter in jollity, gaming and carousing. ... O, America, where is your virtue? O, Washington, where is your courage?

George Washington's army was in no condition to attack anyone. The soldiers were spending each day in their winter quarters not in "jollity, gaming and carousing," but in struggling to find enough wood to burn, clothes to wear, and food to eat, just to stay alive. But the commander in chief could not publicly defend himself against his critics "without disclosing secrets it is of the utmost moment to conceal." He feared that if the British learned of the army's true condition, they would surely come and attack his camp.

So, in their ignorance, his critics faulted him for his inaction, often referring to him as the "American Fabius," after a Roman general famous for avoiding battle until conditions were favorable. James Lovell, a Congressman from Massachusetts, thought "our affairs are Fabiused into a very disagreeable posture." He was disgusted that George Washington, not Horatio Gates, was "the idol of America." General

Lafayette, one of the commander's loyal supporters, thought that many in Congress were "infatuated with Gates ... and believe that attacking is the only thing necessary to conquer." Lafayette wrote to President Laurens:

> All those who talk of storming the lines, of beating G'l Howe, are strangers to our circumstances or desirous to engage G'al Washington in a step where he could fall. ... If you should lose that same man, what would become of the American liberty? Who could take his place? ... G'al Gates do not bear any comparison with our general.

The controversy that historians have labeled the "Conway Cabal" started with Brigadier General Thomas Conway, 45, who was an Irishman, but a thirty year veteran of the French Army. Like so many other European military adventurers, he had gone to Silas Deane in Paris, seeking assurances that Congress would commission him a general in the Continental Army. Conway arrived in the spring of 1777 and proved to be competent enough, but quickly became one of the most hated officers in the army, due to his braggodocio and his constant criticism of his superiors, including General Stirling, who he labeled "a sot, not able to command one hundred" men. When it came to following Stirling's orders, Conway selectively obeyed or ignored them, depending on whether he approved of them. He considered Washington "the perfect gentleman," but his talents for command were "miserable indeed." The vain Conway also had the annoying habit of insulting people. When first introduced to a poorly dressed backwoods officer, he asked the man, "Did Congress see you before they appointed you?"

Thomas Conway was also adept at "stock jobbing," ingratiating himself with individual members of the Congress. He tirelessly lobbied for promotion to major general, over the heads of numerous American brigadiers who had already served in two campaigns before he came over from France. Conway admitted to General John Sullivan, one of his few admirers, that he sought the promotion, "to increase my fortune" and to obtain "sooner the rank of brigadier in the French army." Although, at first, George Washington had been impressed by Thomas Conway as a "man of candor," he quickly became annoyed with Conway's habit of keeping silent during councils of war, then afterwards criticizing the measures taken. By October 1777, Washington's opinion had changed; he now saw Conway as a man whose merit "as an officer and importance in this army exists more in his own imagination than in reality, for it is a maxim with him to leave no service of his own untold, nor to [miss] anything which is to be obtained by importunity."

Horatio Gates's aide-de-camp, James Wilkinson, was the catalyst for the incident that started the controversy, and subsequent myth of a *cabal*, or conspiracy. As mentioned earlier, Gates did not write to the commander in chief to notify him of Burgoyne's surrender at Saratoga, choosing instead to inform only the Congress. He sent the 21-year-old Wilkinson riding south to carry the good news to Congress. Indicative of the effect this news had, Congress voted to accept Gates's suggestion that Lieutenant Colonel Wilkinson be immediately breveted to the rank of brigadier general, simply for carrying the glorious news to them! One of Washington's aides, Lieutenant Colonel John Laurens, commented on the incident:

> There is a degradation of rank and an injustice to senior and more distinguished officers when a man is so extraordinarily advanced for riding post with good news. Let Congress reward him with a good horse for his speed, but consecrate rank to merit of another kind!

In fact, James Wilkinson had taken his sweet time in delivering the momentous news. The young man stopped at Reading to visit with his girlfriend before continuing on to York, where the Congress sat. At every tavern and inn where he stopped along the way, he basked in the praises of patriots, and the numerous toasts they offered up from "the flowing bowl." Wilkinson reveled in his newfound status as one of the heroes of the northern army, conquerors of the pompous Gentleman Johnny Burgoyne.

The night before he reached York, he spent the evening drinking and socializing with several officers from Washington's army, as well as some refugees from Philadelphia, many of them openly critical of the commander in chief's failure to hold the city. Wilkinson, "in his cups," let slip an anecdote about a recent night in which Gates had read aloud to his closest aides and other confidants the contents of a letter he had received from General Conway, listing thirteen reasons why Brandywine had been such a disaster.

The next day, one of those present, Major William McWilliams, an aide to General Stirling, related to him what had transpired. Although McWilliams could only recall one specific item from the Conway-to-Gates letter that Wilkinson spoke of, it was damaging enough to set off the ensuing controversy that would rage for months. General Stirling was happy enough to pass the quote along to the commander in chief, adding a personal note of his own, declaring that, "such wicked duplicity of conduct I shall always think it my duty to detect."

Washington promptly wrote to General Conway, but only to inform him what had been related about his alledged letter to Gates. Washington made no other comment, leaving it up to Conway to react.

>November 9, 1777
>
>Sir: a letter which I receivd last night containd the following paragraph: "In a letter from Genl. Conway to Genl. Gates, he says: 'Heaven has been determind to save your country; or a weak General and bad councellors would have ruind it.'"
>
>I am Sir Yr. Hble Servt.,
>
>George Washington

This initiated a spate of correspondence. Conway sent a fawning, but at the same time ambiguously disrespectful, letter to Washington. Thomas Mifflin, the recently resigned quartermaster general and a harsh critic of Washington, wrote to Horatio Gates, warning him, "An extract from General Conway's letter to you has been procured and sent to headquarters," and might have repercussions because of the "just sentiments" it contained. Alarmed, Gates quickly wrote to Conway, "I entreat you, dear general, to let me know which of the letters were copied off."

Next, Gates wrote to Washington, professing his own innocence, and accusing Washington's aide, Alexander Hamilton, who'd recently been at Albany, of having "stealingly copied" from his correspondence. Keeping with his independent ways, Gates mentioned that he was sending a copy of this letter of his to Washington to Congress.

Annoyed that Gates should feel it necessary to involve Congress, Washington felt it necessary for himself to do the same with all his own correspondence on the subject, including his letters to Gates, and the many insulting letters he began receiving from Conway.

Washington wrote a very long reply to Gates, explaining how the controversy started, and its progress so far, and expressing his shock at learning that Conway was "a corrispondant of yours, much less did I suspect that I was the subject of your confidential letters." He ended the letter by stating that, when he first learned of Conway's remark, he thought Gates had intended, through Wilkinson, to apprise him of it, "to forewarn" him of this "secret enemy ... But, in this, as in other matters of late, I have found myself mistaken."

At the same time all this correspondence, and more, was going back and forth, Congress was finally ready to vote on Conway's request for promotion to major general (he had threatened, otherwise, to resign and return to France). Four weeks before, when George Washington first heard that Congress was considering promoting Conway over 23 more experienced brigadiers, he had written to Richard Henry Lee, the only remaining member of Congress the commander in chief knew well enough to confide in. He explained that such a promotion would precipitate a rash of resignations, and predicted that the offended officers "will not serve under him." In short, the promotion "will give a fatal blow to the existence of the army." Washington was so convinced of this, that he even suggested that he might consider resigning himself.

> I have been a slave to the service; I have undergone more than most men are aware of, to harmonize so many discordant parts; but it will be impossible for me to be of any further service, if such insuperable difficulties are thrown in my way.

However, such was the mood of Congress that, on December 13, 1777, they went ahead with the promotion anyway, over Washington's objections. It should not be inferred from this that many in Congress hoped the commander in chief would resign, so they could appoint Gates in his stead, for Congressman Richard Peters, a month later, confided to General Anthony Wayne that, if it came to a vote between Washington and Gates, Washington would retain his position unanimously. Rather, a majority of Congressmen simply did not believe that Washington would actually resign; and they were determined to retain General Conway, a man of his experience being so rare in the Continental Army. Benjamin Rush had appealed to John Adams before Adams departed Congress for his diplomatic mission to France, "For God's sake, do not suffer him to resign!"

Although the anticipated resignations failed to materialize, fifteen generals and colonels signed a petition to Congress, and Nathanael Greene wrote a letter of his own to President Laurens, protesting the promotions of James Wilkinson and Thomas Conway as without merit. He wanted to acquaint Congress with the "present prevailing discontent among the officers."

> ... If they lose confidence in the justice of Congress ... military ardor will languish, men of honor will decline the service, art & cabal will succeed, and low intrigue will be the characteristic and genius of the army.

Technically, the promoted Conway would not actually be over any of the other generals, since he would serve in a newly created *staff* position, Inspector General of the Army. However, what was significant and ominous about the promotion was that the Inspector General would report directly to the Board of War, a Congressional committee, rather than to the commander in chief. Connecticut's Eliphalet Dyer expressed the mood of Congress when he wrote to Gates, "The army in every department wants a total reform and regulation. We are determined by the blessing of Heaven to have it effected."

And the Board of War would now have three additional members, chosen for the first time from outside Congress: Generals Gates and Mifflin, and Colonel Timothy Pickering. Gates would be the new president of the board. Thus, the Congressional committee charged with overseeing the army's operations was now packed with men hostile to the head of that same army.

By the end of 1777, only two members of the Congress that had voted unanimously to appoint George Washington as commander in chief, back in 1775, were still in Congress. New York's Gouverneur Morris wrote home to John Jay, acknowleging that, "The powerful American Senate is not what we have known it to be." The present membership, down to twenty-one from more than twice that, was described by one observer as "feeble and vacillating," preoccupied with "party feuds." Maryland's Charles Carroll, expressing his disgust, admitted that, "We murder time, and chat it away in idle, impertinent talk." George Washington confided, in a letter to his younger brother, John Augustine Washington, that he "often regretted the ... fatal policy of having our able men engaged in the formation of the more local governments ... leaving the great national concern ... to be managed by men of more contracted abilities."

An intimate old friend of Washington's, Dr. James Craik, wrote to him in mid-January, warning that wherever he traveled he heard gossip that "a strong faction was forming" against him in Congress, and that "the Board of War ... will throw such obstacles and difficulties in your way as to force you to resign."

Those closest to the commander in chief were convinced that a "malignant faction" was actively plotting to supplant him with Gates. Colonel Alexander Hamilton, one of his aides, wrote to New York's governor, calling for "all the true and sensible friends of their country" to join the fight to expose the "monster" of party. John Laurens, Henry Knox, Nathanael Greene, the Marquis de Lafayette, and others were all seeking to discover and expose the "cabaleurs."

Washington kept a journal throughout most of his life, the notable exception being the years he was commanding the Continental Army, so we can not say for sure what his exact thoughts were. However, when writing to his confidants, he would make reference to "my enemies" and once, writing to Lafayette, alluded to Gates as someone practicing "every act to do me an injury." But the commander in chief would not adopt his enemies' tactics; he was determined to stay above it all, and continue his "uniform code of conduct ... regardless of the tongue of slander or the powers of distraction" swirling all around him. He went on to reassure his young French friend, Lafayette:

> We must not, in so great a contest, expect to meet with nothing but sun shine. I have no doubt that every thing happens so for the best; that we should triumph over all our misfortunes, and shall, in the end, be ultimately happy, when, My Dear Marquis, if you will give me your company in Virginia, we will laugh at our past difficulties and the follies of others.

* * * * *

For advice and support at this difficult time, George Washington turned to his trusted advisors, Hamilton, Knox and Greene, but also to this new one, the twenty-year-old Frenchman, Gilbert Motier, the Marquis de Lafayette.

Lafayette had never known his own father. At the Battle of Minden in 1760, the British artillery officer, William Phillips (who Lafayette would oppose in battle, in 1781) fired a cannon ball that took off the head of Lafayette's father. This left two-year-old Gilbert with what eventually would become one of the largest country estates in all of France. At age 9, Lafayette moved with his widowed mother to Paris, where money and connections could be put to use.

At his boarding school, he was the top Latin scholar. Shy and awkward, he was conspicuous for his country accent, ineptness at sports, and lack of noble blood, all combining to make him an easy mark for mockery by the "bloods" at school. By age 16, Lafayette was married off to a 14-year-old bride, daughter of a duke and duchess, the marriage contract having been signed by the older generation of the two families two years earlier, before the couple had even met. Family also arranged for Lafayette to procure a commission in the king's bodyguards, the Black Musketeers that the 19th century novelist Alexandre Dumas would one day bring to everlasting fame.

But Lafayette was not happy. His life was stifled by restrictions placed upon him by his in-laws, with whom he and his bride lived. And they were quick to find fault with him. The temptation to escape and, like so many others had already done, seek glory and honor in America was irresistable. It was the talk of the army, and certainly of the salons. A fellow Frenchman, already in Washington's army, would write about this time, "There is a hundred times more enthusiasm for this revolution in any cafe in Paris than there is in all the United States together."

Though forbidden by order of the king to leave the country, the 19-year-old Lafayette snuck away to the coast, taking with him Baron Johann de Kalb and thirteen other officers of the same mind. There, Lafayette hired a warship and its crew to take him and his friends to America. While still at sea, the idealistic teenager wrote home to his wife, predicting that:

> The welfare of America is intimately bound up with the happiness of humanity. She is going to become a cherished and safe refuge of virtue, of good character, of tolerance, of equality, and of a peaceful liberty.

The ship's captain skirted around the British blockade outside the port of Charleston, South Carolina, and they disembarked 50 miles to the south on June 13, 1777. As soon as he set foot on the shore, Lafayette dramatically raised his hand and pledged to live and die for the cause and ideals of American liberty. The first household they approached nearly fired on them, at first mistaking the fancily uniformed party for a British raiding party, but fortunately one of the frightened defenders spoke French and readily extended them hospitality.

A fews days later, to his delight, Lafayette was well received in Charleston. Before departing that city, he was moved to thank them for their friendship, and to honor them for their successful defense of the city against a British attack the previous year, by paying for new uniforms for the local regiment of South Carolinians. This party of fifteen European officers and their servants then set out, traveling by land 650 miles to Philadelphia, finally arriving on July 27th.

The first Congressman they met who could speak French was James Lovell, who told them curtly:

> French officers are pretty greedy to come and serve us without our asking them. Last year, it is true, we needed officers, but this year we have many, and very experienced ones, too.

It seems that the army and Congress had experienced so many problems with European officers that, by now, they were all disgusted with Silas Deane's having overstepped his authority, promising commissions to virtually every military adventurer who came knocking at his door. The Marquis de Lafayette and his friends were told to please go back to France. But they were not about to do that.

After a few days of behind doors lobbying, Lafayette was asked to send a letter to the president. Congress was impressed with Lafayette's background, his connections to the King of France, and his sincerity. He ended his letter:

> After the sacrifices I have made in this cause, I have the right to ask two favours at your hands: the one is, to serve without pay, at my own expense; and the other, that I be allowed to serve at first as a volunteer.

On July 31st, Congress voted to grant Lafayette the major general's commission that Silas Deane had promised, though it was an honorable commission without a specific command, so as not to antagonize the veteran generals. They would leave any decision on commanding troops up to the commander in chief. Lafayette was grateful and showed it by donating 60,000 francs to the cause, to purchase badly needed supplies for the army. Except for Kalb, all the other officers that came with Lafayette were denied their expected commissions, and eventually returned to France.

Later that day, Lafayette was introduced to the commander in chief at Philadelphia's City Tavern. At first, the Virginian was cautious, having been "plagued and wearied" by the "importunities and discontent" of too many European officers. But he quickly became more receptive to this charming and enthusiastic young aristocrat. George Washington urged the marquis to lodge in the house where he and his "family" of aides and secretaries were staying in town.

The next day, the two mounted their horses and reviewed the army together. The American commander was self-conscious, and apologized for the poor appearance of the army, saying, "We are rather embarassed to show ourselves before an officer who has just left French troops." But the Marquis de Lafayette graciously replied, "I am here, sir, to learn, and not to teach."

What a refreshing change the marquis was to Washington, so unlike the other European officers that Silas Deane and Congress had sent him. Reacting to a specific request by Benjamin Franklin to do so, George Washington invited the young Frenchman to look upon him as a "friend and father." What was equally important to Lafayette was that the American commander treated him with respect and looked upon him as a mature adult. This all made a lasting impression on Lafayette, who had been treated as a cipher by his father-in-law, the Duc D'Ayen. Lafayette became totally enamored of Washington and cherished their friendship, which would grow and last a lifetime.

Though he was not an aide-de-camp, Lafayette was welcomed into Washington's family. He rejected Conway's overtures toward him, and instead, became protective of this American commander he so strongly admired. On January 6, 1778, he wrote to his wife in France, explaining why he would not be home soon:

> My presence is more necessary at this moment to the American cause than you can possibly conceive. Many whose ambitious views have been frustrated have raised up some powerful cabals. They have endeavoured, by every sort of artifice, to make me discontented with this revolution, and with him who is its chief. They have spread as widely as they could the report that I was quitting the continent. ... I cannot in conscience appear to justify the malice of these people. If I were to depart, many Frenchmen who are useful here would follow my example. ...
>
> General Washington, in the place he occupies, is liable to be surrounded by flatterers or secret enemies; he finds in me a secure friend in whose bosom he may always confide his most secret thoughts, and who will always speak the truth. Not one day passes without his holding long conversations with me, writing me long letters, and he has the kindness to consult me on the most important matters. A peculiar circumstance is occurring at this moment which renders my presence of some use to him; this is not the time to speak of my departure.

* * * * *

Other officers who were equally loyal to George Washington, and angered by all the gossip, took it upon themselves to seek out the gossipers. General Cadwalader tried unsuccessfully to lure Mifflin into a duel. Nathanael Greene's aide, Major John Clark, spread the word in York that, "a few ounces of gunpowder, diffused through proper channels, will answer a good purpose." And Colonel Daniel Morgan, the brawny rifleman from Washington's home state of Virginia, accosted the Board of War's secretary, Richard Peters. Morgan shook with rage and nearly came to violence, as he informed Peters that camp talk implicated the secretary in the cabal. Peters denied it, swearing it to be "the most villainous of falsehoods." Another member of Congress observed, one "dares not speak one's mind too freely."

By mid-winter, it became apparent that virtually all the top level officers in the army were staunch supporters of the commander in chief. And the soldiers, hearing the rampant rumors of a possible vote in Congress to replace the commander, got word to one visiting Congressman: "No Washington, no army."

Everyone seemed to want to distance themselves from Thomas Conway. Lafayette noted that Conway's fellow French officers would no longer speak to him. When Conway went to Washington with his commission as inspector general to ask for duties to perform, the commander icily refused to give him any. So Conway took up residence in York, where he spent his time complaining about Washington. Soon Congress was seeing him for what he was, as they read copies of his insulting letters to Washington, including one of December 31st in which Conway sarcastically equated "the great Frederick in Europe" with "the great Washington on this continent." The aide John Laurens became enraged that Conway would so insult the commander in chief, knowing that he could not risk jeopardizing the cause by challenging Conway to a duel. John wrote to his father, President Laurens, on January 3, 1778:

> [Conway's] last letter which is a most insolent attempt at what the French call *persiflage* or humoring a man,

affects the Gen'l very sensibly. It is such an affront as Conway would never have dared to offer if the General's situation had not assured him of the impossibility of its being revenged in a private way. The Gen'l therefore has determined to return him no answer at all.

President Laurens, after reading Conway's insulting letter, thought that "Gen. Conway was guilty of gross hypocrisy or gross & unpardonable insult." Congress decided to send Conway out of the country, assigning him to a new expedition, a planned "irruption into Canada."

This ill-conceived expedition was the brainchild of Horatio Gates, President of the Board of War. Though George Washington privately considered it "a child of folly," he made no objections to the proposal. "As it is the first fruit of our new Board of War," he wrote, "I did not incline to say anything against it." Washington always tried to stick to his philosophy that, in a truly democratic republic, the military must defer to the leadership provided by the civilian government.

Apparently, Gates had conceived the idea of a second invasion of Canada even before his appointment to the Board of War, for he already had preparations well on the way. Colonel Timothy Bedel was raising militia and funds for it among the New England states. And General Jacob Bayley was starting work on a frontier road from Co'os, New Hampshire (present day Newbury) across Vermont to the northern end of Lake Champlain, just south of Fort St. Jean.

Now the expedition Gates had been secretly preparing would be executed under the auspices of the Continental Congress. That body appointed Lafayette to head up the mission, with Generals Thomas Conway and John Stark reporting to him. Lafayette left Valley Forge with some misgivings, reluctant to be drawn away from Washington at this critical time. He agreed to the command only if Conway was replaced as his second by Johann Kalb. Congress agreed to send him Kalb, but did not remove Conway as his second.

Lafayette rode to Albany, the staging ground for the invasion of Canada, and discovered a "hell of blunders, madness and deception."

Thomas Conway was already there, directing preparations for the invasion in a manner suggesting he was the prime mover and Lafayette only a figurehead. The expedition was steeped in problems, including insufficient recruitment, money and supplies, such as snowshoes, as well as low morale and pessimism among all the officers. Everyone on the scene advised Lafayette to cancel the expedition, if he could. Lafayette "found a spirit of dissatisfaction every where; every eye seems to say to me, 'where are you going to bring those unhappy wretches?'" So, on February 19, 1778, he wrote to President Laurens to express objections to the campaign, and to suggest, instead, an attack on New York.

While waiting for a reply, Lafayette received a letter from Horatio Gates, mentioning that the Board of War might ask Congress to recall both he and Kalb, and leave Conway in charge of the expedition, under direct supervision of Gates as head of the Northern Department. Suddenly, "the great scheme" became apparent to Lafayette: the whole expedition was a plot by Gates and Conway to steal the laurels, and propel Gates into the position of commander in chief of all continental forces. Perhaps Gates, if events went well, would even personally take over from Conway. Hadn't Gates, just the year before, taken the reins from Philip Schuyler when the tide was beginning to turn against Burgoyne, just in time to reap the laurels for himself as the "Hero of Saratoga?" If Gates did the same with this expedition, adding another success to Saratoga, how could Congress refuse to promote him?

So Lafayette wrote a strong letter of protest to President Laurens, accusing "General Conway and the Board of War of deception and treachery." However, before his letter arrived, Congress had soured on the whole expedition, and decided to cancel it. In March, they recalled Lafayette and Kalb to Valley Forge; removed Gates from the Board of War, and sent him back to Albany; and reassigned Conway to a relatively obscure post, Fishkill, New York. There, he would be second in command to Major General Alexander McDougall, one of George Washington's staunchest supporters. Thomas Mifflin, for his part, resigned in disgust from the Board of War.

To protest his recent treatment, Conway submitted his resignation, expecting Congress to refuse it and give him some more useful command. This time, to his mortification, Congress called his bluff. Gouverneur Morris happily informed Washington, "no opposition was made to accepting his resignation." Maryland's Charles Carroll bluntly informed Thomas Conway that anyone who did not support George Washington should leave the army.

Angry and humiliated, Conway lingered in America, gossiping about Washington. Finally, on July 4, 1778, General John Cadwalader decided to force Conway into a duel by accusing him of cowardice at Germantown, saying he had left his brigade and hidden in a barn (actually, during the retreat, out of sheer exhaustion, he had stopped there for a short rest). Despite the fact that Cadwalader was known to be the most deadly shot in the army, Conway immediately demanded satisfaction. In the ensuing duel, Conway fired first, but missed. Cadwalader hesitated, still holding his pistol by his side, as a gust of wind swept the field. "Why do you not fire?" Conway demanded. To which Cadwalader grimly replied, "We came not here to trifle. Let the gale pass, and I shall do my part." Conway then turned to squarely face him, saying, "Then you shall have a fair chance of performing it well." After the wind subsided, Cadwalader raised his pistol and sent a bullet through Conway's mouth, passing out the back of his neck. Conway fell, face forward, onto the ground. Cadwalader walked forward, looked down contemptuously at his victim, and declared, "I have stopped the damned rascal's lying tongue, at any rate."

Thinking his wound was fatal, Conway sent off one last letter to George Washington:

> Sir, I find myself just able to hold the pen during a few minutes, and take this opportunity of expressing my sincere grief for having done, written, or said any thing disagreeable to your Excellency. My career will soon be over; therefore, justice and truth prompt me to declare my last sentiments. You are in my eyes the great and

> good man. May you long enjoy the love, veneration, and esteem of these States, whose liberties you have asserted by your virtues.

But Thomas Conway survived, returned to France, and eventually served as governor of the French colonies in India. He later fought against the armies of the French Revolution, and died in exile in 1800.

Hurt feelings were assuaged by the end of winter, as everyone seemed to be calling for a return to sanity. By now, Washington had seen copies of letters to his close associates from Congressmen trying to set his mind at ease. Elbridge Gerry, of Massachusetts, replied to an earlier letter from General Henry Knox asking if there were indeed persons in Congress plotting to remove the commander. Gerry thought these "groundless rumours" must have been started by army officers disgruntled over promotions denied or delayed. He wrote back in early February to reassure his friend Knox and, indirectly, the commander in chief:

> I have not yet been able to make any discoveries that can justify a suspicion of a plan's being formed to injure the reputation of, or remove from office, the gentleman hinted at in your favor of Jan'y the 4th ... the character of this worthy officer is high in Congress.

President Henry Laurens wrote on January 12th to his son, John, one of Washington's aides:

> I think the friends of our brave and virtuous General may rest assured that he is out of the reach of his enemies, if he has an enemy, a fact of which I am in doubt of. I believe that I hear most that is said and know the outlines of almost all that has been attempted, but the whole amounts to little more than tittle tattle, which would be too much honored by repeating it.

Laurens went on to estimate Washington's supporters in Congress as "so large a majority as 9 in 10." President Laurens, wanting to end the controversy, had a meeting with Horatio Gates. Afterwards, he would write, "I discovered an inclination in him to be upon friendly terms with our great and good General." Gates convinced Laurens that he had never been involved in any cabal, and that he disapproved of Conway's sentiments expressed in the infamous letter that had precipitated the controversy.

Horatio Gates wrote to George Washington, apologizing and expressing his hope that "no more of that time, so precious to the public, may be lost upon the subject of General Conway's letter. ... I solemnly declare that I am of no faction." Washington wrote back on February 24th, agreeing "with the desire you express of burying [the matter] hereafter in silence and, as far as future events will permit, oblivion."

There is no evidence that Horatio Gates ever became an active partner in the alleged cabal. The former British officer chose to sit back and await events. It is very possible that, in the fall of 1777 - after Burgoyne's surrender - Gates may have been hopeful of an appointment to supplant Washington. A few days after the surrender, Gates, perhaps giddy with the praise that was pouring in, confidentially told his fellow Virginian, Daniel Morgan, that he had heard reports of unrest among Washington's officers, many of whom would resign unless he was replaced as commander in chief. From Morgan's reply, it is evident that Gates misjudged him.

> I have one favor to ask of you, which is never to mention that detestable subject to me again; for under no other man than Washington will I serve.

As for the Congress replacing the commander in chief, it apparently never came close to a vote. Connecticut's Eliphalet Dyer declared that there was "never the most distant thought of removing Genll. Washington, nor even one expression in Congress looking that way."

Thus ended the "Conway Cabal." The historian Jonathan Rossie summed up the cabal as "a French concoction, which, like souffle, was mostly air." Though it caused George Washington a great deal of distress while it lasted, in the end he benefitted from it. The three principal cabaleurs - Conway, Mifflin and Rush - were discredited, and each resigned his position in the army. George Washington's position as commander in chief was now more secure than ever, and he would be virtually immune from criticism for the rest of the war.

CHAPTER EIGHT
THE BRITISH IN PHILADELPHIA

"Another year's campaigning is finished and all that we have accomplished, with the loss of a great many men, is the taking of Philadelphia ... In balance, the conquest of a single city ... the many people lost during the expedition, and with those lost at Saratoga ... makes the scale tip in favor of the enemy. Everyone here attributes the capture of the Northern Army to General Howe."

- *Platte Grenadier Battalion Journal,*
New York, October 22, 1777.

The campaign of 1777 came to a close in December when, the week before Washington marched his army to Valley Forge, Howe brought his own army fifteen miles out of Philadelphia to offer battle at Whitemarsh. However, the rebel army was well prepared, having dug in on high ground. They had been warned by Lydia Darragh, a patriot woman who, having overheard British officers discussing the planned strike, talked her way past the British sentries by saying she needed to take grain to a gristmill outside of town. Howe spent three days maneuvering and skirmishing, in the process taking a "severe drubing" of 89 killed and wounded at the hands of Daniel Morgan's recently arrived riflemen, they having marched from Saratoga. Concluding that the strong rebel position "prevented any hope of success," Howe turned his army around and marched it back to Philadelphia.

The aborted effort at Whitemarsh would be Sir William Howe's last attempt to beat George Washington. Howe informed his superior in London that, "this army, acting upon the defensive, will be fully employed to maintain its present position." Though he came to learn that much of the rebel army at Valley Forge was ill or starving, he felt that alone "did not justify an attack on that strong position during the severe weather." Memories of his disastrous attack against entrenched Americans on Breed's Hill, back in 1775 - when he had stood alone on the battlefield, his aides lying dead or wounded all around him, and experienced "a moment I never felt before" - were still too vivid in his mind. He would not sacrifice his army again.

Sir William Howe and his brother, Admiral Lord Richard Howe, had failed to end the war on their own terms. As a dissenting member of Parliament's House of Commons, William Howe had objected to this war against fellow Englishmen, and he'd only reluctantly agreed to go to North America and fight in it when his cousin, King George III, told him it was an order, not a request. So William Howe had left Nottingham for America, after explaining to his constituents that he "could not refuse without incurring the odious name of backwardness to serve my country in distress."

The Howes had attempted to implement a humane policy of limited warfare - beat the rebels on the field of battle, but do not annihilate them; rather, allow them to retreat; and do this repeatedly until, eventually, they become disillusioned with the futility of the rebellion. But this policy had not succeeded. And now, it appeared that the war would go on indefinitely, for surely, after Burgoyne's defeat, France would come in on the side of the rebels.

For William Howe, there was still the gnawing realization that, overall, the campaign of 1777 had been a failure. To his dismay, the capture of Philadelphia had not been decisive. The rebel Congress had simply relocated; its ragtag army was still in the field and, as usual, would be reinforced come spring, in time for the next campaign.

A review of the correspondence of their officers shows that the Howe brothers were alone in their assessment of how to end the rebellion. Everyone else felt that the rebel *army* - not cities or territory - was what must be conquered. The previous year, Ambrose Serle had noted a popular saying of the rebels: "If Great Britain cannot conquer us, she cannot govern us." And the rebel General Nathanael Greene, writing from Valley Forge, noted that, because "they cannot conquer us ... the limits of the British government in America are their out-sentinels." The Howe brothers' policy of territorial conquest had failed.

It was time to step down and let someone else, perhaps someone more ruthless, try his hand at putting down the rebellion. William Howe would return to Parliament, where he knew he would have to defend himself against his critics, for surely there would be a Parliamentary inquiry, blaming him for Burgoyne's loss of an army. On the night of October 22nd, the same day that the attack at Red Bank had failed so miserably, General Howe wrote to Colonial Secretary Lord George Germain:

> From the little attention, my Lord, given to my recommendations since the commencement of my command, I am led to hope that I may be relieved from this very painful service, wherein I have not the good fortune to enjoy the necessary confidence and support of my superiors ... I humbly request I may receive his Majesty's permission to resign the command.

William Howe now awaited the pleasure of the king's response, expecting that his resignation would be accepted and he could return to his country estate in Nottingham, and his seat in Parliament. Until then, he would enjoy the comforts of winter, the social season in Philadelphia, which was the largest city in North America, and only surpassed in England by London itself. William Howe's buxom and adoring mistress, Mrs. Loring (wife of his commissary of prisoners), enjoyed the drinking and gambling as much as he did, sitting alongside him at the faro table each evening. He also enjoyed the friendship of his subordinate officers, and the fawning attention of the city's many loyalists.

The tranquil life of Philadelphia that winter was interrupted on January 5th by David Bushnell, an annoying Yankee from Connecticut.

Sixteen months before, Bushnell had tried unsuccessfully to blow up Admiral Richard Howe's flagship with his *Turtle*, a "water machine" of curious invention. The *Turtle*, a one-man boat, moved below the surface of the water, powered by human pedaling, and was armed with a detachable time-bomb. Bushnell had failed in his sabatage mission in 1776, but now he was back, this time with a new invention: floating mines. In March, Boston's *Continental Journal and Weekly Advertiser* printed a letter received from Francis Hopkinson, a Congressman from New Jersey:

> This city [Philadelphia] has lately been entertained with a most astonishing instance of the activity, bravery, and military skill of the royal navy of Great Britain. ...
>
> Some time last week, two boys observed a keg of a singular construction floating in the river opposite the city. They got into a small boat, and attempting to take up the keg, it burst with a great explosion and blew up the unfortunate boys.
>
> On Monday last, several kegs of a like construction made their appearance. An alarm immediately spread through the city. Various reports prevailed, filling the city and the royal troops with unspeakable consternation. Some reported that these kegs were filled with armed rebels, who were to issue forth in the dead of the night, as the Grecians did of old from their wooden horse at the siege of Troy, and take the city by surprise. Others said they were charged with combustibles ... to consume all the shipping. ...
>
> The battle begun, and it was surprising to behold the incessant blaze that was kept up against the enemy, the kegs. Both officers and men exhibited the most unparalleled skill and bravery on the occasion, whilst the citizens stood gazing as solemn witnesses of their prowess. From the *Roebuck* and other ships of war, whole

broadsides were poured into the Delaware. In short, not a wandering chip, stick, or drift log but felt the vigor of British arms.

The action begun about sunrise and would have been completed with great success by noon had not an old market woman, coming down the river with provisions, unfortunately let a small keg of butter fall overboard, which floated down to the scene of action. At the sight of this unexpected reinforcement of the enemy, the battle was renewed with fresh fury; the firing was incessant till the evening closed the affair.

The kegs were either totally demolished or obliged to fly, as none of them have shown their heads since. It is said his Excellency Lord Howe has dispatched a swift sailing packet, with an account of this victory, to the court of London. In a word, Monday, the fifth of January, 1778, must ever be distinguished in history for the memorable BATTLE OF THE KEGS.

Francis Hopkinson immortalized the event in a song that became popular with the troops at Valley Forge, *British Valour Displayed: Or, The Battle of the Kegs*. Sung to the tune of *Yankee Doodle*, it included one verse that alluded to William Howe's refusal to come out of the city and offer battle to his enemy at Valley Forge:

> Sir William, he, snug as a flea
> Lay all this time a-snoring;
> Nor dreamed of harm, as he lay warm
> In bed with Mrs. Loring.

The city's leading loyalists tried in vain to persuade General Howe to lead his army out of the city, march it to Valley Forge, and defeat the rebels, once and for all. Their desires were expressed in a verse written by a loyalist and published in American and English newspapers in the spring of 1778:

> Awake, arise Sir Billy,
>   There's forage in the plain.
> Ah, leave your little filly,
>   And open the campaign.
>
> Heed not a woman's prattle
>   Which tickles in the ear,
> But give the word for battle
>   And grasp the warlike spear.

Like so many loyalists, the British Captain John Andre had hoped that taking Philadelphia would not stop General Howe from continuing to do battle with his Virginian foe. But Andre was disappointed, as he found that, by the middle of December, "The system became totally defensive." Another year's campaigning had not produced an end to the war. Discouraged, Andre confided his thoughts to his journal:

> Affairs are not yet at an end. Washington will quit the field [for the winter] with a more respectable army than last year. Will he appear again in the spring, recruited in the same proportion?

For Captain Andre, an aide-de-camp to General Grey, the winter was a time of very little military activity, allowing him to write home and reassure his mother, "I am in a very quiet station." However, Andre kept busy, for his talents were much in demand. Like many another officer, in his free time he was an amateur dramatist, one of "Howe's Thespians." Lieutenant John Peebles noted in his journal, "The performers are gentlemen of the army and navy & their mistresses. The gentlemen do their parts well, but the ladies rather deficient." A total of thirteen plays were put on during the winter, with the proceeds from ticket sales benefitting widows and orphans of

British soldiers killed in the war. Besides acting in these plays, Andre painted the sets, composed rhyming prologues, designed the invitations, etc. His artistic talents were indispensable.

Captain John Andre was also a popular guest at numerous teas hosted by the most eligible young loyalist belles in town. He was a handsome flirt. Though 27, he still had boyish features that included long eye lashes, and an "almost feminine gentleness." Andre could entertain the ladies by speaking in French or Italian, playing the flute, singing, reciting poetry, or, if requested, writing a poem or sketching a portrait for a particular admirer.

One was seventeen-year-old Peggy Shippen. In 1779, she would marry a rebel general, Benedict Arnold, and the next year help her old friend, John Andre, arrange Arnold's defection to the British side. Their scheme, in 1780, to hand over the Hudson River fortress at West Point as well as the visiting General Washington, would be discovered and aborted at the last moment. Though the traitorous Benedict Arnold would manage to escape to the British lines, John Andre, captured in civilian clothes and carrying damning correspondence on his person, would be held as a spy. George Washington's offer to exchange Andre for Arnold would be rejected, and Andre would hang as a spy.

Andre's unfortunate fate was still in the distant future. For now, in the winter of 1777-1778, the British and Hessian officers had enough "assemblies, concerts, comedies, clubs and the like," as one Hessian officer noted, "to make us forget there is any war, save it is a capital joke." Many a Philadelphia belle caught "scarlet fever" that winter, as the scarlet coated officers came calling. At the end of February, Mrs. William Paca, exiled from the city because she was the wife of a Congressman, received a letter from her loyalist friend in the city, Rebecca Franks:

> You can have no idea of the life of continued amusement I live in. I can scarce have a moment to myself. I have stole this [time] while everybody is retired to dress

> for dinner. ... Most elegantly am I dressed for a ball this evening at Smith's, where we have one every Thursday. You would not know the room, 'tis so much improved.
>
> The dress is more ridiculous and pretty than anything that ever I saw: great quantity of different coloured feathers on the head at a time, besides a thousand other things. The hair dressed very high. ...
>
> Oh how I wish Mr. P. would let you come in for a week or two - tell him I'll answer for your being let return. I know you are as fond of a gay life as myself - you'd have every opportunity of raking as much as you choose ... I've been but three evenings alone since we moved to town. ... I must go finish dressing, as I'm engaged out to tea.

One is left to wonder whether the British and Hessian officers realized the long-lasting effects they would have on the inhabitants. The jager captain, Johann Ewald, recorded an enlightening experience he had on January 30, 1778:

> I went today to a Quaker meeting next to my quarters, partly out of curiosity ... Everybody was somber, and there was a hushed silence everywhere. I walked as softly as my boots, spurs and big sword would permit, and stood for more than half an hour as quiet as a post. I was just about to leave, when suddenly an aged woman got up and asked the assembly to pay attention to her, because the Holy Spirit had impelled her to say the following:
>
> "My admonition is addressed to my sex. In these frightful times, which we have deserved by our sins, our land has been overrun by different foreign peoples. I hear very bad things of our wives and daughters ... said to receive and pay visits to these soldiers. I know that

some are not even ashamed to walk around with these people during the day. I pray you, mothers and fathers, stop these vices. Because these people are transients, you cannot take legal steps against them by our laws. If your daughters keep company with them, consider that you will have to accept to your own shame what they will leave behind for you. This is not good."

Then the matron sat down. Again there was silence for a while, whereupon the assembly left the place of devotion. I went to my quarters. My curiosity was satisfied, but I was not exactly edified.

News of General Howe's resignation saddened his officers. General James Pattison noted that, "his loss is universally regretted." Captain John Andre proposed that they put on a *fete* to honor the departing commander in chief. Andre declared they should call it a *Mischianza*, an Italian word signifying a medley, for it would feature a "variety of entertainments" the like of which America had never seen before.

The officers determined to put on a joust, for the favors of "ladies selected from the foremost in youth, beauty and fashion." It would be a "tournament according to the customs and ordinances of ancient chivalry." Fourteen officers would dress as knights from the Crusades, each with an accompanying lady dressed as a Turkish princess. Andre was among twenty-one officers who subscribed more than three thousand pounds to finance the production. In addition, according to a Hessian officer, "The great English shop of Coffin and Anderson took in 12,000 pounds sterling for silk goods and other fine materials, which shows ... how elegantly the ladies were dressed."

Those people lucky enough to receive Andre's ornately designed invitations assembled at Redoubt Number 1 at "three o'clock in the afternoon" of May 18th and "embarked in flatboats and passed down the Delaware River with musical accompaniment." They were rowed only a half mile, stopping at the landing of the confiscated estate of a rebel in exile, Thomas Wharton, whose mansion and grounds had been completely done over to accomodate this extravaganza. A lady in town, corresponding with the wife of the rebel Colonel Theodorick Bland, describes their arrival:

> At length, we reached the place of destination ... The house stands about three hundred yards from the river. Here we landed, and in a lane formed by grenadiers and guards we proceeded about halfway to the house ... A triumphant arch in honor of Lord Howe engaged our attention. Neptune with his trident was engraved thereon and two sisters guarded it with drawn swords; they were placed in little niches formed for that purpose. On each side of this arch were seats for the ladies, steps, one above another, and carpets thrown over the whole. ...
>
> Fourteen young ladies were dressed alike: white Poland dresses of Mantua with long sleeves, a gauze turban spangled, and sashes around the waists. Seven of them wore pink sashes with silver spangles, and the others, white with gold spangles; handkerchiefs of gauze spangled in the same manner. Those of the pink and white were called the Ladies of the Blended Rose, the white and gold were of the Burning Mountain. These ladies, with all the others, were seated on these steps, when a herald from the Blended Rose made his appearance.

Captain John Andre, one of the Knights of the Blended Rose, would later use watercolors to make a beautiful painting, and write a detailed account of the night, presenting both as souvenirs to Peggy Chew, who was his partner at the Mischianza. From Andre's account:

> [The White Herald] ... after a flourish of trumpets, proclaimed the following challenge: "The Knights of the Blended Rose, by me their herald, proclaim and assert that the Ladies of the Blended Rose excel in wit, beauty

and every accomplishment those of the whole world; and should any Knight or Knights be so hardy as to dispute or deny it, they are ready to enter the lists with them and maintain their assertions by deeds of arms, according to the laws of ancient chivalry." ...

[The Black Herald arrived and] ordered his trumpets to sound, and then proclaimed defiance to the challenge in the following words: "The Knights of the Burning Mountain present themselves here, not to contest by words, but to disprove by deeds, the vainglorious assertions of the Knights of the Blended Rose, and enter these lists to maintain that the Ladies of the Burning Mountain are not excelled in beauty, virtue or accomplishment by any in the universe." ...

After they had [entered] the lists and made their obeisance to the Ladies, they drew up fronting the White Knights; and the Chief of these having thrown down his gauntlet, the Chief of the Black Knights directed his Esquire to take it up. The Knights then received their lances from their Esquires, fixed their shields on their left arms, and making a general salute to each other by a very graceful movment of their lances, turned round and, encountering in full gallop, shivered their spears. In the second and third encounter they discharged their pistols. In the fourth they fought with their swords.

At length, the two Chiefs, spurring forward into the centre, engaged furiously in single combat, till the Marshal of the Field rushed in between the Chiefs and declared that the Fair Damsels of the Blended Rose and Burning Mountain were perfectly satisfied with the proofs of love and the signal feats of valour given by their respective Knights; and commanded them to desist from further combat.

The participants and guests then proceeded through the second ornate arch, this one honoring General Howe, under which each knight dismounted and, on bended knee, received a favor his lady unpinned from her turban. When everyone reached the mansion's gardens, they drank "cooling liquors" and looked skyward, where Howe's chief engineer, Captain John Montresor, put on twenty different demonstrations of fireworks. Then they all went inside for dancing, followed at midnight by a sumptuous meal, which included exotic West Indian fruits rushed to the site by the navy. Andre concludes his account:

> Toward the end of the supper, the Herald of the Blended Rose, attended by his trumpeters, entered and proclaimed the king's health, the queen, royal family, the army and navy, with their respective commanders, the knights and their ladies, and the ladies in general. Each of these toasts were followed by a flourish of music. After supper, we returned to the ballroom and continued to dance until four o'clock.

Evidently, the effort had all been worthwhile, for Captain Andre observed on the countenances of the Howe brothers, both general and admiral, "a generous emotion, [to] answer the undissembled testimony of our love and admiration." Some, of course, disapproved. Admiral Howe's secretary, Ambrose Serle, was appalled at the "folly and extravagance" of the Mischianza. One old artillery major thought, "The Knights of the Burning Mountain are tomfools, and the Knights of the Blended Rose are damned fools!" Mrs. Henry Drinker, whose husband had been taken away from her by the rebels for his anti-war writings, was outraged. She wrote in her journal that night:

> This day may be remembered by many for the scenes of folly and vanity. How insensible do these people appear, while our land is so greatly desolated, and death and sore destruction has overtaken and impends over so

many.

Having been given his grand send-off on May 18th, Sir William Howe turned over command of the army to Sir Henry Clinton on the 24th before boarding a ship that would take him home to England. Clinton, who Howe had left in charge at New York in 1777, was the king's second choice for Howe's successor. His first choice was Lord Jeffrey Amherst, who had been so effective in the previous war against the French, but who, once again, as he had done in 1775, declined the king's request to partake in this unpopular war.

Amherst did, however, agree to provide some analysis of the situation. In mid-January, he told the cabinet that, if the French entered the war, continuing an "offensive land war" in America would require 30,000 new recruits. Such an expense being impracticable "under our present circumstances," future military operations should therefore be "principally naval, to distress [American] trade and prevent their supplies from Europe."

While the king and his ministers were mulling over Amherst's advice, the long anticipated Franco-American alliance finally became a reality. It speeded up development of a new military strategy. This new war with France meant new objectives, including conquest of the Sugar Islands. The land war against the American rebels would now be of "secondary importance." In March, King George III was formally notified of the "faithless and insolent conduct of France," and he immediately wrote to Prime Minister Lord North, stating his conviction that, "it is a joke to think of keeping Pensilvania, for we must form from the army now in America a corps sufficient to attack the French Islands." Colonial Secretary Lord Germain informed the new commander in chief, General Sir Henry Clinton:

> [The King,] in consequence of the advice of his most confidential servants, has taken the resolution to avenge the insulted honour of his crown and vindicate the injured rights of his people by an immediate attack upon

the French possessions in the West Indies.

Clinton was instructed to evacuate Philadelphia and divide up his army. Three thousand troops would be needed to maintain control of the Floridas. Another five thousand would be needed for a Caribbean campaign, starting with the seizure of St. Lucia, a French naval base in the West Indies. Clinton was also told to take the remainder of his army at Philadelphia back to New York. If he could not very quickly "bring Mr. Washington to a general action," he should "give up every idea of offensive operations" and use his army to maintain a defensive war: protect the naval bases at New York and Newport, Rhode Island, and send forth raiding parties along the coast, particularly against the New England seaports that had "annoyed much" the British shipping - nearly 500 merchant ships had already been taken by rebel privateers since the start of the war. Furthermore, if Clinton found it impossible to defend New York, he should withdraw to Newport, and, if that post proved untenable, he should give Newport up, too, and move all his forces to Halifax, Nova Scotia.

General Clinton was stunned by this new strategy, which he labeled "imbecility." He now considered Britain's chances of winning back the colonies an "impossibility." The impending evacuation of Philadelphia made the army's quartermaster-general, Sir William Erskine, feel "miserable" and "ashamed of the name of a Briton."

In May, as General Howe packed and otherwise prepared to leave for England, he took time out to meet with one of the city's chief magistrates, representing the loyalists of the city. Howe advised him

> to tell them to make peace with the States, who he supposed would not treat them harshly; for it was probable, on account of the French War, the troops would be withdrawn.

This shocking news "soon circulated about the town," filling the loyalists with "melancholy on the apprehension of being speedily deserted; now a rope was, as it were, about their necks, and all their property subect to confiscation." The loyalist leader, Joseph Galloway, discussed it with his good friend from England, the admiral's secretary, Ambrose Serle, who felt "horror and indignation" at this shameful and unnecessary retreat, especially when he "reflected upon the miserable circumstances of the rebels ... who might soon be crushed by spirited exertions." From Ambrose Serle's journal:

> Friday, [May] 22d. A confirmation of the sad intelligence of yesterday was communicated to Mr. Galloway. ... It filled my poor friend, as might be expected, with horror and melancholy ... now left to wander like Cain upon the earth without home and without property ...
>
> I now look upon the contest as at an end. No man can be expected to declare for us when he cannot be assured of a fortnight's protection. Every man, on the contrary, whatever his primary inclinations, will find it his interest to oppose and drive us out of the country.
>
> I endeavored to console, as well as to advise my friend. I felt for him and with him. Nothing remains for him but to attempt reconciliation with what I may now venture to call the United States of America ... O Thou righteous God, where will all this villainy end!

Because the new war against France would require huge resources, Britain must, according to Prime Minister Lord North, "get out of the dispute [with America] as soon as possible." Never before had the king and his ministers considered anything other than a military solution to the American rebellion, but now they sought a diplomatic one. Lord North persuaded Parliament to authorize a conciliatory offer. Peace commissioners were appointed to present the offer to the rebel Congress. And, unlike the half-hearted attempt made in September, 1776, these commissioners would actually have something to offer besides amnesty.

Among the concessions to be made, should the Congress agree that the former colonies would return their allegiance to King George III: an immediate cease fire; pardons to all individual rebels; recision of all objectionable laws passed since 1763; no British military forces to be allowed on American soil without permission of Congress; Congress to be recognized as a legitimate legislative body; the American colonies to have a voice, but no vote, in Parliament; and, likewise, British observers to sit in the Congress and the colonial legislatures. In sum, this would virtually be full self-government for the American colonies. As to the sticky point of American independence, the commissioners' secret instructions stipulated that independence could be *discussed*, in order to keep the negotiations moving along, but it must not be *granted*. The King made it very clear that, "to treat with independence can never be possible." He wrote to Lord North:

> Should America succeed in that, the West Indies must follow them ... Ireland would soon ... be a separate state, and this island be reduced to itself, and soon would be a poor island indeed.

The new peace commission was called the Carlisle Commission, named after its leader, Frederick Howard, Earl Carlisle. Carlisle and the other commissioners sailed for Philadelphia in April, expecting to offer "terms of peace to a defeated adversary from the walls of his conquered capital." Announcements providing the gist of their proposals arrived in America before the commissioners had even left England. Congress shrewdly made no effort to suppress their publication, but rather assisted in widely disseminating them. At the same time, leading patriots were enlisted to write editorials and pamphlets denouncing the conciliatory offer. For example, Governor William Livingston submitted a series of letters, each in a different hand, to the *New Jersey Gazette*, to create an impression of widespread opposition to North's conciliatory offer. The patriot writers ridiculed the offer as just another ruse by Parliament to subject Americans to its former tyrannical rule, and claimed that Parliament would renege on all its promises as soon as the Americans laid down their arms.

On the sixth of June, Carlisle and the other commissioners landed at Philadelphia and declared to the generals and loyalist leaders, "The only method of putting an end to this disastrous war [is] by liberal, specific, and intelligible offers of reconciliation, supported at the same time by the most active and spirited military operations." However, such was not to be the case. Clinton informed the commissioners that he was in the final phase of preparations to evacuate the city; he had been instructed to return to New York, where he would have to wage a defensive war with a depleted army. The commissioners were "greatly astonished" at this news. And they were infuriated that Clinton's packet had left London a full month before they themselves had embarked, yet those directives "had industriously been kept a secret from us." Carlisle bitterly vowed that, once he returned to London, "those who contrived the cheat must answer for the consequences." Carlisle and the other commissioners saw that this new miltiary strategy would "render the Commission both ineffective and ridiculous," because they would be negotiating from weakness, not strength.

> That which we had always looked upon as the great instrument which was to secure us success, the active and offensive course of military operation, was no longer to support our proceedings ... our offers of peace were [now] too much the appearance of supplications for mercy from a vanquished and exhausted state.

The commissioners, in Carlisle's words, decided that this new situation "permitted none of the protracting arts of negotiation ... we were all convinced that we had no other part to take but at once to display every concession and every inducement which our country had empowered us with." They even made offers that they were not authorized to, such as Parliamentary representation, but it was all to no avail. New York's patriot Governor George Clinton declared,

"Lord North is two years too late with his political maneuvers." Connecticut's Governor Trumbull thought the commissioners' terms, if offered in 1775, "might have been accepted with joy and gratitude." George Washington, apprehensive about the offer - which he termed a "dangerous game" - wrote to John Banister:

> They are endeavoring to ensnare the people by specious allurements of peace. ... Nothing can be more evident than that a peace on the principles of dependence, however limited, after what has happened, would be to the last degree dishonourable and ruinous. ...
>
> Nothing short of independence, it appears to me, can possibly do. A peace on other terms would, if I may be allowed the expression, be a peace of war. The injuries we have received from the British nation were so unprovoked and have been so great and so many, that they can never be forgotten.

Though Washington refused the commissioners' request for safe passage to York to meet with Congress, he did agree to make sure their correspondence reached Congress.

There was a lot of optimism on the British side that the conciliatory offer would be well received. Germain wrote to Clinton, telling him what his loyalist refugee advisors, claiming to know the "disposition of the inhabitants," had assured him:

> The generality of the people desire nothing more than a full security in the enjoyment of all their rights and liberties under the British Constitution. ... the generous terms held out to them will be gladly embraced ... [and] supersede the necessity of another campaign.

True, the offer was a good one, but its timing was extremely poor. The members of Congress, like Americans everywhere, were still digesting the sensational news of the military alliance with France; the Continental Army had survived another winter, was presently being reinforced, and was stronger and more confident; the French fleet was expected soon; and people were already talking about the war coming to a favorable conclusion within the next six months.

Nevertheless, many loyalists and officers in Philadelphia thought that such "very favorable terms" as these would certainly be accepted by the rebel Congress. A Hessian officer, writing in the journal of the Jager Corps, reflected on this optimism and the outcome:

> Everyone was so completely convinced that peace would result and so certain had this belief taken hold, that we were astounded and amazed by Congress' scornful refusal of everything which in the least curtailed independence.

The British soldier Thomas Sullivan thought that it was fitting - his government's proposals were received by the Congress "with as much coolness as the American Petitions had been received formerly by the Parliament of Great Britain." After the members of Congress voted unanimously to reject the offer, President Laurens wrote back to Carlisle, explaining that the Congress would be ready to consider

> a treaty of peace and commerce ... when the King of Great Britain shall demonstrate a sincere disposition for that purpose ... [by] an explicit acknowledgment of the independence of these states, or the withdrawing his fleets and armies.

Until then, Laurens informed one of the other commissioners, "the good people" of America would persevere in defending themselves, and if necessary, retire "westward of yonder mountains" to continue fighting from there until independence was assured.

Congressman W. H. Drayton, from South Carolina, tried to soothe

Carlisle's feelings by explaining the futility of granting anything short of independence. America, in its continental expanse, was "formed for empire [and] must naturally arrive at it." Drayton went on to describe what America would be like under Carlisle's proposed system:

> Having [once] tasted of it, she will ever be anxious to possess it again; having by arms acquired a power, but short of independence, she will increase in reputation and ability to become independent, and this will increase her desire to be so.

Commissioner George Johnstone, former Governor of West Florida, was not yet ready to give up. He recalled that their instructions had stipulated, "if a treaty with Congress failed, the Commissioners should apply to bodies of men, or individuals." So he used the wife of the commission secretary as a liaison. This woman, Mrs. Ferguson, approached Joseph Reed, the Presdient of Pennsylvania's Executive Council. From Reed's account:

> Mrs. Ferguson then went on to say that Governor Johnstone expressed great anxiety to see me, and particularly wished to engage my interest to promote the object of their misison, viz. a reunion between the two countries, if it was consistent with my principles and judgment; and in such case, it could not be deemed improper or unbecoming in Government to take a favourable notice of such conduct; and in this instance I might have 10,000 pounds sterling and any office in the colonies in his Majesty's gift.
> I found an answer was expected, and gave one: "That I was not worth purchasing, but such as I was, the King of Great Britain was not rich enough to do it." By this time the evening was pretty far advanced, and no reply being made, I rose ... and left the house, with a mind

much agitated with this new and unexpected scene.

Reed brought the bribery attempt to the attention of Congress, which expressed its "most pointed indignation" by breaking off further communication, and ordering the following resolution published in the newspapers: "Resolved, That Congress will not in any degree negotiate with the present commissioners in America for restoring peace."

Discouraged, the commissioners wrote back to London, asking permission to return home. In the meantime, they would sail with Lord Howe for New York. In October they would leave America for good, after issuing a final manifesto, what Lord Carlisle termed "a last dying speech of the Commission." When New Jersey's Governor William Livingston received his parchment copy, he fashioned a kite from it for his son to play with. George Washington considered Prime Minister North's conciliatory bills "an insult to common sense," knowing, as North should have, that "a treaty had actually been signed" with France. How "he could expect that such an undisguised artifice would go down in America, I cannot conceive."

Britain had finally come up with a sincere and generous conciliatory offer. But it had failed, and King George III would not make another attempt. He was determined now to forego further diplomatic efforts until the military situation was resolved. He wrote to North, on August 12, 1778:

> Further concession is a joke ... We must content ourselves with distressing the rebels, and not think of any other conduct till the end of the French [war], which, if successful, will oblige the rebels to submit.

CHAPTER NINE
THE BRITISH RETREAT
ACROSS NEW JERSEY

"I have no doubt but if we overtake them we possess a very happy chance."

- *General Lafayette.*

"They did not leave, they vanished." So wrote a resident of Philadelphia, describing the British evacuation in the wee hours of June 18, 1778. For the loyalists, and for Quakers such as Mrs. Henry Drinker, life would be different, now that "there was not one redcoat to be seen in town." The rebels were back, and citizens who were not for the cause had best keep their opinions to themselves. Elizabeth Drinker would record in her journal two weeks later:

> July 2. The Congress came in today - firing cannon on the occasion.
>
> July 4. A great fuss this evening, it being the anniversary of Independence - firing of guns, sky rockets, etc. Candles were too scarce and expensive to have an illumination, which perhaps saved our windows.
>
> A very high head-dress was exhibited through the streets this afternoon, on a very dirty woman, with a mob after her with drums, etc., by way of ridiculing that very foolish fashion.

To prevent price gouging by merchants, and acts of vengeance against loyalists, the city was temporarily put under military rule.

Benedict Arnold, formerly the army's best field general but now relegated to less active commands because of his Saratoga leg wound, occupied the city on June 19th with a regiment of continentals.

The civilian refugees also returned, and found that the enemy had left the city "one promiscuous scene of ruin." Henry Knox, the artillery general, at first had hoped to find his wife some lodging in the city, "but it stunk so abominably that it was impossible to stay there." One particularly disgusting practice of the occupying troops had been to board their horses inside the refugees' houses, and cut holes in the floor, through which their servants could shovel the manure into the cellar. Such actions, reflected a disillusioned loyalist named Robert Morton, showed that the citizens of Philadelphia "appeared contemptible in the eyes of men who have uniformly despised the Americans as a cowardly, insignificant set of people."

Occupation by the British Army had turned many a loyalist into a patriot, just as John Adams had predicted a year earlier, when he wrote that, "There are impurities [loyalist sentiments] here which will never be so soon or so fully purged away as by that fire of affliction which Howe enkindles wherever he goes."

A returning civilian recorded some interesting impressions, later printed in Boston's *Continental Journal and Weekly Advertiser*:

> Houses are destroyed and redoubts built on the spots where some of them formerly stood. The timber has been all cut down ... an abatis made of fruit trees extends from Delaware to Schuylkill. ...
>
> Coming into the city, I was surprised to find that it had suffered so little, but the morals of the inhabitants have suffered vastly. The enemy introduced new fashions ... [the gentleman's] hat is now amazingly broad-brimmed and cocked very sharp. ... [The ladies'] hair is dressed ... in such a manner as to appear too heavy to be supported by their necks ... a northwester would certainly throw these belles off their center. ...

> I cannot yet learn whether the cork rumps have been introduced here, but some artificial rumps or other are necessary to counterbalance the extraordinary natural weight which some of the ladies carry before them. ... Indeed, many people do not hesitate in supposing that most of the young ladies who were in the city with the enemy and wear the present fashionable dresses have purchased them at the expense of their virtue.

Though the new British commander in chief felt that to "retreat with such an army is mortifying," Clinton really had no choice. "My instructions are positive; I cannot misunderstand them, nor dare I disobey them." Unlike his predecessor, William Howe, whose two and a half years as commander in chief had been noteworthy for his indolence, Henry Clinton lost no time in setting his army in motion. Clinton quickly put "all the heavy baggage, as well as the tents, sick and wives aboard" the relatively few ships he had at his disposal, then prepared his army for a march to New York.

Clinton wrote to Lord Germain, explaining that, despite orders to take his army by sea, he "found it impracticable ... as there are not transports enough to receive the whole at once," and he would not make himself vulnerable to his enemy by dividing his army. He decided to disobey orders and postpone sending the assigned detachments to Florida and the West Indies until the whole army safely reached New York. The bulk of his army started the slow march across New Jersey on June 18th, bringing with them some light field pieces and 1,500 wagons loaded with provisions and baggage.

To reduce the ill effects of plundering the inhabitants while on the march, Clinton tried to limit the number of camp followers:

> Commanding officers to take two women per company, provided they are known to be good marchers, as no carriages will be allowed for them or their baggage. ... The women of the Army always to march upon the

flanks of the baggage of their respective corps, and the provost marshal has received orders to drum out any women who shall dare to disobey this order.

Complicating evacuation plans was the large number of loyalist refugees and all their baggage. Lord Carlisle estimated that 3,000 refugees boarded the ships that sailed from Philadelphia. Clinton would not leave these people, "whose attachment to government has rendered them objects of vengeance to the enemy."

Captain John Andre, too, was apprehensive over the likely fate of any loyalists who did not go with the army, for surely, the returning committee-men would exercise "very great rigor against all persons who have befriended us." Among those staying was Andre's partner from the Mischianza, Peggy Chew. Her father, Benjamin Chew, had gravely told the family that, no matter who ruled it, America was their country, so the family would stay here and try to retain their estate, Cliveden. John's courtship of Peggy ended with the army's departure. On June 17th, when they parted for the last time, he pressed a folded paper into her palm. Later, unfolding it, she read these lines:

> If at the close of war and strife
>   My destiny once more
> Should in the varied paths of life
>   Conduct me to this shore;
>
> Should British banners guard the land
>   And factions be restrained;
> And Cliveden's mansion peaceful stand,
>   No more with blood be stained --
>
> Say! Wilt thou then receive again,
>   And welcome to thy sight,
> The youth who bids with stifled pain
>   His sad farewell tonight?

Clinton also put aboard the ships two Hessian regiments that he suspected would be decimated by desertions if they were allowed to march across New Jersey. Lieutenant Feilitzsch had already recorded in his journal, as early as two months before, that "the soldiers desert in large numbers. This happens with every patrol." Several factors were responsible for their desertion rate having increased recently. The Hessians, as hired mercenaries, had no personal attachment to this war between Englishmen, particularly ever since Howe had sent so many of their countrymen to be slaughtered at Red Bank in October. And they could barely tolerate the "confounded pride and arrogant bearing of the English, who treat everyone that was not born on their ragamuffin island with contempt."

Another factor was the rebels' continuing propaganda campaign designed to encourage Hessians to desert. The day after Howe's army landed at Head of Elk, back in August, "a Pennsylvanian" went among the Hessians distributing "many thousand copies" of a broadside, printed in both English and German, enticing them to desert. In January, 1778, Congress authorized up to 30,000 acres be allocated for Hessian deserters. Individuals would receive acreage and livestock, the amounts dependent on their rank.

Of course, a man would also need a wife to help him establish himself in this new land. Pennsylvania, with its large German speaking population, could provide *die werdende braute*. An investigation in March, 1778, into the desertion of three Hessian grenadiers discovered they'd been influenced by three local women. The army had by now been encamped in the same place for many months, so contact with the inhabitants was inevitable, especially for those soldiers who repeatedly patrolled the same routes, frequented the same taverns, etc. And these Pennsylvanians had such appealing customs! Friedrich von der Lith:

> A young stranger when he first comes into a house is invited to dinner in a friendly manner. If the master of the house has one or more daughters, after the table has

been cleared he offers that the stranger should also stay at his place and pass the night in bed with his daughter.

This offer is, quite naturally, seldom refused, if the young lady is good looking as well. The father himself brings the two to bed without further formalities ... This wonderful practice is called in English, "bundle."

The only inconvenience of it is that the stranger ... if such a night has consequences, must either marry the young lady or at least support her together with the child.

Before the end of the winter, General Knyphausen was reporting to the Landgraf of Hesse-Cassel that many of his soldiers had requested permission to marry Americans. On December 13, 1777, one of our British diarists, Thomas Sullivan, married "Sarah Stoneman, an inhabitant of the city of Philadelphia." The next day, Chaplain Philipp Waldeck performed a double ceremony for another couple: "the baptism of the child, and the marriage." The chaplain was pleased that, "It is customary ... among the Americans for the minister to kiss the bride at the conclusion of the ceremony."

During the night that Clinton's army evacuated Philadelphia, many British and Hessian soldiers hid themselves in cellars, attics and elsewhere until the army and fleet had disappeared. A few hours later, a party of continental light horse, commanded by Captain Allen McLane, triumphantly rode down the streets "with drawn swords in hand" and reclaimed the city. They reported finding dozens of enemy soldiers, men who offered no resistance.

On the march across New Jersey in June, advance American parties following closely on the heels of Clinton's army would report taking in hundreds of deserters. One of these men would be Thomas Sullivan. He had tried before, without success, back in 1775. Having just arrived in Boston, the twenty-year-old Irishman, "seeing America under arms ... and examining the reason," concluded that, "they were striving to throw off the yoke under which my country sunk." By June 25,

1778, Thomas Sullivan was determined to seize the moment and "gain that freedom which every heart should wish for, i.e., being their own masters." His recollection of his second desertion attempt:

> A breath of freedom still glowed in my breast ... like a lingering disease, it broke out at last; being partly roused to it by the ill usage I received (undeservedly) when I was in the 49th battalion, and partly on account of my being married to a young woman that was born in America, whom I knew wished me to be clear of the army.
>
> Those and a few more reasons induced me ... to live a more retired, regular and easy life, in regard to my soul and body ... the army in general was a repository for all manner of vice. ... [If a man endeavours] to practice his duty towards GOD he will be derided and laughed at, hated by some, while others load him with reproaches.
>
> In order to put my design in execution, I learnt the hour our battalion ... were to march off their ground; being a quarter before four in the morning. After I gave ... directions to my wife ... to keep clear of the column, I told her the resolution I had taken ... to free myself of the English service, or lose my life in the attempt. ...
>
> As the out sentries were called in, the picquets followed the battalion, this party excepted, and I set off to my hut and from thence slipt into a wood, where I remained untill the column got upon their march.
>
> The troops being gone, I left the wood and saw my wife standing at the door of a waste house at some distance, whom I approached ... we could see the rear of the division at about 200 yards distance from us. ...
>
> I met an old man, who cautioned us against a set of people called Tories ... He also informed me which route to take, in order to avoid any danger.
>
> After making a short halt under a shade, and taking

some refreshment, we struck off across the country, and after a tedious and troublesome march, through woods and marshes ... we met Colonel Morgan's rifflemen ...

I want words to express the joy and gladness with which my wife was seized, upon seeing the American troops, which she expressed to me in the strongest terms, saying at the same time, that we were safe and out of danger. ... I returned thanks to the Almighty ...

June 28th. We arrived at Philadelphia, where upwards of eight hundred deserters arrived before us, the most part of which, having three days provisions and passes, went towards Reading. ...

July 28th. Upon my departure from Philadelphia, I left my wife there, with directions to follow me [to the army] as soon as I wrote for her ... to my great satisfaction she reached the [White] Plains this day. Any man that tasted the sweets of matrimony ... [and] a contented life may conceive the joy and pleasure I felt in meeting ...

By the first week of June, George Washington, through his network of spies, had been apprised of the British preparations to evacuate the city, but despite "the most diligent pains," he could not discover Clinton's intended route. He posted observation parties in every likely path. To the south, Smallwood's brigade was still at Wilmington; for the southwest, he sent a party to Chadd's Ford, in case the British returned the way they had come. To cover the east, he sent William Maxwell's brigade of light infantry to Mount Holly, with orders to cooperate with Moylan's light horse and New Jersey militia under General Philemon Dickinson. If Clinton started marching across that state, they should observe the march, cut off stragglers whenever opportunities arose, collect deserters, "give the enemy some annoyance" by felling trees, taking up bridges, filling wells with earth, etc., but avoid a general engagement. "And when you find that it is needless to pursue any further," he instructed Maxwell, "you are to file off and gain the North River as quick as possible." Knowing Clinton would soon be in New York, Washington intended to relocate his army along the Hudson, "in order to protect communications between New England and the South."

The British peace commissioners unwittingly alerted Washington as to the planned timing of the evacuation, when they demanded of their laundrywoman that all their laundry be ready by June 16th. She sent her son to sneak out of Philadelphia and make his way to Valley Forge with the intelligence.

Washington promptly called a council of war on June 17th, to ask his top generals whether he should attack the enemy while on the march (by now he had realized that Clinton did not have enough transports to go by sea). Two were for an attack, a few others were for following and harassing them on the march, but the majority sided with Charles Lee, who was "passionately opposed to strong measures." Tempers flared as Lafayette and Wayne resented the disparaging remarks that Lee (a former British officer) made about the continentals' fighting abilities, compared to the British. Losing control of his council, Washington curtailed all further discussion and asked each man to submit his own thoughts in writing. Nathanael Greene immediately forwarded his opinion, concluding, "People expect something from us, and our strength demands it."

The next morning, June 18th, a citizen named George Roberts rode into camp with the news that Clinton's whole army had crossed over into New Jersey during the night. Within an hour, a courier from Captain Allen McLane's Light Horse arrived to confirm the intelligence. That night, an advance division under Lee, Lafayette and Wayne was on the move. Jeremiah Greenman recorded in his journal on June 19th, "Last night about twelve oclock att the beet of *the Genl.* struck our tents & marcht." Washington followed in the morning with the rest of the army, except for the invalids to be left in camp and the regiment sent with Benedict Arnold to take possession of Philadelphia.

The army's two divisions crossed at Coryell's Ferry (present day New Hope, PA), north of Trenton. Traveling lighter than the enemy, they would catch up with Clinton ten days later at a place called Monmouth Courthouse, after marching eighty miles.

Burdened by their uncomfortably hot and tight uniforms, and an average load of sixty pounds on the back of each man, the regulars of Clinton's army suffered more than their lighter clad, less equipped pursuers. Dr. Johann Schoepff was kept busy on this march, treating cases of heatstroke, noting that among its deadly effects, "blood gushes from the mouth and nostrils." He worried about this "remarkable" heat and fatigue:

> Enveloped as our men are in heavy woolen garments and tight leggings, and carrying the entire weight of a gun, sixty cartridges, knapsack, and rations, they cannot but suffer doubly from all the discomforts of such days.

Each morning the army rose at 3 a.m., so as to accomplish most of the marching before the heat became intolerable. The last two weeks of June that year in New Jersey were notable for many unusually hot and sultry days, filled with scorching sunshine punctuated by severe thunderstorms and downpours that drenched the suffering marchers. Soldiers made note of the sandy soil retaining the heat of the sun more than other soils would. At the end of the seventh day of marching, Jacob Piel recorded that "almost half of our troops fell along the way due to the heat," many of them died of heatstroke; the others were helped back up and kept marching. Occasionally, woods offered a respite of shade, but the trees cut off the breezes and were home to swarms of biting mosquitoes.

The march was conducted "in the height of the season of cherries." Clinton's thirsty soldiers "could not climb the trees, but universally cut them down" to get at the fruit. On June 22nd, George Washington's detailed marching instructions for his own army also mentioned the fruit trees (could it be that the soldiers of both armies were plundering the orchards?).

> ... the guards [should be] kept to their duty and all damage to the fruit trees prevented, of which the whole road hitherto exhibits such shameful proof.
>
> Commanding officers of companies will see that their men fill their canteens before they begin the march, that they may not be under the necessity of running to every spring and injuring themselves by drinking cold water when heated with marching.
>
> Each brigade is to furnish an active-spirited officer and twenty-five of its best marksmen immediately. These parties to join Colonel Morgan's corps, and continue under his command till the enemy pass through the Jerseys, after which they are to rejoin their regiments ...
>
> *The General* to beat at 3 o'clock in the morning, and the Army march at 4 o'clock precisely. ...

On June 24th, Clinton and his army reached Allentown. By now he was aware that Washington's main army was closing in. Clinton was also receiving reports (false ones) that claimed Gates was marching an army from the upper Hudson to converge with Washington's in the hill country around Princeton and block his path to Amboy. So Clinton decided to alter the remainder of his march from his intended northerly direction to a more easterly one, aiming now for Sandy Hook.

The previous night, while staying in the village of Crosswicks, the British commander in chief had had a bottle or two, then fell into a fitful sleep, according to Mrs. Bunting, at whose house he stayed that hot, muggy night.

> [Clinton] had an attack of nightmare caused by the carouse of the evening, and, probably imagining that the Yankees were upon him, had started from his bed, and rushing through the door, which was opened on account of the heat, dashed down the hill. Before the astonished sentinel could decide whether he had seen a ghost or

not, his noble commander was floundering knee deep among the mud and mallows of the little creek.

The plunge awakened him, and his loud outcries brought officers and soldiers rushing from their tents in full expectations of finding themselves attacked by the Rebel army. The shouts and curses, the confusion, the rushing here and there of half-dressed men, formed a scene at once alarming and ridiculous.

But the cause being at length discovered, the discomfited General was led back to his quarters, and with Mrs. Bunting's aid was cleansed, and, half stupefied as he still was, placed again in the clean, comfortable bed which he occupied. Order was restored in the camp and silence reigned unbroken till *Reveille* aroused the slumbering host.

Dickinson's militia, Maxwell's light infantry, and Moylan's light horse continued to harass Clinton's slowly moving army, its baggage train stretching out over twelve miles. Typical of entries recorded during this oppressive march were these from the Jager Corps journal:

> The Jaegers skirmished constantly with an enemy scouting party, which slowly fell back, giving resistance at every defile, woods or bridge, and tore up every bridge, and caused whatever other harassment they could. ... Today ... due to the unbearable heat, we lost three men. The march was very tiring, and as we were the last troops and constantly engaged with the enemy, and because of the exhausted and ruined wells, suffered severely from the shortage of water; many of the Jaegers fell on the road and were put on the officers' horses in order to be carried along with us, as we were not allowed any wagons. This happened frequently on the retreat across the Jerseys.

Back in Philadelphia, Benedict Arnold had raised 100 patriotic townsmen and sent them forward to the army, along with a regiment of continentals that Arnold no longer needed in the city. They arrived on June 23rd. By the 28th, official returns would total 13,424 men, approximately the same strength as Clinton's army. The new recruits brought with them hundreds of badly needed musket cartridges. They had been made by "the virtuous ladies of Philadelphia," painstakingly wrapping the valuable gunpowder inside pieces of paper torn from copies of Gilbert Tennent's sermons on defensive warfare, saved since the French and Indian War and found in Benjamin Franklin's printing room.

On the 24th, a near total eclipse of the sun occurred. Private Joseph Plumb Martin noted that, "Had this happened upon such an occasion [with a battle imminent] in 'olden time' it would have been considered ominous ... but we took no notice of it." At 9:00 that morning, George Washington called his generals to yet another council of war. In the opinion of Anthony Wayne, any council of war was "the surest way to do nothing." As he had done at Valley Forge on June 17th, Charles Lee argued that, "It would be the most criminal madness to hazard a general action at this time." Rather, the army should "keep at a comfortable distance from the enemy" and be content with "annoying them by detachment." Lee swayed a majority of the generals to his opinion.

* * * * *

After Washington, Major General Charles Lee was the highest ranking general in the entire Continental Army. Although only 47, Lee was the most experienced of all the American generals, having been a lieutenant colonel in the British forces, and later a general in those of Poland. Lee naturally had an exalted opinion of European professionals, whether Hessian or British. Lafayette would later comment on Lee, "He always expressed contempt of the American soldiers, and usually spoke of them with a sneer." Lee had once offered his expert opinion to the Continental Congress: "It is in vain for Congress to withstand British troops in the field." He told Washington that risking "a decisive action in fair ground" against regulars would be "impossible," and anyone who says otherwise is talking "nonsense."

An overbearing, abusive officer, Lee was fond of using satire when criticizing officers, such as Washington, who stood in the way of his further advancement. Though he was arrogant, crude in his language, and often exhibited peculiar behavior (such as having his dogs sit in chairs and dine at his table), Charles Lee "was able to impress everyone with the idea of his military genius, skill and experience." Years later, Alexander Hamilton would comment that General Lee had the "preconceived and preposterous notion of his being a very great man." Thomas Paine, showing his greater skill with words, said Charles Lee was "above all monarchs, and below all scum."

In the campaign of 1776, Lee had undeservedly claimed laurels for himself after the successful defense of Fort Sullivan in Charleston harbor. (Lee actually had taken no part in the battle; Colonel Moultrie repulsed a concerted attack by the British Navy and Army, after ignoring Lee's pre-battle order to evacuate the fort.) Later that year, during the Continental Army's retreat across New Jersey following the fall of Fort Washington, Lee belatedly agreed to come to the army's aid by marching his division from White Plains to New Jersey. On the way, on December 13, 1776, Lee was captured by a British patrol; they found him in bed with a tavern wench two miles from his camp.

While being held in New York, Lee heard that Howe had written to London, asking permission to hang him as a traitor, since Lee was a former British officer. So, to save his own hide, Lee tried to win favor with his captors. First, he wrote to friends in Congress, asking that delegates be sent to New York to negotiate with the Howe brothers, who were still serving as peace commissioners. Congress refused. John Adams labeled Lee's idea "an artful strategem," and William Gordon chastised Lee for "suffering himself to be made a pawn of by the Howes." Lee then wrote down a plan on how to win the war by invading Maryland, and submitted it to General Howe. Though he did not sign the document, it would be discovered in Howe's papers in 1860, filed as "Plan of Mr. Lee, 1777." As it turned out, Lee's efforts to save himself from execution were unnecessary, for word came from London stating that, because Lee had resigned his commission before coming to Virginia in 1772, he should be treated as a prisoner of war.

George Washington worked hard to negotiate Charles Lee's exchange, knowing that the campaign season was about to begin. Despite some personal misgivings about Lee's personality, he respected Lee's military experience. On April 5, 1778, Lee arrived at Valley Forge, where the commander in chief made much ado about his return to the army. Colonel Elias Boudinot, Commissary of Prisoners:

> All the principal officers of the army were drawn up in two lines, advanced of the camp about two miles ... the music[ians] of the camp attended. The General, with a great number of the principal officers and their suites, rode about four miles on the road towards Philadelphia and waited until General Lee appeared. General Washington dismounted and received General Lee as if he had been his brother. He passed through the lines of officers and the army, who all paid him the highest military honors, to Headquarters, where Mrs. Washington was and there he was entertained with an elegant dinner, and the music playing the whole time.

Lee lost no time in, once again, disgracing himself, according to Boudinot, who continues his account of Lee's arrival at Valley Forge:

> A room was assigned to him back of Mrs. Washington's sitting room and all his baggage was stowed in it. The next morning, he lay very late and breakfast was detained for him. When he came out, he looked dirty, as if he had been in the street all night. Soon after I discov-

ered that he had brought a miserable dirty hussy with him from Philadelphia, a British sergeant's wife, and had actually taken her into his room by a back door, and she had slept with him that night.

Boudinot had spent an evening with Lee in New York, after arranging his exchange. At that time, Lee confided to Boudinot his opinions of the commander in chief as being "so weak" and unduly influenced by "the worst of advisors." Lee told Boudinot "that Gen'l Washington was ruining the whole cause." He then went on at length, asserting "the improbability of our troops under such an ignorant commander in chief, not fit to command a sergeant's guard, ever withstanding British grenadiers and light infantry." When Boudinot approached General Washington to enlighten him about Charles Lee, the commander curtly cut him off before he could start, telling him there had already been too much divisiveness and he would not listen to any more; Boudinot then decided to keep his suspicions to himself.

* * * * *

At the council of war on June 24th, Washington offered the command of the advance division to Lee, "since his seniority would have entitled him to the command," it being closest to the enemy. But Lee declined it, saying such harassing actions were more fit for "a young volunteering general," meaning Lafayette. So Washington gave the command to Lafayette, who had argued that it "would be disgraceful and humiliating to allow the enemy to cross the Jerseys in tranquillity." But soon, according to Alexander Hamilton:

> General Lee very inconsistently reasserted his pretensions. The matter was a second time accommodated. General Lee and Lord Stirling agreed to let the Marquis command. General Lee, a little time after, recanted again and became very importunate. The General, who

had all along observed the greatest candor in the matter, grew tired of such fickle behavior, and ordered the Marquis to proceed.

Within 24 hours after the council, General Washington received letters from Greene, Lafayette and Wayne, each of them expressing their reservations about the pacifist approach that the majority, influenced by Lee, had voted for (i.e., harassing, but not confronting, the enemy). This was just the advice that Washington, who too often showed an embarassing deference to the more experienced Charles Lee, was looking for; it agreed with his own desire to not let Clinton reach New York unmolested. So, late on the 25th, he sent General Charles Scott with 1,500 men, as well as Colonel Daniel Morgan and his 600, ahead to reinforce Lafayette's advanced division.

Washington also sent new orders for the Frenchman to attack "by detachment, and, if a proper opening should be given, by operating against them with the whole force under your command." Within 24 hours, Lafayette was sending back encouraging reports that "deserters come in amazing fast," and, as to Clinton's army, "I have no doubt but if we overtake them we possess a very happy chance."

Despite his youthfulness, Lafayette had Washington's confidence, having recently shown his leadership abilities under pressure. On May 20th, two days after the Mischianza, Lafayette had led a raiding party of 3,000 to Barren Hill, just north of Philadelphia. The British soon learned of his whereabouts, and General Howe planned to trap "the boy." With the Schuylkill River at Lafayette's back, and two large British columns closing in on his front, Howe was so confident of trapping Lafayette's detachment that he sent out invitations to "dine with the marquis" the coming evening.

But Lafayette was warned of the trap at the last minute, and used a clever ruse to elude it. A small hillock and copse of woods shielded his retreat, one company at a time hurrying to ford the river, while a small covering party of infantry, horse, and Oneida Indians feigned an attack on General James Grant's approaching column. Grant stopped his own march to form his column into battle lines, then waited for the arrival of the other British column coming from the other direction. This allowed Lafayette time to cross his main body, and his covering party quickly followed. When the British reached the riverbank, moments too late, they helplessly watched the last of Lafayette's forces reaching the far bank. Lafayette would write that the British "were very tired and ashamed, and laughed at for their bad luck."

On June 26th, Clinton's two divisions, which had been marching on separate roads, reunited at Freehold, also known as Monmouth Courthouse, it being the county seat. From Lieutenant Feilitzsch's journal:

> 26 June - At five o'clock [a.m.] we marched; as usual, the rear guard. The enemy had disturbed us during the night up until we marched. We went about twelve miles. The enemy harassed us the entire day. I lead a patrol off to one side. The heat was terrible. It was an extremely tiring day. Would to God it is the last one. The place where we halted is called Upper Freehold.

Knowing they were in the path of the advancing armies, the fifteen households of Freehold fled to surrounding villages. The sheriff also left, and headed for Morristown with his fifty prisoners, removing them from the "gaol" in the basement of the courthouse.

Because his pursuing continentals were already rain-soaked by 9:00 a.m., Washington halted them at Mount Holly, resting them there for the remainder of the day. This meant that, by the end of the day, Clinton's army had stretched their lead over Washington's division to 20 miles. With this breathing room, the unremitting weather, and a need to rest and do some foraging for fresh meat and water, Clinton decided to stay in Freehold the night of the 26th, as well as the whole next day and night. On the 27th, another day of thunderstorms and near 100 degree heat, the main division of continentals marched thirteen miles to narrow the gap. They would finally catch up and clash with Clinton the next day, in what would be known as the Battle of Monmouth.

CHAPTER TEN
MONMOUTH
JUNE 1778

"Tell the Philadelphia ladies that the heavenly, sweet, pretty redcoats, the accomplished gentlemen of the guards and grenadiers have humbled themselves on the plains of Monmouth. The Knights of the Blended Rose and Burning Mountain' have resigned their laurels to rebel officers, who will lay them at the feet of those virtuous daughters of America who cheerfully gave up ease and affluence in a city, for liberty and peace of mind in a cottage."

- *General Anthony Wayne, writing to Richard Peters after the Battle of Monmouth.*

By noon on the 27th, the main army had reached Cranbury, eight miles west of Monmouth Courthouse. Washington called his top generals together and, asking for no opinions, informed them that he would take personal responsibility for his decision to bring on a general engagement with Clinton's rear guard. The advanced division, three miles ahead at Englishtown, would initiate the action the next morning, "as soon as the enemy has marched," and he would bring up the main army to support it.

The day before, Charles Lee, having seen that a battle was imminent, had gone to the commander in chief and demanded the advanced division for himself, saying otherwise "both myself and Lord Stirling will be disgrac'd." Washington was in a quandary: on the one hand, he had Lafayette, an energetic, charismatic young general who wanted to fight; and on the other hand, he had Lee, his most senior general, who was demanding the position, despite his earlier emphatic assertions against engaging the enemy. Washington wrote to his good friend, Lafayette, explaining that he felt for "Gen'l Lee's distress of mind," and must give him the command. To justify the change of command, he made the advanced division even larger, and thus in need of a more senior general to lead it. Washington asked Lafayette to stay, as Lee would need his help with such a large division.

Washington ordered Lee to convene a council of his own generals later that same day, "to concert some mode of attack." Lee held the council, but neither offered nor solicited any battle plans. He told them it was impossible to plan a battle, because of lack of intelligence concerning the enemy's strength and dispositions, and that the probable field of battle was "far from being reconnoitered." Afterwards, Lee made no efforts to have anyone reconnoiter that night, nor talk to any inhabitants concerning the terrain, etc. He announced that he was resolved to proceed cautiously the next morning and "act according to circumstances." Such were his unsatisfying words to Lafayette, Anthony Wayne, William Maxwell, and Charles Scott. Later, two days after the confusing battle, Scott and Wayne would write a joint letter to Washington, complaining bitterly that, "no plan of attack was ever commun- icated to us."

Lee's other commanders - Colonel Moylan of the light horse, the militia General Philemon Dickinson, and Colonel Daniel Morgan of the rifle corps - were miles away, on Clinton's left and right flanks, and had not been summoned to the meeting. Lee sent Dickinson written orders to take his 800 militia as near as possible to the enemy and continue to serve as his eyes concerning all enemy movements. Neither the militia nor the light horse would take an active part in the battle. To Colonel Morgan, Lee wrote a note saying he should march his men to Monmouth Courthouse and attack the enemy's right flank as soon as they broke camp. However, throughout the entire battle day, Morgan, with the 600 best marksmen in the Continental Army, failed to make an appearance, and thus left Lee's right flank "in the air." Why this happened is partly explained in a subsequent letter Morgan wrote:

29th June 1778. ... General Lee wrote me yesterday at one o'clock in the evening, he intended to attack the enemy's rear this morning and ordered me to attack them at the same time on their right flank. ...

Evidently, Lee, understandably tired at such a late hour, had dated his note to Morgan "1:00 in the evening, June 28," meaning a.m., but Morgan thought Lee meant p.m. During the day, Morgan, hearing the sounds of battle, would send a rider to find Lee and ask for orders. Arriving on the battlefield at the start of the confused retreat, the messenger would first encounter a very exasperated General Anthony Wayne. Wayne would ask where Morgan was. The messenger's answer: three miles from here, and are there any orders for him? Instead of sending the messenger on to Lee, Wayne would reply, "Tell Morgan to govern himself accordingly." So, unaware of how desperately he was needed, Morgan would stay put and continue waiting, in vain, for orders from Lee.

On the day of the battle, June 28th, Clinton had the larger of his two divisions, Knyphausen's, with all the train of baggage, on the road by 4:00 a.m., heading east. Clinton then rode west to personally reconnoiter the enemy, and only observed a detachment of 1,000 from Lee's division on the road to Freehold. His scouts had told him that the rest of the rebels' advanced division was still at Englishtown, and their main division, under Washington, was three miles further west. Persuaded by this intelligence that Washington was not planning a large scale attack, Clinton told Cornwallis to have his division follow Knyphausen's, set out at 10:00 a.m., and leave a covering party of 2,000 behind, near the courthouse.

Clinton believed that Washington, "after having always hitherto so studiously avoided a general action, would not now give in to it," especially since "the late alliance with France ... and the near approach of a superior French [naval] squadron gave him strong reason to expect that the wishes of the colonies were on the eve of being accomplished without his risking so hazardous an experiment." Nevertheless, Clinton had "hopes that Mr. Washington might be tempted ... to measure his strength with me in the field." Clinton had "little doubt respecting the issue of a general and decisive action with them," should Washington dare bring it on. A British victory now might force either the French King to back out of the treaty, or the rebel Congress to treat with the peace commissioners.

At 11:30 a.m., when his main division had advanced as far as Englishtown, Washington dismounted and wrote a brief note to Henry Laurens, to inform the Congress that a battle was about to commence. Earlier, at about 5:00 a.m., he'd sent a message ahead to Lee, telling Lee to "bring on an engagment or attack as soon as possible, unless some very powerful circumstance forbid it." He added that the main body of troops "had thrown aside their packs and was advancing to his support." An hour later, Washington had sent Lee another message, to "annoy the enemy as much as in his power, but at the same time to proceed with caution and take care the enemy dont draw him into a scrape." By the time Lee received this second message, the enemy would be trying to do exactly that.

Lee moved his forces past Tennent Meetinghouse, three miles west of the courthouse, and crossed the first of three ravines that would come into play this day. This was the "west morass," a swampy area whose narrow causeway in the middle offered the only passage for artillery. He led his army over this causeway, then continued down the road, in the direction of the village, its big courthouse the only significant landmark. General Dickinson rode over and, pointing back to the narrow causeway, warned General Lee, "you are in a perilous situation." Lee, never receptive to unsolicited advice or criticism, curtly told the militia general that he would "make the best of it."

For the past five days, Private Joseph Plumb Martin's company had been part of the advanced division, following closely on the heels of Clinton's army. Some days, they'd arrived upon the British "camping ground within an hour after their departure from it," then had to halt "an hour or two to give the enemy time to advance, our orders being not to attack them unless in self-defence." Now they would finally have their chance, according to Martin's captain, "a brave man [who] feared nobody nor nothing." The captain spoke to his company:

> "Now, you have been wishing, for some days, to come up with the British. You have been wanting to fight - now you shall have fighting enough before night."
>
> The men did not need much haranguing to raise their courage ... when some of the [invalids'] arms were about to be exchanged with those who were going into the field, they would not part with them. "If their arms went," they said, "*they* would go with them at all events."

Lee had pushed the troops forward in starts and stops all morning, as he tried to react to each new piece of intelligence. Though the enemy could not be seen, Dickinson insisted they had not yet left. This contradicted what several inhabitants, acting as self-appointed scouts, had reported. Lee, petulant as always, accused Dickinson of giving him false reports; the militia general defended himself in equally heated terms. At last, Lee told Dickinson he suspected Clinton marched most of his army, only leaving a covering party. "I am determined," he declared, "to march on and ascertain with my own eyes the number, order, and disposition of the enemy, and conduct myself accordingly." Lee spurred his horse forward, and his division of the army followed.

Lee soon received a report that an enemy force had moved forward to flank him on his left. He had his troops hurriedly turn back and recross the ravine, only to find out that the troops off to the left were a party of Dickinson's militia.

So again they advanced, crossed the west morass and the middle ravine, and marched into the village of Freehold. One quarter mile to the right of Lee's main body, his right flank was suddenly charged by the Queen's Rangers, a 300 man force of mounted Tories. Colonel Butler's 9th Pennsylvania Regiment, despite orders to hold their fire, brought up their guns and gave the Tories a single, tremendous volley. It halted their charge, killing several, and wounding their leader, Lt. Colonel John Simcoe, in the arm. His horse was also hit in the volley and, frightened, ran off with him. The Tories fired off their pistols as they turned and rode away. In present day Freehold, a monument stands to commemorate where this initial skirmish took place.

Lee's forces cautiously advanced toward the courthouse, observing near it a small party of British dragoons, which soon retreated before them. The Americans passed the courthouse and a third ravine, the "east morass." Now, out on an open plain, Lee spotted what he took to be all the forces Clinton had left behind, 500 or 600, composed of British dragoons and, to their rear, light infantry. Eleazer Oswald took his battery of four guns off to the left, after Lee cautioned him to stick to the woods, for he did not want the enemy to know yet that he'd brought artillery along. Lee next ordered Anthony Wayne to go forward and attack the enemy with Butler's Pennsylvania regiment and Colonel Jackson's detachment of Massachusetts men.

However, Jackson's men, just arrived from Philadelphia (these were the continentals that Benedict Arnold had sent forward), had only 13 or 14 cartridges apiece in their cartouche boxes. General Lee instructed one of his aides to go with one of Jackson's sergeants and collect one cartridge from each man in all the nearby units, so that Jackson's men could be well prepared for action. Then they set out at the quick step, and, after nearly a mile of hard marching, nearly caught up with Butler's regiment, just as Wayne ordered Butler to march his regiment out of the woods. Butler's Pennsylvanians moved through an orchard and into the open plain to engage the enemy.

The British dragoons charged Butler's regiment. Two years before, at White Plains, just such a cavalry charge as this had turned the American flank and led to a British victory. A courier came galloping over to Jackson and, amidst many expletives, begged him to form his men in battle line and come to Butler's aid, or they'll all be cut to pieces. Jackson quickly formed them, and they left the shade of the woods to rush to Butler's support. Butler calmly told his men that, this time, they must remain cool and hold their fire until the last possible moment, when he would give them the word to fire, then to let them have it. This they did, and the dragoons, according to Clinton's report of the battle, "did not wait the shock, but fell back in confusion upon their own infantry," riding right through them.

Both British parties retreated, and Anthony Wayne ordered Butler to pursue them. But, after going two or three hundred yards, Butler's men were forced by a battery of British three-pounders to fall back to the east morass. It was not yet 11:00 a.m., but the temperature had already risen to 96 degrees.

Looking ahead to the right, Anthony Wayne observed British and Hessian grenadiers not seen before. He ordered a party forward to meet them. In the meantime, he sent back word to Lee that the enemy totaled 1,500 to 2,000, not the 5 or 600 they'd thought. But Lee had nearly 4,000 Contintentals, so he formulated a plan to catch them in a pincers movement, a strategy he had once used effectively in the Polish Army. Lee sent an aide, Captain Mercer, riding forward to tell Wayne to "annoy them with a few loose cannon shot." Lee hoped that Wayne would deliver "a feint or show" to draw the enemy forward while he, himself, led the bulk of his forces far to the left, around the east morass, to eventually come sweeping down on them.

Lee did not send any forces to the right, to protect Wayne's right flank, because he still expected Morgan's riflemen to make their appearance there. He did send Generals Scott and Maxwell far to the left to protect his own westward march around the east morass. To protect Wayne's left flank from the enemy in front, Lee sent Lafayette forward with a detachment, after confidently declaring, "My dear Marquis, I think those people are ours." He expected to surround and capture the enemy's entire rear guard of 2,000, who would be "caught in a forceps." About this time, a messenger arrived from Washington, and Lee told him to tell the Virginian the good news. "By God! I will take them all!"

But Lee did not explain his grand scheme to anyone; instead, he gave his subordinates clipped, short commands for moving their troops here and there. Lieutenant Colonel John Laurens, an aide to Washington but with Lee that morning, later recalled that, "One order succeeded another with rapidity and indecision." Since Lee had not revealed his plan to any of his subordinate generals, they would spend this critical phase of the battle making their own decisions and acting independently of each other.

Lee's plan soon began to fall apart. He and Lafayette left the main column that was marching to the left, and rode ahead to some high ground to have a look around. Three-fourths of a mile in their front, just now coming over Briar Hill, they saw a new, even larger British force. Led by Clinton himself, it consisted of 4,000 troops from the column of Lord Cornwalllis, called back from their march by Clinton's order.

Clinton, from atop Briar Hill, saw that, because of Morgan's absence, the rebel right was unprotected. Clinton "made a disposition to turn it." He was confident that he was not overreaching himself. He did not think Washington would be "incautious" and "blockheaded enough to sustain Lee" by crossing the west morass, for "I should have catched him between two defiles." Clinton directed Cornwallis to make a thrust against Lee's right. The British column marched off the hill, down the road that led toward the courthouse.

Seeing this, Lafayette suggested to Lee that he be allowed to lead a flank attack against them. Lee was appalled. "Sir," he replied, "you do not know British soldiers; we cannot stand against them; we shall certainly be driven back at first, and we must be cautious." Lafayette answered with feeling, "It may be so, General, but British soldiers have been beaten and they may be again; at any rate, I am disposed to make the trial." Then Lafayette rode off. Before leading his troops to the right, to support Wayne and counter this thrust, Lafayette prudently sent an aide riding back in search of Washington, to tell him to hurry forward, he was needed on the field. John Laurens also sent back two riders with similar urgent messages.

With the east morass at his back, Lafayette decided to seek higher ground. Meanwhile, Generals Scott and Maxwell had marched their brigades far to the left, around the ravine, as Lee had told them to do. Now, on this high ground, Scott rode his horse over to Maxwell's. Pointing out the British brigades pouring down Briar Hill, and then moving his finger to the right where Lafayette's troops were apparently retreating (actually, an oblique march toward higher ground to the rear), Scott declared, "We must get out of this place!" Maxwell then ordered his own brigade "to face to the right about, and march back." Both brigades turned around and marched to the rear, repassing the east morass.

This was at the same time that Lee's messenger, Captain Mercer, was riding their way, trying to deliver a message to Scott that he should stop moving to the left, but hold his ground and wait for Lee bringing up the other brigades. When the aide arrived on the high ground, he could find neither Scott nor any troops. He returned to Lee, who was moving with his main force along one bank of the east morass. Told the astonishing news about Scott and Maxwell, Lee vehemently exclaimed, "They have retired without orders!" He then turned to an aide and remarked that this "might prove the ruin of the day." Lafayette now observed Scott and Maxwell retreating and, after firing off several rounds of artillery fire, ordered his own troops to follow suit. Seeing this, the exasperated Lee remarked to an aide that this was another example of unauthorized withdrawal.

Now Lee's only thoughts concerned how he could safely withdraw his troops across the ravines. Facing an enemy superior in numbers by at least 3 to 2, his own division scattered, and the main army still more than an hour's march away, it surely would be folly to try to stop the retreat here. Lee also noticed that Clinton's cavalry numbered 5 or 600, and he had only a handful of horsemen to oppose them, since Moylan's light horse was miles ahead, harassing Knyphausen's baggage train. The British cavalry, their horses fresh after resting the last day and a half at Freehold, would surely come thundering down on his flanks if he tried to make a stand. To his rear, Lee's troops would bunch up while attempting to cross the narrow causeway leading over the middle ravine and west morass. That annoying militia general,

Dickinson, had been right - he was indeed "in a perilous situation."

Lee wisely ordered a retreat of all his scattered forces, an order he would be vilified for later. It was a slow and orderly retreat, the men too tired and hot to run. Captain Stephen Olney, of Rhode Island:

> The heat of the day was so intense that it required the greatest efforts of the officers to keep their men in the ranks, and several of my company were so overcome and faint ... that they said they could go no further. But, by distributing about half a pint of brandy, which I happened to have in my canteen ... I made out to get them along.

By 1:00 p.m., his troops were starting to pass Tennent Meetinghouse, but George Washington rode on ahead. He began encountering soldiers heading back toward Englishtown. Puzzled, he stopped each one that came near him, and demanded an explanation. One boy, a fifer, explained that the army was in retreat. Washington, whose last report from Lee had predicted capture of the entire British rear guard, thought the boy was lying, and told him that he would be whipped if he told such a tale to another soul. Moments later, wanting to be sure the boy kept quiet, Washington ordered a light horseman to take the boy into custody. Then one of the aides spoke up, pointing out that "a countryman" (Thomas Henderson) had just minutes earlier come along with the same tale; there just might be some truth to the boy's story. Pondering this, the commander in chief frowned and spurred his horse onward.

Private Joseph Plumb Martin, though in the advanced division, had not seen any action yet.

> The first cleared land we came to was an Indian cornfield, surrounded on the east, west and north sides by thick tall trees. The sun shining full upon the field, the soil of which was sandy, the mouth of a heated oven

seemed to me to be but a trifle hotter than this ploughed field; it was almost impossible to breathe. We had to fall back again as soon as we could, into the woods.

By the time we had got under the shade of the trees and had taken breath ... we received orders to retreat ... Grating as this order was to our feelings, we were obliged to comply.

We had not retreated far before we came to a defile, a muddy, sloughy brook [the middle ravine]. While the artillery were passing this place, we sat down by the roadside. In a few minutes the commander in chief and suite crossed the road just where we were sitting. I heard him ask our officers "by whose order the troops were retreating," and being answered, "by General Lee's," he said ... "D--n him." ... he seemed at the instant to be in a great passion.

Lee led his remaining forces back to the west side of the east morass. Here Wayne rode over and begged Lee to give him enough troops to make a stand. Lee, a shocked look on his face, answered, "Poh! Poh! It is impossible!" Lee told Wayne that they must continue falling back, and look for better ground than this to make a stand. A villager named Peter Wykoff, who, though not in uniform, was a captain in the Monmouth County militia, came up to General Lee. He said he lived nearby and knew the country well, and wanted to know whether he could be of service to the general, regarding the lay of the land. At first, he suggested Comb's Hill, but Lee said they didn't have time to lay boards over the swampy ground at its foot, to facilitate the movement of artillery. So Wykoff suggested a lesser rise on the far side of the middle ravine. This is where Lee was leading the division when he encountered Washington.

The Virginian reined in his large white horse - a gift, three days before, from Governor William Livingston - and exclaimed, "My God, General Lee! What are you about?" Charles Lee said nothing; just stared back, a quizzical expression on his face. The tall Virginian, impatient for an answer, angrily glared at his second. When he spoke next, the tone of his voice indicated he was fighting to control his temper. "I desire to know, sir! What is the reason, whence arises this disorder and confusion?"

Lee, flustered by his commander's unfriendly manner, could only stammer, "Sir? Sir?" To which Washington repeated, "What's all this confusion for? And what is the cause for this retreat?" Composing himself, Lee sat straight in the saddle and, as calmly as he could, answered, "I see no confusion but what has arose from my orders not being properly obeyed." Lee went on to say that it was not in the interest of the army or America to have a general action brought on, and that he did not desire to attack the whole British Army, they had a far greater number of cavalry. And furthermore, "You know that all this was against my advice." To which, Washington blurted out, "Whatever your opinion might have been, sir, I expect my orders to be obeyed!"

Washington did not question Lee about the enemy's strength and disposition, but turned from him and immediately began to issue orders to a nearby officer, with an aim toward bringing a halt to the retreat. Seeing this, General Lee spoke out, "Sir! These troops are not able to meet British grenadiers!" General Washington, his face red from rage, glared at the man, and replied, "Sir, they *are* able, and by God, they *shall* do it!" No longer able to keep hold of his temper, George Washington cursed his highest ranking subordinate general. One witness claims he called Charles Lee a "damned poltroon." General Scott, years later, was asked if Washington ever swore; his answer:

> Yes, once. It was at Monmouth, and on a day that would have made any man swear. Yes, sir, he swore on that day till the leaves shook on the trees. Charming! Delightful! Never have I enjoyed such swearing, before or since. Sir, on that memorable day, he swore like an angel from Heaven!

Washington then told Lee he would personally take command of Lee's division. Private Martin recalls that "the General took a view of the enemy," then "returned and ordered the two Connecticut brigades to make a stand at a fence, in order to keep the enemy in check, while the artillery and other troops crossed" the causeway to higher ground in the rear, near the Tennent Meetinghouse. Having calmed down somewhat, he then returned and asked the dazed Lee, "General, will you take command in order to give me time to make a disposition of my army?" Lee said he would do so, and would be "one of the last to leave the field." Washington rode back and hurried on the main army, still coming down the road from Englishtown.

In his absence, Lee for an hour oversaw a courageous defense against the elite of the British Army. This part of the battle, along the middle ravine, was a stop-gap effort to hold off the enemy while Washington organized the main army along a rise of ground just west of the west morass. Lee rode back and forth, encouraging the men and directing the fight, which at times involved bayonet charges on both sides and hand-to-hand combat. The aides, Alexander Hamilton and Joseph Laurens, were injured when their horses were shot and fell beneath them. General Clinton's own life was nearly taken when an American colonel took aim at him. Clinton's two adjutants spurred their horses to protect the commander. The rebel's bullet hit the horse of Captain William Sutherland, while the other adjutant, Lt. Thomas Lloyd, reached the rebel and ran him through with with his sword.

The British dragoons and waves of grenadiers and light infantry charged a party of Connecticut and Rhode Island troops who had taken shelter behind a hedgerow. Lieutenant Colonel Jeremiah Olney led the Americans in a heavy fire and follow-up bayonet charge that forced the British back. Afterwards, finding his party too far forward, isolated, and in danger of being flanked, Olney decided to fall back. He brought Eleazer Oswald's battery with him, the sweating gunners, stripped to the waist, struggling in the heat to bring off the field pieces. All the time, they were being bombarded by the first few British batteries to come up and take position on some high ground in the center of the battlefield. It was during this action that Olney's second, Major Simeon Thayer, lost an eye from the windage of a passing cannon ball. Joseph Plumb Martin relates an incident he later heard about:

> A woman whose husband belonged to the artillery and who was then attached to a piece in the engagement attended with her husband at the piece the whole time. While in the act of reaching a cartridge and having one of her feet as far before the other as she could step, a cannon shot from the enemy passed directly between her legs without doing any other damage than carrying away all the lower part of her petticoat. Looking at it with apparent unconcern, she observed that it was lucky it did not pass a little higher ... [then she] continued her occupation.

This pregnant woman, Mary Ludwig Hayes, won immortal fame that day as "Molly Pitcher." She was the wife of a private in a Pennsylvania artillery unit, and in this particular action had been going back and forth to a nearby well (now known as the Molly Pitcher Well), carrying pitchers of water to the artillerists and the wounded. They would call out to her, "Molly! Pitcher!" She continued doing this until her husband was shot down. An officer then ordered the gun taken to the rear, but Molly adamantly refused to allow it, insisting that she would "avenge his death" by fulfilling his duties for the remainder of the action. Dr. Albigence Waldo remarks that:

> She immediately took up his gun and cartridges [and], like a Spartan heroine, fought with astonishing bravery, discharging the piece with as much regularity as any soldier present. This a wounded officer, whom I dressed, told me he did see himself, she being in his platoon, and assured me I might depend on its truth.

When the commander in chief returned, he saw Lee ushering the last remnant of his division, Oswald's battery of guns, over the west morass causeway. Lee followed them across, true to his prediction that he would be one of the last to leave the field of battle. Now Washington asked Lee to gather his scattered forces and reform them in the rear. A little while later, Washington thought better of it, and sent Steuben to do the business. When Steuben caught up with Lee and explained it to him, Lee acquiesced, saying that he was glad to be relieved, for he was very tired. Some of Lee's troops stayed behind, including those of Wayne, who craved action and begged Washington to let his brigade stay and fight.

Later in the afternoon, Lee would return to the battlefield to accost Washington, wanting an explanation for why he had impugned his character earlier, when he'd told Lee that he "should not have undertaken" the command if he did not "think it proper to risk so much." Washington, not wanting to discuss it further, turned away from the man and rode off to continue directing the battle. Lee turned his own horse around and returned to his quarters at Englishtown. Two days later, Lee would demand a court martial to clear his name.

Washington rode his new white horse back and forth across that battlefield until the horse dropped to the ground and died, and the big Virginian had to mount a spare, his favorite "chestnut mare," brought forward by his slave, Billy Lee. Lafayette later recalled Washington's leadership that afternoon:

> His presence stopped the retreat ... his fine appearance on horseback, his calm courage, roused to animation by the vexations of the morning, gave him the air best calculated to excite enthusiasm ... He rode all along the lines amid the shouts of the soldiers, cheering them by his voice and example and restoring to our standard the fortunes of the fight. I thought then, as I do now, that never had I beheld so superb a man.

The battle became a more even contest, as more and more American units arrived. General Steuben watched his former pupils move up "with as much precision as on ordinary parade, and with the ... intrepidity of veteran troops." The army's left column, under General Stirling, halted and took post on a wide slope just short of the west morass, not far past the Tennent Meetinghouse. Washington personally commanded the center, where Wayne's brigade took post.

To cover his right flank, Washington had earlier sent Nathanael Greene instructions, while still on the march from Englishtown, "to file off by the new [Tennent] Church two miles from Englishtown" and take the road that went from Allentown to the courthouse. This road ran behind Comb's Hill. Greene and Henry Knox, moving along that road, saw the steep hill and decided to ride up it and have a look at the battlefield. Knox immediately recognized it as the perfect place to set up his batteries. Comb's Hill was steep, it had a gulley in its front, a brook protected three-fourths of its base, and it commanded much of the battlefield.

Clinton established his own artillery, under General James Patterson, on a smaller rise of ground nearly a mile away, about halfway between Comb's Hill and the courthouse. Nathanael Greene recalled that the opposing "artillery kept shot and shells flying as thick as hail" until 6:00 p.m.

Clinton found himself in "an exposed position," his enemy having attained superior numbers and holding the higher ground. He wanted to withdraw from the field and catch up with his main body, but was forced to "press the business further" in order to "cover the retreat of the light troops and horse, whose ungovernable impatience only had carried them too far" and were in a crossfire from the guns of both Knox and Stirling.

To extricate them, Clinton tried to flank Stirling's position by leading a thrust against the American left. A strong force of grenadiers and Highlanders crossed the middle ravine several hundred yards upstream from the causeway. Lieutenant Colonel Edward Carrington poured artillery fire into the leading British ranks as they struggled through the west morass, but they managed to reach an orchard that provided shelter and shade.

The pressure against Stirling's left was relieved when the 1st Virginia and the 1st and 3rd New Hampshire Regiments, "between 3 and 4 oclock," moved to the left through some woods and counterattacked this British detachment. "His Excellency," Colonel Joseph Cilley would later write, "ordered me ... to go and see what I could do with the enemy's right wing, which was formed in an orchard in our front." Private Joseph Plumb Martin was recruited to go with them:

> The weather was almost too hot to live in, and the British troops in the orchard were forced by the heat to shelter themselves from it under the trees ... [allowing] our detachment an opportunity to look about us. Colonel Cilly of the New Hampshire Line passed along in front of our line, inquiring for General Varnum's men, who were the Connecticut and Rhode Island men belonging to our command. We answered, "Here we are." He did not hear us in his hurry, but passed on. In a few minutes he returned, making the same inquiry. We again answered, "Here we are." "Ah!" said he, "you are the boys I want to assist in driving those rascals from yon orchard."
>
> We ... joined another, the whole composing a corps of about 500 men. We instantly marched towards the enemy's right wing, which was in the orchard ... keeping behind the bushes. When we could no longer keep ourselves concealed, we marched into the open fields and formed our line. The British immediately formed and began to retreat to the main body of their army. ... we pursued ... I singled out a man and took aim directly between his shoulders. They were divested of their packs. He was a good mark, being a broad-shouldered fellow.

What became of him, I know not; the fire and smoke hid him from my sight. ... I hope I did not kill him, although I intended to at the time.

By this time our whole party had arrived, and the British had obtained a position that suited them ... they returned our fire ... and had a small piece of artillery, which the soldiers called a grasshopper. We had no artillery with us. The first shot they gave us from this piece cut off the thigh bone of a captain, just above the knee, and the whole heel of a private in the rear of him.

We gave it to poor Sawney (they were Scotch troops) so hot that he was forced to fall back and leave the ground they occupied. When our commander saw them retreating and nearly joined with their main body, he shouted, "Come, my boys, reload your pieces, and we will give them a set-off." We did so and gave them the parting salute, and the firing on both sides ceased. We then laid ourselves down under the fences and bushes to take breath, for we had need of it. ... the heat of that day, none can realize it that did not feel it.

Next, Cornwallis led a thrust against the American right. Knox's artillery fire stopped their charge. Cornwallis regrouped and turned his attention to the American center. Covered by Knox above, Wayne's Pennsylvania regiments showed the discipline instilled in them at Valley Forge, as they crossed the west morass causeway to counterattack, pushing back the British grenadiers, who were soon after reinforced and, in turn, forced the Pennsylvanians to fall back. They soon halted and tenaciously held their ground behind a hedgerow fence.

The British assault was led by the grenadiers, under Lt. Colonel Henry Monckton, a brave officer who had already suffered battle wounds at Long Island and Brandywine. One of his colleagues claimed that Monckton's recklessness in battle was the result of his having squandered away his personal fortune at the gambling tables.

The grenadiers came on, responding to Monckton's command, "Forward to the charge, my brave grenadiers!"

With bayonets fixed on the ends of lowered muskets pointed at the rebels they hated so, the sweating regulars charged as fast as they could, though by now lightheaded and panting from the heat. Above them, the terrible sun was a fireball in a cloudless sky. Wayne's line was supported by Knox's artillery, the guns sighted by Lt. Colonel du Plessis. Perfectly posted on Wayne's right, atop Comb's Hill, they did "prodigious execution," sending enfilade fire down the ranks of the oncoming British. In his memoir of the battle, Clinton noted, "one round shot struck the muskets from the hands of an entire platoon."

Behind the hedgerow, Anthony Wayne went up and down the line, shouting, "Steady! Steady! Wait for the word, then pick out the king-birds!" At forty yards, he gave the command, and a volley crumpled the charging redcoats. Dozens of these brave grenadiers fell down to the dusty ground, including "the high sergeant," a soldier who, at seven feet four inches, was the tallest in the entire British Army. Monckton fell, too, close to the hedgerow. Seeing this, Captain William Wilson's company, led by Lieutenant David Ziegler, leaped out and engaged the handful of grenadiers that stood their ground while the others fled. After some fierce hand-to-hand combat, the Pennsylvanians overcame the grenadiers and picked up Monckton's body, as well as his regiment's colors, and brought both triumphantly back to their comrades behind the hedgerow.

Soon after this action, General Wayne, observing more British units preparing to flank him on both the left and right, ordered a withdrawal across the creek. The next day, they would give Monckton a military burial in the Tennent Meetinghouse yard.

The British attacks against the American left and right having both failed, the battle now turned into a draw. By four o'clock, most of the infantry action was over. One soldier recalled they were told to "sit down and rest themselves," while the big guns had their duel. For the next two hours, most of the infantry on both sides would rest and watch the artillery demonstrations. Some of the local inhabitants had come back from hiding by now and sat atop the church roof, watching the spectacle. From up there, they saw a British cannon ball land and bounce between the gravestones until it hit a man sitting atop one of them, killing him.

It had been one of the longest battles of the war, and a battle of detachments. Monmouth, in General Lee's words, was fought "in pieces, and by dint of fighting in a variety of places, in the plain and in the woods, advancing and retreating, the enemy were at last worn down." By six o'clock Clinton had maneuvered his forces so as to protect his withdrawal from the field, falling back to the far side of the east morass. Joseph Clark recorded in his journal that, at this point, "the day being so excessively warm & the enemy so handsomely drubbed already, they did not attempt to meet us again."

The Americans had shown a military discipline never before exhibited, and the British had displayed the awesome courage they were famous for, marching into the face of blazing muskets while suffering deadly crossfire from rebel artillery. Because the rebels remained on the field of battle, they claimed victory, but Clinton had achieved what he wanted to in this rear guard action - ensuring the safe progression of his army and all its baggage to the coast. In fact, in the entire march across New Jersey, he did not lose a single wagon.

At Sandy Hook, the British Navy, daily expecting the arrival of a hostile French fleet, was anxious to ferry Clinton's army across to New York, so they could then prepare to meet the French squadron. Years later, Clinton would write that he could have made more "attempts ... upon Washington ... but when you recollect the critical situation of New York, and the fleet, & that we had not 48 hours provision, it was not a time to play the Quixote or experiment."

Near the end of the afternoon, Washington had sent detachments out to circle around and strike the British left and right flanks, but they "did not reach the ground till night came on. The attack was, therefore, delayed until morning. But the enemy retreated about midnight." This attempt to flank the enemy was too little, too late. During the heat of the action in the afternoon, Washington had been conservative.

Except for the detachments under Cilley and Wayne that had been counterattacks to British thrusts, he had kept his army safely on the high ground behind the west morass. A British officer named Charles Stedman, who would later write a history of the war, concluded that General Washington

> should have endeavoured to turn one of General Clinton's flanks. Had he succeeded, that part of the British army must have been destroyed ... the American General suffered the important occasion to pass by, when he might have terminated the war by one great and decisive effort.

At 12:30 in the afternoon, during Lee's retreat to the middle ravine, Washington had received a message from Colonel Daniel Morgan, and sent back the following reply:

> I have just received your letter by the dragoon. As your corps is out of supporting distance, I would have you confine yourself to observing the motions of the enemy, unless an opportunity offers of intercepting some small parties; and by no means to come to an engagement with your whole body unless you are tempted by some very evident advantage.

If Washington had called up Daniel Morgan's rifle corps, well rested and the very best marksmen in the army, they might have turned the tide of the battle, just as they had at Saratoga nine months before. By not using them, or others, in an ambitious pincers movement, such as Lee had tried but failed to do, Washington showed that he was more cautious than Lee. But Lee would be the one blamed for letting a victory slip away.

In the words of Private Martin, Clinton "gave us the slip" during the night, and within a week's time his army was safely back in New York.

Washington let them go. Having slept on the ground, beneath an apple tree, George Washington arose the next morning and, seeing no break in the weather, knew a forced march would not be possible. His army was greatly fatigued, and reports were coming in showing that, of the 106 American deaths on the battlefield the day before, 37 had been from heatstroke. On the British side, Clinton reported 124 dead, 59 were from heatstroke, though the Americans would report burying 251 enemy dead. Washington knew his army needed to rest and refresh themselves. Most of all, they needed fresh water to refill their canteens. Jeremiah Greenman's journal noted two days after the battle, "Such a number of solders that water is almost as scares as liquor & what is got is very bad indeed."

Lieutenant Archilaus Lewis, adjutant in a Massachusetts regiment, recorded the General Orders of June 30th in his orderly book, while the army recuperated at Englishtown:

> ... The men are to wash them silves this after noon and appear as deacent as posiable - 7 oclock this evening is appointed that we may publickly unite in thanksgiving to the Supreme Disposer of Human Events, for the victoray which was obtained on Sunday over the flower of the British Armey. ...

After Monmouth, the Continental Army rested for a week, then marched to White Plains, north of British-occupied New York. George Washington noted the irony: "after two years manoeuvring ... both armies are brought back to the very point they are sent out from," back in October 1776. Neither was the irony lost on London's *Evening Post*, always quick to satirize the British Army's commanders:

> Here we go up, up, up,
> And here we go down, down, downy.
> There we go *backwards* and *forwards*,
> And here we go round, round, roundy.

On July 4, 1778, the army celebrated the second anniversary of independence, as well as their recent victory on the battlefield. Many of the continentals now considered victory in the war inevitable. Colonel Thomas Clark wrote home to North Carolina:

> The wisdom of Congress and the conduct of General Washington have waded through innumerable difficulties, but what can not a country do when its liberties are at stake. Our independence is now, I think, firmly established, by which Britain has lost her right hand.
>
> We have a fine army, well disciplined, well armed and accoutered; what can they not do in this situation, when they have performed wonders without any of them. ... It is supposed [the British] are about to leave New York. They are like the wandering Israelites equally cursed by their maker. This campaign, I think, will deprive them of any foot hold in America.

Joseph Cilley, writing from White Plains on July 22nd to Thomas Bartlett, also had a favorable prediction:

> I think Clinton is brought himself into a fine hobble. He has now a strong French fleet in his front and General Washington in his rear. I think we shall Burgoyne him in a few weeks, which God grant may be the case.

However, the much anticipated, climactic Franco-American victory in New York would not take place. In fact, Monmouth would be the last major engagement in the North, and the last time that the American and British commanders in chief would oppose each other. The war would now shift to the South and feature secondary armies from both sides. Only the war's final large scale engagement, three years later, would see Washington's main army involved again. He would march his army all the way to Yorktown, Virginia, to engage a British southern army under Lord Cornwallis, while the outfoxed and cautious Sir Henry Clinton stayed behind in New York, leaving Cornwallis to his fate, the fate of a nation.

* * * * *

Besides the confidence boost that the Battle of Monmouth gave to the Continental Army, it resulted in the most sensational court martial of the war. Not even the Conway Cabal had generated so much excitement in the army. On July 2nd, Washington instructed the army's adjutant, Colonel Alexander Scammel, to arrest Major General Charles Lee. The warrant that he handed to Lee listed three charges: "disobedience of orders in not attacking the enemy," "misbehavior before the enemy by making unnecessary, disorderly and shameful retreat," and expressing "disrespect to the commander in chief in two letters." At first, Charles Lee considered this act of Washington's to be "madness," but he resolved to put up a good defense.

General Stirling served as president of the court, sitting alongside eight colonels and four generals, none of them from Lee's advanced division of the army. The trial started on July 4th and lasted several weeks, over several sites, as the army slowly moved to White Plains. Lee's outrageous testimony belittled and insulted George Washington's character and actions. This was an approach that Lee may have predicted in his insulting letter of June 30th, when he had told Washington that he looked forward to the "opportunity of shewing to America the sufficiency of her respective servants." By ridiculing Washington, Lee forced the court to choose between himself and Washington, not a wise thing to do so soon after the Conway Cabal.

Before the trial, Nathanael Greene had predicted "a slight censure," since the evidence against Lee was not very strong. The early 20th century historian, Sydney George Fisher, like many others who studied the court testimony, concluded:

An impartial view of all the evidence of the witnesses at the court-martial afterwards held, together with the account of the battle given by the British, fail to show that Lee was in fault. His retreat seems to have been both fortunate and necessary. At the moment when Washington met him, he had brought the troops out of a bad strip of country about two and a half miles in length, in which all the positions were favorable to the British, and he had just reached a good position to make a stand.

But Charles Lee was found guilty of all three counts, and sentenced to a one year suspension from the army. The decision, along with the recorded testimony, was sent to Congress, so that body could vote on whether to uphold or overrule the court. On December 5th, the state delegations voted six to two to uphold the court (four delegations were evenly split, and one abstained altogether). The individual votes were 16 to uphold, 7 to overrule. Several Congressmen abstained, perhaps wanting to overrule, but not doing so because it would, in effect, be giving the commander in chief a vote of no confidence. Two years later, after receiving a bitter and insolent letter from Charles Lee, Congress would make the one year suspension a permanent one.

Several Continental Army officers, including Nathanael Greene, would later write of "the error of the sentence." Sir Henry Clinton would write that, had Lee not retreated, "his whole corps would probably have fallen ... before Mr. Washington's main army could possibly be near enough to support him." A consensus of many British officers' opinions was reflected in the Tory Jemmy Rivington's *Royal Gazette*: Lee had saved the rebel army at Monmouth from certain defeat, the court's decision was purely a partisan vote to save George Washington from embarassment. The contemporary Whig historian, Reverend William Gordon, who published the first history of the war in 1786, concluded that Lee should have been found guilty only of the third charge, disrespect to the commander in chief. "Several are of opinion," he wrote, "he would not have been condemned on these [first] two, had it not been for his desrespectful conduct toward Washington."

Kicked out of the army, Charles Lee retired to his backwoods Virginia home (what would become Shephardstown, West Virginia), to live in seclusion with his servant and his beloved dogs. True to his idiosyncratic nature, the home resembled a barn more than a home; it was almost completely empty inside, with hand-drawn chalk lines on the floor, dividing it into hypothetical rooms. Charles Lee would spend the remaining four years of his life writing damning letters about Washington and other generals.

Before he left for Virginia, he was called to the "field of honor" by one of Washington's aides, John Laurens, for his insults to the commander in chief. In a wood four miles outside Philadelphia, they fired at each other from fifteen feet apart, Lee receiving a slight wound in his right side. He then said to Laurens, "You may fire at me all day, sir, if it will amuse you. What I have said I am not disposed to recall." Both men grimly began reloading, but were stopped by the intercession of Laurens's second, Alexander Hamilton.

Just before he died, Charles Lee would travel to Philadelphia and take lodgings in an upstairs room at the Conestoga Wagon Inn. One newspaper account claimed that his final words, in the throes of death, were a shout: "Stand by me, my brave grenadiers!" Thus would end a life which was a "history of disputes, quarrels and duels in every part of the world." George Washington, on hearing of Lee's demise, wrote a letter of condolence to Lee's sister in England.

Charles Lee was buried in the yard of Philadelphia's Christ Church. This was against his wishes. In his will, he had stipulated that his body must not be buried near any church, for "I have kept so much bad company while living, that I do not choose to continue it when dead."

BIBLIOGRAPHY

Primary Sources

Adams, Charles Francis, *Familiar Letters of John Adams and His Wife, Abigail Adams*. New York: Hurd and Houghton, 1876.
Anderson, Enoch, *Personal Recollections of Captain Enoch Anderson, an officer of the Delaware Regiments in the Revolutionary War*. Edited by Henry Hobart Bellas. Historical and Biographical Papers of the Historical Society of Delaware, vol. 2, no. 16, 1896.
Andre, Major John, *Major Andre's Journal*. Edited by C. DeW. Willcox. Tarrytown, NY: William Abbatt, 1930.
Balderston, Marion, and David Syrett, editors. *The Lost War, Letters from British Officers during the American Revolution*. New York: Horizon Press, 1975.
Bauermeister, Carl Leopold, *Revolution in America, Confidential Letters and Journals 1776-84 of Adjutant General Major Bauermeister of the Hessian Forces*. Edited by Bernhard A. Uhlendorf. New Brunswick, N.J.: Rutgers University Press, 1957.
Boudinot, Elias, *Journal, or Historical Recollections of American Events During the Revolutionary War*. Philadelphia: Bourque, 1884.
Bradford, William, "Letter," Massachusetts Historical Proceedings, vol. 13, 1874.
Burgoyne, Bruce E., translator and editor, *Enemy Views, The American Revolutionary War as Recorded by the Hessian Participants*. Bowie, MD: Heritage Books, 1996.
Burnett, Edmund C., editor, *Letters of Members of the Continental Congress*. Washington, DC: Carnegie Institute, 1923.
Clinton, Henry, *The American Rebellion, Sir Henry Clinton's Narrative of his Campaigns, 1775-82*. Edited by William B. Wilcox. New Haven: Yale University Press, 1954.
Commager, Henry Steele, and Richard B. Morris, editors, *The Spirit of 'Seventy-Six, The Story of the American Revolution as told by the Participants*. New York: Harper & Row, 1975.
Darlington, William, "Letter," Historical Society of Pennsylvania Bulletin, 1845.
Drinker, Mrs. Henry, "Journal," Pennsylvania Magazine of History and Biography, vol. 13, 1889.
Eelking, Max von, *The German Allies in the American Revolution, 1776-1783*. Baltimore: Genealogical Publishing Co., 1969.
Ewald, Johann, *Diary of the American War, A Hessian Journal*. Translated and edited by Joseph P. Tustin. New Haven, CT: Yale University Press, 1979.
Ferguson, James, *Two Scottish Soldiers*, Aberdeen, Scotland, 1888.

Franks, Rebecca, "Letter of Rebecca Franks, 1778," Pennsylvania Magazine of History and Biography, vol. 16, 1892.
Greene, Nathanael, *The Papers of Nathanael Greene*. Edited by Richard K. Showman, et al. Chapel Hill, NC: University of North Carolina Press, 1980.
Greenman, Jeremiah, *Diary of a Common Soldier in the American Revolution 1775-83*. DeKalb, IL: Northern Illinois University Press, 1978.
Hamilton, Alexander, "Letters describing the Battle of Monmouth," Pennsylvania Magazine of History and Biography, vol. 2, 1878.
Hunter, Sir Martin, *The Journal of General Sir Martin Hunter*. Edited by Anne Hunter. Edinburgh, Scotland: The Edinburgh Press, 1894.
Lafayette, Gilbert Motier Marquis de, *Lafayette in the Age of the American Revolution, Selected Letters and Papers*. Edited by Stanley J. Idzerda. Ithaca, NY: Cornell University Press, 1979.
Laurens, Henry, *The Papers of Henry Laurens*. Edited by David R. Chestnut, et al. Columbia, SC: U. of South Carolina Press, 1990.
Lee, Francis B., editor, *New Jersey Archives, 1778*. Trenton, NJ: The Murphy Publishing Co., 1903.
Mackenzie, Frederick, *Diary of Frederick Mackenzie*. Cambridge, MA: Harvard University Press, 1930.
Martin, Joseph Plumb, *Private Yankee Doodle*. Edited by George F. Scheer. New York: Little, Brown, 1962.
McDonald, Hugh, *A Teen-ager in the Revolution*. Harrisburg, PA: Historical Times, 1966.
McMichael, James, "Diary of Lt. James McMichael, of the Pennsylvania Line, 1778-1778." Pennsylvania Magazine of History and Biography, vol. 16, 1892.
Muenchhausen, Friedrich Ernst von, *At General Howe's Side 1776-78*. Translated and edited by Ernst Kipping, and annotated by Samuel Smith. Monmouth Beach, N.J.: Philip Freneau Press, 1974.
Murray, James, *Letters from America 1773-80*. Edited by Eric Robson. Manchester, England: Manchester University Press, 1951.
Ryan, Dennis P., editor, *A Salute to Courage, The American Revolution as Seen Through Wartime Writings of Officers of the Continental Army and Navy*. New York: Columbia University Press, 1979.
Scheer, George F., and Hugh F. Rankin, *Rebels and Redcoats*. Cleveland: World Publishing Co., 1957.
Serle, Ambrose, *The American Journal of Ambrose Serle, Secretary to Lord Howe 1776-78*. Edited by Edward H. Tatum. San Marino, CA: Huntington Library, 1940.
Sullivan, Thomas, *From Redcoat to Rebel, The Thomas Sullivan Journal*. Edited by Joseph Lee Boyle. Bowie, MD: Heritage Books, 1997.

Townsend, Joseph, "Letter," Historical Society of Pennsylvania Bulletin, 1846.
Waldo, Albigence, "Valley Forge 1777-1778, Diary of Surgeon Albigence Waldo, of the Connecticut Line," Pennsylvania Magazine of History and Biography, vol. 21, 1897.
Washington, George, *The Writings of George Washington*. Edited by Jared Sparks. Boston: Russell, Odiorne and Metcalf, 1834.
Weedon, George, *Valley Forge Orderly Book of General George Weedon*. New York: Dodd, Mead & Co., 1902.
Wheeler, Richard, *Voices of 1776*. New York: Crowell, 1972.
Wister, Sarah, "Journal of Miss Sally Wister," Pennsylvania Magazine of History and Biography, vol. 9, 1885.
Wright, Esmond, *The Fire of Liberty*. London: Folio Society, 1983.

Secondary Sources

Anderson, Troyer Steele, *The Command of the Howe Brothers During the American Revolution*. New York: Oxford University Press, 1936.
Atwood, Rodney, *The Hessians, Mercenaries from Hessen-Kassel in the American Revolution*. Cambridge, England: Cambridge University Press, 1980.
Billias, George Athan, *Elbridge Gerry, Founding Father and Republican Statesman*. New York: McGraw Hill, 1976.
Blumenthal, Walter Hart, *Women Camp Followers of the American Revolution*. Philadelphia: George S. MacManus Co., 1952.
Bobrick, Benson, *Angel in the Whirlwind, The Triumph of the American Revolution*. New York: Simon & Schuster, 1997.
Davis, Burke, *George Washington and the American Revolution*. New York: Random House, 1975.
Eastby, Allen G., "The Baron," American History Illustrated, Nov/Dec 1990, vol. XXV, no. 5.
Fisher, Sydney George, The Struggle for American Independence. Philadelphia: 1908.
Flexner, James Thomas, *George Washington in the American Revolution*. Boston: Little, Brown, 1967.
Flexner, James Thomas, *The Traitor and the Spy, Benedict Arnold and John Andre*. New York: Little, Brown, 1953.
Gottschalk, Louis, *Lafayette in America*. Chicago: University of Chicago, 1975.
Griffith II, Samuel B., *In Defense of the Public Liberty*. Garden City, NY: Doubleday, 1976.
Gruber, Ira D., *The Howe Brothers and the American Revolution*. New York: Atheneum, 1972.

Hibbert, Christopher, *Redcoats and Rebels, The American Revolution Through British Eyes*. New York: Norton, 1990.

Higginbotham, Don, *The War of American Independence, Military Attitudes, Policies & Practice, 1763-89*. New York: MacMillan, 1971.

Hughes, Rupert, *George Washington*. New York: Morrow, 1930.

Jackson, John W., *The Pennsylvania Navy 1775-81, The Defense of the Delaware*. New Brunswick, NJ: Rutgers University Press, 1974.

Jackson, John W., *With the British Army in Philadelphia 1777-1778*. San Rafael, CA: Presidio Press, 1974.

Kapp, Friedrich, *The Life of John Kalb*. New York: Henry Holt & Co., 1884.

Kipping, Ernst, *The Hessian View of America 1776-83*. Monmouth Beach, NJ: Philip Freneau Press, 1971.

Leckie, Robert, *George Washington's War, The Saga of the American Revolution*. New York: Harper Collins, 1992.

Lowell, Edward J., *The Hessians and the other German Auxiliaries of Great Britain in the Revolutionary War*. New York: Harper Brothers, 1884.

Lundin, Leonard, *Cockpit of the Revolution, The War for Independence in New Jersey*. Princeton, NJ: Princeton University Press, 1940.

Marshall, Douglas W., and Howard H. Peckham, *Campaigns of the American Revolution, An Atlas of Manuscript Maps*. Ann Arbor, MI: University of Michigan Press, 1976.

Marshall-Dutcher, Joan, "Winter at Valley Forge," American History Illustrated, Nov/Dec 1990, vol. XXV, no. 5.

Miers, Earl Schenck, *Crossroads of Freedom, The American Revolution and the Rise of a New Nation*. New Brunswick, NJ: Rutgers University Press, 1971.

Mintz, Max M., "Horatio Gates, George Washington's Rival," History Today, 7/76.

Mitchell, Broadus, *The Price of Independence, A Realistic View of the American Revolution*. New York: Oxford University Press, 1974.

Moomaw, William H., "The Denouement of General Howe's Campaign of 1777," English Historical Review, vol. 79, July 1964.

Murphy, Orville T., "The Battle of Germantown and the Franco-American Alliance of 1778," Penn. Magazine of History and Biorgraphy, vol. 82, 1958.

Nelson, Paul David, *General Horatio Gates*. Baton Rouge, LA: Louisiana State University Press, 1976.

Nelson, Paul David, *General James Grant, Scottish Soldier and Royal Governor of East Florida*. Gainesville, FL: University Press of Florida, 1993.

Pancake, John S., *1777, Year of the Hangman*. University, AL: University of Alabama Press, 1977.

Pearson, Michael, *Those Damned Rebels, The American Revolution as Seen Through British Eyes*. New York: Putnam's Sons, 1972.

Peckham, Howard H., "Sir Henry Clinton's Review of Simcoe's Journal," William and Mary College Quarterly, vol. 21, October 1941.

Reed, John F., *Campaign to Valley Forge, July 1, 1777 - December 19, 1777*. Philadelphia: University of Pennsylvania Press, 1965.

Robinson, Joseph A., "British Invasion of the Chesapeake," in *Chesapeake Bay in the American Revolution*. Edited by Ernest M. Eller. Centreville, MD: Tidewater Publishers, 1981.

Robson, Eric, *The American Revolution In Its Political and Military Aspects*. New York: Norton, 1966.

Rossie, Jonathan Gregory, *The Politics of Command in the American Revolution*. Syracuse, NY: Syracuse University Press, 1975.

Royster, Charles, *A Revolutionary People at War, The Continental Army and American Character, 1775-83*. New York: Norton, 1979.

Smith, Page, *A New Age Now Begins, A People's History of the American Revolution*. New York: McGraw-Hill, 1976.

Smith, Paul H., *Loyalists & Redcoats, A Study in British Revolutionary Policy*. Chapel Hill, NC: University of North Carolina Press, 1964.

Smith, Samuel Stelle, *Fight for the Delaware 1777*. Monmouth Beach, NJ: Philip Freneau Press, 1970.

Smith, Samuel Stelle, *The Battle of Brandywine*. Monmouth Beach, NJ: Philip Freneau Press, 1976.

Smith, Samuel Stelle, *The Battle of Monmouth*. Monmouth Beach, NJ: Philip Freneau Press, 1964.

Stryker, William S., *The Battle of Monmouth*. Edited by William S. Myers. Princeton, NJ: Princeton University Press, 1927.

Stryker, William S., *The Forts on the Delaware in the Revolutionary War*. Trenton, NJ: John Murphy Publishing Co., 1901.

Tebbel, John, *Turning the World Upside Down, Inside the American Revolution*. New York: Orion Books, 1993.

Thayer, Theodore, The Making of a Scapegoat, Washington and Lee at Monmouth. Port Washington, NY: Kennikat Press, 1976.

Trussell, John B., *Birthplace of an Army, A Study of the Valley Forge Encampment*. Harrisburg, PA: Pennsylvania Historical and Museum Commission, 1976.

Tucker, Glenn, *Mad Anthony Wayne and the New Nation*. Harrisburg, PA: Stackpole Books, 1973.

Ward, Christopher L., *The War of the Revolution*. New York: MacMillan, 1952.

Whitridge, Arnold, "Baron von Steuben, Washington's Drillmaster," History Today, July 1976.

Willcox, William B., "British Strategy in America, 1778," Journal of Modern History, June 1947.

INDEX

ADAMS, Abigail 52 92 John 11 52 74 92 94 106 146 184 196
ALLEN, James 54 94
AMHERST, Jeffrey 173
ANDERSON, 169 Enoch 6 32-33 38 59 67
ANDRE, 167 172 Capt 166 172 John 19 48-49 51 54 76 94 98 126 166-167 169-170 186
ARMSTRONG, 61 64-66 "Hickory Shins" 64
ARNOLD, Benedict 81 139 167 184 191 195 206
ASHLIN, Lee 13
AUSTIN, Jonathan 105
BANISTER, John 178
BARTLETT, Thomas 223
BAUERMEISTER, Carl Leopold 21 Maj 45 50 89 102
BAYLEY, Jacob 154
BEDEL, Timothy 154
BLAND, Col 25 Theodorick 24 170
BORRE, Pruedhomme de 31
BOUDINOT, 198 Elias 197
BRADFORD, William 91
BRANTLY, John 64
BROGLIE, Charles Francis de 109
BROOKS, John 121
BROWN, 34 Joseph 33
BUNTING, Mrs 193-194
BURGOYNE, 2 4-5 7 9 13 20 56 71 74 92-93 95 105 143 155 158 162-163 Gen 1 6 95 105 "Gentleman Johnny" 1 144
BUSHNELL, 164 David 163
BUTLER, 206-207 Col 205
CADWALADER, Gen 153 John 156
CAMPBELL, 19 Capt 19
CARLETON, Guy 5
CARLISLE, 176-177 179-180 Earl 176 Lord 181 186
CARRINGTON, Edward 216
CARROLL, Charles 147 156
CATTELL, Jonas 78
CHARLES, King Of Spain 106
CHEW, 62 64-65 68 Benjamin 61 186 Peggy 170 186
CHEYNEY, Thomas 24

CHIPMAN, Nathaniel 139
CILLEY, 221 Joseph 217 223
CILLY, Col 217
CLARK, John 153 Joseph 35 37 120 220 Oliver 79 Thomas 223
CLINTON, 174 177-178 185-188 190-195 199-209 216 219-220 222-223 Gen 174 213 221 George 177 Henry 5 173 185 224-225
COFFIN, 169
CONWAY, 34 140 144-145 152 154 156 159 224 Gen 144-146 154-155 158 Thomas 32 129 142-143 146 153-155 157
CORNWALLIS, 18 22 25 27 29 45 51 61 67 102 203 208 218 Gen Lord 102 Lord 19-20 26 29 103 208 224
CRAIK, James 139 147
CRESSWELL, Nicholas 3
DARLINGTON, William 33
DARRAGH, Lydia 161
DAVID, Ebenezer 109 Rev 109
DAYEN, Duc 152
DAYTON, Elias 46 65
DEANE, Silas 92 105 142 150-151
DERLITH, Friedrich von 187
DICKINSON, 194 205 210 Gen 204 Philemon 190 202
DONOP, 78-82 84-85 87 90 Carl von 4 71 77 Col 80-81 86 88-89 Count 92 Ens 80
DRAYTON, 180 W H 179
DRINKER, Elizabeth 183 Mrs Henry 172 183
DUMAS, Alexandre 149
DYER, Eliphalet 147 158
ELLERY, William 121
ELLIS, Dick 78 Joseph 78
ELMER, Ebenezer 32
ERSKINE, William 174
EWALD, 26 83 Capt 52 80 82 Johann 25 28 37 58 62 68 80 83 87 89 168
EWING, George 133
FEILITZSCH, 95 Heinrich Carl Philipp 8 Lt 8 95 117 187 200
FERGUSON, 21 Mrs 180 Patrick 22 38
FISHER, Sydney George 224

FLEURY, Col 96 Francois Louis Teissedre 94 Lt Col 98-99
FOULKE, "Aunt" 125
FRANKLIN, 106 129 Benjamin 91 105-107 128-129 151 195 Dr 105
FRANKS, Rebecca 167
FRAZER, Persie 24
FREDERICK, The Great 131 153
GALLOWAY, Joseph 175 Mr 175
GATES, 5 20 53 56 102 140 142 144 146-148 193 Gen 75 102-103 106 142 147 Horatio 2 74-75 93 139 141 143 145 154-155 158
GEORGE III, King Of England 43 79-80 90 162 173 176 179-180
GERMAIN, 4 178 George 2 163 Lord 5 13 173 185
GERRY, Elbridge 52 157
GORDON, William 196 225
GRANT, 66 Gen 65 James 199
GREENE, 15 33-35 54 57-58 61 65-66 82 84-85 88 93 103 199 Christopher 81 Col 81 83 85 88 92-94 Gen 135 Nathanael 5-6 23 40 53 102-103 122 146 148 153 162 191 216 224-225
GREENMAN, Jeremiah 138 191 222
GREY, 50 66 Charles 48 Gen 49 166 "No Flint" 48
HAGEN, Lt 28
HAINS, Capt 63
HALE, Lt 36
HAMILTON, Alexander 9 53 75 129 145 148 196 198 213 226
HAMMOND, Andrew 7
HANDEL, 137
HANNIBAL, 55
HARCOURT, William 87
HAWKINS, John 36
HAYES, Mary Ludwig 214
HAZELWOOD, 72 76 Comdr 76 90-91 103 John 71
HAZEN, 31 Col 23 Moses 23
HECTOR, Edward 35
HENDERSON, Thomas 210
HENRY, Patrick 140
HETH, William 68-69
HOFFMAN, 28-29
HOPKINSON, Francis 164-165
HOWARD, Fredrick 176
HOWE, 2 5-6 12-16 18-19 22 29-30 33 37 39-40 42 44-45 47-48 50 52-55 58 60 64-69 72-78 82 87 93 95 102 106 141 161 172 184 187 196 199 Adm 7 90 98 172 G 46 Gen 1 3-4 6-7 12-13 19 23 37 42 48 55 60-61 68 71 78 81 87 89 94-95 99-100 124 142 161 163 165-166 169 172 174 197 199 Lord 99 165 170 181 Mr 134

HOWE (cont.)
Richard 3 90 162 164 "Sir Billy" 166 Sir Wm 29 165 William 1-3 7 11 19 41 51 71 104 112 138 161-163 165 173 185
HUMPTON, Col 49
HUNTER, Martin 55 58 60
JACKSON, 206 Col 136 206
JARVIS, Stephen 22
JAY, John 147
JOHN, Laurens 143
JOHNSON, James 27 Mary 127
JOHNSTONE, George 180 Gov 180
KALB, 151 155 Baron 54 Johann de 109 116 149 154
KEMBLE, Stephen 4
KENNEDY, Dennis 120
KNOX, 62 218 Gen 45 62 Henry 62 112 148 157 184 216
KNYPHAUSEN, 18-22 33 35 38 45 203 209 Gen 14 17-22 26 188 George 17
LAFAYETTE, 16 38 124 142 148-155 191 195 198-202 207-209 215 Adrienne 52 Gen 141 183 Marquis 9 34 52 148 150-151
LAURENS, 158 179 Henry 129 140 157 204 John 108 129 134 148 153 157 208 226 Joseph 213 Pres 142 146 153-155 158 179
LEE, 140 191 196 198-199 202-213 215 221 Arthur 105 Billy 112 215 Charles 16 191 195 197-199 201 211 224-226 Gen 196-198 202-204 206 211-212 220 Mr 197 Richard Henry 145
LEWIS, Archilaus 222
LIDDY, 125
LIVINGSTON, William 176 181 211
LLOYD, Thomas 213
LORD, Cornwallis 27
LORING, Mrs 163 165
LOUIS XVI, King Of France 2 105-107 136-137 150
LOVELL, James 141 150
MACKENZIE, Frederick 4
MARREL, John 136
MARSHALL, Christopher 141
MARTIN, 205 Alexander 67 Joseph Plumb 57-58 89 95 100-101 108 110 116 122 195 204 210 214 217 Pvt 97 111 123 213 221
MAXWELL, 20-22 38 62 194 207-209 William 190 202 "Scotch Willie" 20
MCDONALD, 67 Hugh 42 44-46 64 67 93 118
MCDOUGALL, Alexander 155
MCGRATH, William 136
MCKAY, William 118
MCLANE, Allen 188 191
MCMICHAEL, James 9 46 56 67 138

MCPHERSON, Capt 28
MCWILLIAMS, William 144
MEASES, James 120
MERCER, Capt 207 209
MIFFLIN, 147 153 159 Thomas 122 144 155
MINNIGERODE. Lt Col 84
"MOLLY PITCHER," 214
MONCKTON, 219 Henry 218
MONTRESOR, 77 Capt 93-94 John 9 76 172
MORGAN, 20 203 207-208 Col 190 193 202 Daniel 153 158 161 199 202 221
MORRIS, Gouverneur 147 156
MORTON, Robert 103 184
MOTIER, Gilbert 148-149
MOULTRIE, Col 196
MOYLAN, 190 194 209 Col 202
MUENCHHAUSEN, 15 67 98 104 Capt 9 16 30 39 45 81 93 99 Friedrich 5 18 60 95
MUHLENBERG, "Devil Pete" 35 Peter 35
MURRAY, 15 James 15
MUSGRAVE, 62 Col 62-63 68 Thomas 61
NASH, Francis 64 Gen 64
NOAILLES, Viscount de 106
NORTH, Lord 106 173 175-176 178 Prime Minister 181
OLNEY, 214 Capt 86 Jeremiah 80-81 213 Stephen 83 86 210
OSBORNE, George 79
OSWALD, 215 Eleazer 206 213
PACA, "Mr P" 168 Mrs William 167
PAINE, Thomas 69 91 196
PATTERSON, James 216
PATTISON, James 169
PEEBLES, John 166
PETERS, Richard 146 153 201
PHILLIPS, William 148
PICKERING, 54 Timothy 38 41 53 147
PIEL, Jacob 192
PLESSIS, 85 Chevalier Demauduit Du 81 88 Lt Col 219
PONCEAU, Pierre Du 131 135 138
PORTAIL, Louis Du 107 Louis Le Begue De Presle Du 112
POTTER, Asa 84
POTTS, Isaac 112
PRISSA, "Cousin" 125
PRUSSIA, King Of 128
PULASKI, 67 Casimir 108 Count 35
PUTNAM, 102 Israel 6 9
RALL, Col 55
REED, 181 Joseph 180
RIVINGTON, Jemmy 225
ROBERTS, George 191
ROSS, Adj Gen 26 James 23

ROSSIE, Jonathan 159
RUEFFER, Carl 79-80 Carl Friedrich 11 Ens 12 89 100-101
RUSH, 159 Benjamin 140 146
SCAMMEL, Alexander 132 224
SCHOEPFF, Johann 192
SCHUYLER, Philip 155
SCOTT, 209 Charles 199 202 Gen 207-208 212 William 29
SEATON, 126
SERGEANT, 141 Jonathan 140
SERLE, Ambrose 7 9 14 162 172 175
SHIPPEN, Peggy 167
SIMCOE, John 206
SMALLWOOD, 61 65-66 190 Gen 108 124-125
SMITH, 168 Col 76 92 Samuel 76 94
SPEAR, James 23 Maj 23
STARK, John 154
STEDMAN, Charles 221
STEPHEN, 25 30-31 66 Adam 65 67
STERLING, 87 Col 87
STEUBE, 128
STEUBEN, 129-133 135 137 215 Baron 133 137 Friedrich 128 133 134 Gen 120 216
STIRLING, 25 30-31 64-65 142 216-217 Gen 30 61 93 142 144 216 224 Lord 201
STODDERT, Maj 125-126
STONEMAN, Sarah 188
STUART, Alexander 80 Maj 80 82
SULLIVAN, 25 30-33 57-58 61 65 Gen 30 John 23-24 142 Thomas 21 25 35 45 80 179 188
SUTHERLAND, William 213
SWEETZER, 86
TALLMADGE, Benjamin 62
TENNENT, Gilbert 195
THAYER, Simeon 214
TILLY, Mr 125-126
TODD, Jonathan 113
TOWNSEND, 27 "Brother" 27 Joseph 26 36
TRUMBULL, Gov 178
VARNUM, Gen 217 James 109
VERGENNES, Comte de 106-107
WADSWORTH, Jeremiah 122
WALDECK, Philipp 188
WALDO, Albigence 114 134 214 Dr 118-119
WALKER, Benjamin 130
WARREN, Adm 48
WASHINGTON, 3 5-6 9-10 14-19 22-26 28 33-34 37-38 42-47 50 53-54 56 61-62 64-66 69 74-75 95 102 105 109 113 121-122 124 137 142 144-146 148-149 152 156-158 161 166 191 193 196 199-204 207-208 212-213 215-216 220-222 224 226 "Clever" 62 Gen 2 9 13 16 23 27 34 39 41 43-44 50 54 64 68 92-93

WASHINGTON (cont.)
 108 112 115 119 124 127-128 130 134 138-
 139 141-142 152 158 197-199 221 223 George
 16-18 20 24 35 51-52 54-55 68 71 73 92 95
 103-104 106 108 122 128-129 136 138-141
 143 145 147-148 151 153-156 158-159
 161 167 178 181 190 192 195 197 210 212 222
 224-226 John Augustine 147 Martha 112 Mr
 27 174 204 225 Mrs 135 197
WAYNE, 36 48-50 59-60 65-67 102 191 199 208
 211 215-216 218-219 221 Anthony 23-24 35
 47 50 58 69 108 118 146 195 201-203 206-

WAYNE (cont.)
 207 219 Gen 49 59 219
WEEDON, Gen 40 69
WHARTON, Thomas 169
WHITALL, Job 79
WHYTE, Robert 99
WILKINSON, 144-145 James 143 146 Lt Col 143
WILSON, William 219
WISTER, Sally 125-127 Sarah 124
WYKOFF, Peter 211
YORKE, Joseph 90
ZIEGLER, David 219

www.ingramcontent.com/pod-product-compliance
Lightning Source LLC
Chambersburg PA
CBHW071428150426
3191CB00008B/1083